IMAGES
*of America*

# NORMAN
## 1889–1949

**On the Cover:** This panoramic view of downtown Norman, captured by M.M. Marables around 1910, shows the banking corner at the intersection of East Main Street and Peters Avenue. The first bank to occupy the northwest corner was the Commercial Bank in 1889, a branch of the Newton, Kansas, Commercial Bank. The institution closed its branch offices in the economic depression of 1898. The building was soon occupied by Citizens Bank, which was formed by Norman businessmen. In 1910, the bank building was home to First State Bank. Today, First Fidelity Bank occupies the northwest corner of East Main Street and Peters Avenue. (Cleveland County Historical Society.)

IMAGES
*of America*

# NORMAN
# 1889–1949

Sue Schrems and Vernon Maddux on behalf
of the Cleveland County Historical Society

ARCADIA
PUBLISHING

ISBN 978-1-4671-1048-8

Published by Arcadia Publishing
Charleston, South Carolina

Printed in the United States of America

Library of Congress Control Number: 2013934787

For all general information, please contact Arcadia Publishing:
Telephone 843-853-2070
Fax 843-853-0044
E-mail sales@arcadiapublishing.com
For customer service and orders:
Toll-Free 1-888-313-2665

Visit us on the Internet at www.arcadiapublishing.com

*This book is dedicated to the pioneer families of Norman and Cleveland County, Oklahoma.*

# Contents

# ACKNOWLEDGMENTS

Every time I hear the engineer blow the whistle as the Santa Fe freight train makes its way through central Norman, I think of those hardy pioneers who built this beautiful town on the dry, barren prairie. The sound of the train is the one constant that ties present-day Norman to its early years. Many of those pioneer families left their histories and photographs to the Cleveland County Historical Society after its founding in 1967. From the paper and photographic archives, we have complied this history. I want to thank the membership of the Cleveland County Historical Society, who donated their artifacts, their time, and their financial support to the society and to the Moore-Lindsay Historical House Museum. I would also like to thank the City of Norman Town Council for its continued financial support of the Moore-Lindsay House. Last, but certainly not least, I would like to thank the curator of the Moore-Lindsay House, Erin Smith, and the board of the Cleveland County Historical Society for their dedication and their efforts to preserve the history of Norman.

The photographs in this book are credited to the following institutions: Cleveland County Historical Society (CCHS); Western History Collection, University of Oklahoma (WHC); Carl Albert Congressional Archives, University of Oklahoma (CACA); Dickerson Research Center, National Cowboy Museum (NCM); Oklahoma Historical Society (OHS); and Special Collection, University of Nevada–Reno Library (UNR).

# INTRODUCTION

On the morning of April 22, 1889, in Purcell, Indian Territory, the fireman on the special Atchison, Topeka & Santa Fe (AT&SF) train, overloaded with passengers, started shoveling coal from the tender to the firebox; the engineer, waiting for the beginning of the Oklahoma land run, was getting up steam for the trip north into the unassigned lands. Those in Purcell not riding the train waited anxiously along the South Canadian River. And at the northern edge of the unassigned lands, settlers on horseback and in wagons waited along the Oklahoma-Kansas border at Arkansas City. People from all walks of life—young and old, men and women, southerners and northerners, rich and poor—anxiously waited to make the "run" for their 160 acres of free land accorded them under the United States Homestead Act of 1866. As the hour of noon approached, all waited to make the mad dash into the available region. By nightfall, settlers had staked their claims and pinned their hopes on a new beginning in a new territory called Oklahoma.

Like many towns located along the AT&SF route through central Oklahoma, Norman was an overnight town populated immediately after the opening of the territory. Several factors contributed to making Norman a prosperous town in the late 19th and early 20th centuries: it was a commercial center for the surrounding agricultural area; it was a station on the Santa Fe Railroad; it was the county seat; and it was the home of the University of Oklahoma.

The springs at Bishop Creek played an important role in the location and the name of the town known as Norman, Oklahoma. Today, Bishop Creek meanders through central Norman neighborhoods, quietly making its way to the South Canadian River. Because of this once-natural oasis in the middle of a semiarid region, the spring was well known to Native Americans and to thirsty cowboys off the Arbuckle Trail. In 1870, it became known to Abner Ernest Norman, the namesake of the town. A.E. Norman was part of Theodore H. Barrett's engineering company, hired by the US Land Office to survey western Oklahoma, which included all of Cleveland County. Abner Norman was the supervisor for Barrett's crew; their responsibility was to survey the area from the Red River to north of the Canadian River. While surveying what is now Cleveland County and the future town of Norman, the crew camped at a spring surrounded by a grove of trees. The camp became known as Norman's Camp when a crewmember carved "Norman" on one of the trees by the spring. The spring was located just south of today's intersection of Classen Boulevard and East Lindsey Street. After Abner Norman completed his survey in 1873, he moved back to his home state of Kentucky, married, and worked at various business enterprises, never returning to the town that bears his name.

Shortly after Norman's survey crew left the area, Chickasaw rancher Montford T. Johnson built a dugout near the spring to provide shelter for his cowboys. The riders were assigned the task of protecting the rancher's cattle. For 10 years at "Dugout Creek," as they called it, Johnson's men kept cattle safe from hungry wolves and away from the other herds moving up the Arbuckle Trail. The Arbuckle was an eastern feeder trail to the Chisholm Trail, which ran west near present-day Tuttle, Oklahoma.

Until 1879, the area now known as Oklahoma was designated Indian Country and was not opened to settlement. But, pressure to open the lands was put on the US Congress by businessmen, bankers, newspapermen, and most of all, by railroad interests. After the Civil War, government subsidies to railroads motivated many companies to establish lines west of the Mississippi River. The Missouri, Kansas & Texas Railroad Company (MKT) was the first railroad to lay track into Indian Country, with a line from Kansas to Muskogee and eventually to Denison, Texas. In 1871, the Atlantic & Pacific Railroad Company (A&P) laid track into the Cherokee Nation. By 1882, the railroad line extended to Tulsa, which was then called Tulsey Town, in the Creek Nation.

The AT&SF received authorization from Congress to build a branch of the Santa Fe across the unassigned lands of Indian Territory in 1884. The railroad authorized a survey along a 100-mile corridor from Kansas to Texas to determine the best route. The decision to build the line through the unassigned lands in central Oklahoma was influenced by the likelihood that this land would be opened to non-Indian settlers in the near future. The railroad survey crew stayed at "Norman's Camp" near the spring, where Johnson's cowboys had built their dugout. On September 1, 1886, at Arkansas City, Kansas, railroad crews started preparing the bed and laying track to the south into the unassigned lands of Indian Territory. The crews finished just past Norman's Camp on April 15, 1887. While crews laid track south from Kansas, other crews started laying track north from Gainesville, Texas; the two tracks met at Purcell, Oklahoma, on April 26, 1887. The rail line ran within a quarter of a mile of Norman's Camp.

The railroad crews also decided the location of station houses along the rail route. Since Norman's Camp at Dugout Creek was a familiar location, a station house and siding were established nearby, and the name Norman became attached to the station. In 1887, the railroad built a house for telegraph operator W.E. Thomas, who occupied the house at this lonely location for 18 months before moving on. That year, the first passenger train passed through Norman Station, on a route from Galveston, Texas, to Kansas City, Missouri. By April 17, 1889, the first Santa Fe agent, Andrew Kingkade, along with his wife and four-year-old son, moved into the station house at Norman.

Three weeks before the run, Santa Fe engineers designated four towns along the rail route through the unassigned lands: Guthrie, Oklahoma City, Kingfisher, and Norman. Draftsmen for the company then plotted the four townsites. Accordingly, surveyors oriented the streets of Norman at right angles to the railroad tracks. They also named the streets, many after employees of the railroad and after Native Americans, such as Muskogee, Tonhawa, Comanche, and Apache.

On April 22, 1889, the day of the land opening, James M. Bishop, Albert C. McCord, and Jeptha M. Chastain filed on the quarter section that contained Norman's Camp. The issue of three claimants had to be decided at a hearing at the land office in Guthrie, Oklahoma. Chastain withdrew his claim; Bishop and McCord waited four years for the matter to be settled. The US Land Office determined that Bishop was the rightful claimant. The spring and creek, first known as Norman's Camp, then Dugout Creek, now became known as Bishop's Creek. By 1972, 100 years after Abner Norman completed his survey of the area that would include the town of Norman, the spring and grove of trees were eliminated; town officials authorized covering up the spring and relocating the creek.

# *One*

# Growth of a Town

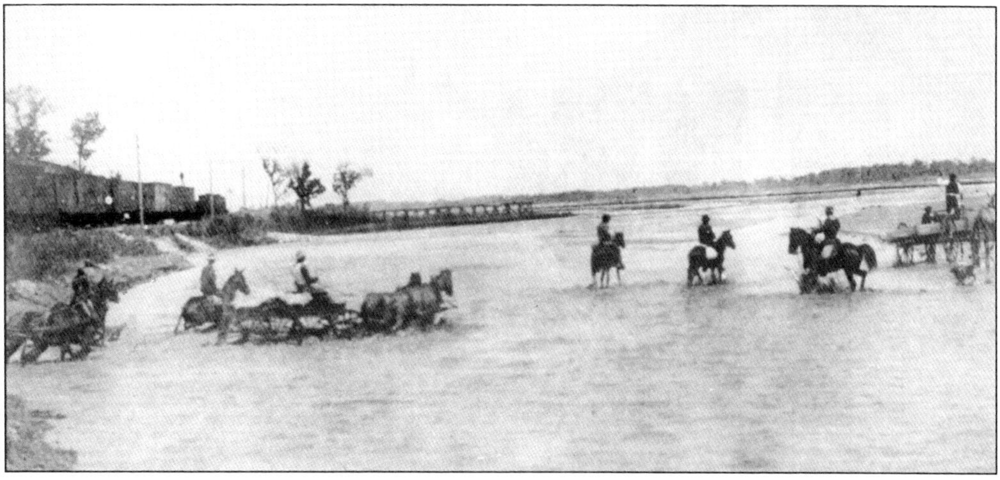

On March 23, 1889, the US Congress passed an Indian Appropriations Act authorizing Pres. Benjamin Harrison to open two million acres of public land for settlement. The Homestead Act of 1862 permitted settlers to claim 160 acres of public land. On April 22, land seekers lined up for the run into the unassigned lands in central Oklahoma. (CCHS.)

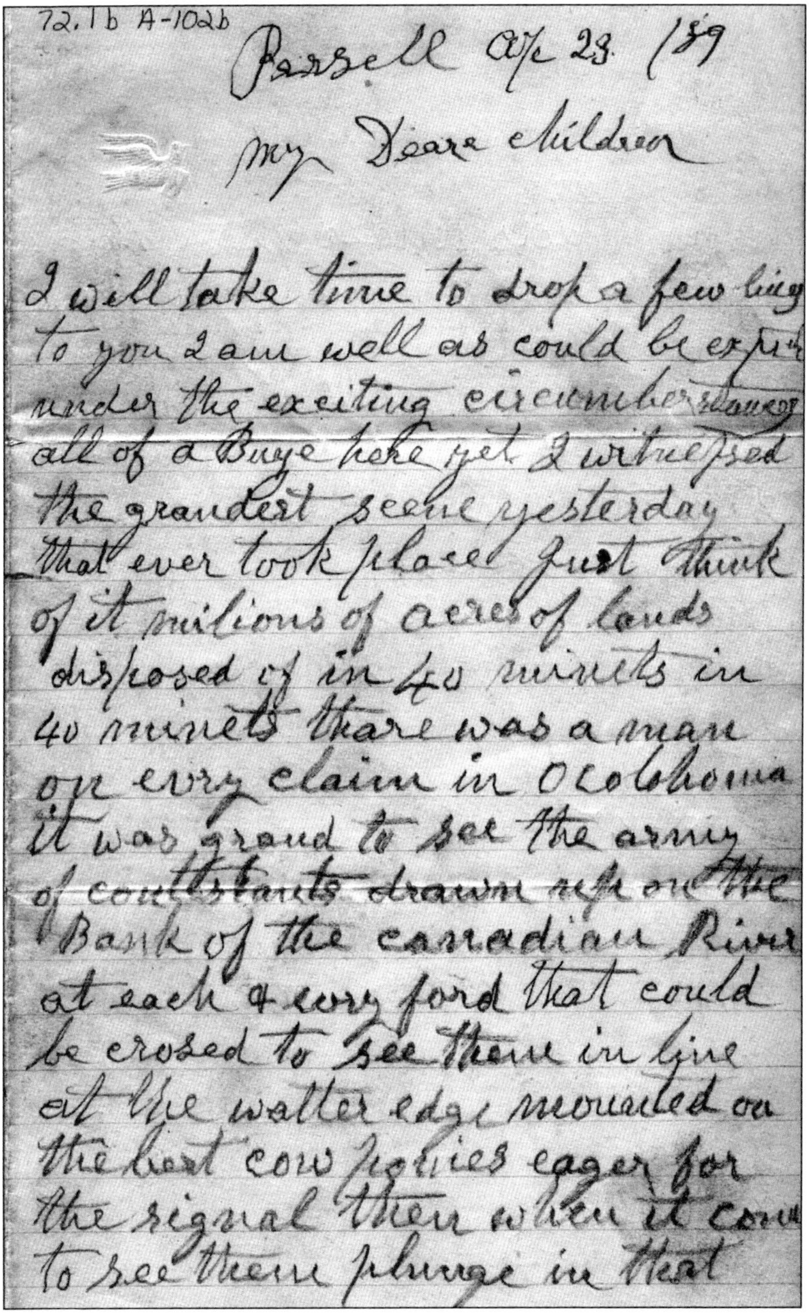
72.1b A-102b

Purcell Ap 23 189

My Deare Children

I will take time to drop a few lins
to you I am well as could be exp
under the exciting circumberstances
all of a Buge heke yet I witnessed
the grandest scene yesterday
that ever took place just think
of it milions of acres of lands
disposed of in 40 minets in
40 minets thare was a man
on evry claim in Ocolohoma
it was grand to see the army
of contestants drawn up on the
Bank of the canadian River
at each & evry ford that could
be crosed to see them in line
at the watter edge mounted on
the best cow ponies eager for
the signal then when it com
to see them plunge in that

In 1889, Purcell was a sleepy railroad town of 200 people established along the Santa Fe tracks in the Chickasaw Nation. The town was a gathering place for those who planned to make the run into the unassigned lands. Over 2,000 people crowded into the town in the spring of 1889 to await the land opening on April 22. Many of them passed their time by gambling in the street. J.W. Galbraith wrote to his family from Purcell the day after the run. The letter, shown here, reads in part: "I could see them for six miles. There was one widow lady who made the race from this point; she had one mile to make, she make it like a hero. She jumped off her pony, raised her flag, and fired off her pistol, as much as to say I am lord and master of this ranch." (CCHS.)

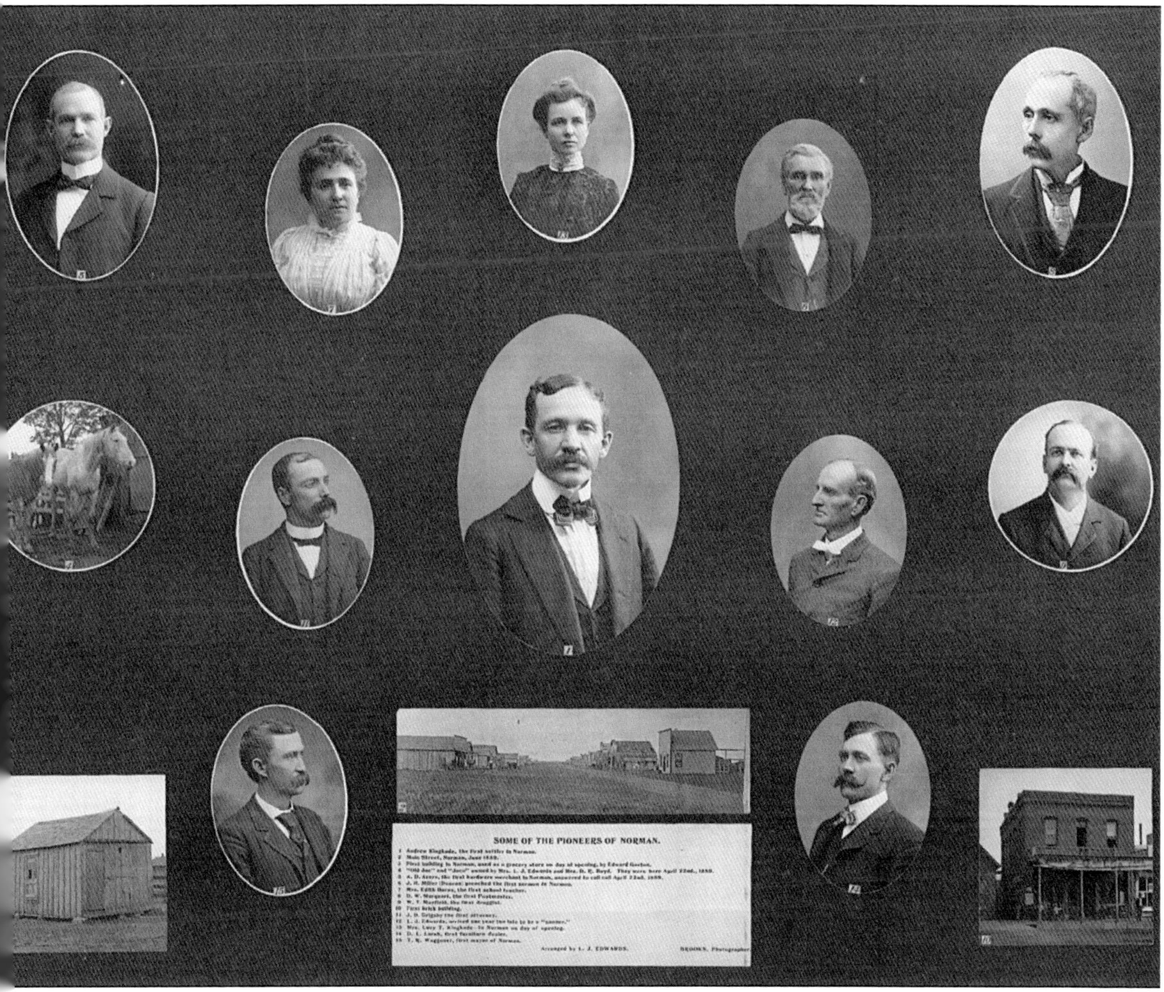


L.J. Edwards was an early Norman businessman and civic leader and, perhaps, Norman's first historian. He compiled this collage of the men and women who made an impact on Norman's early development. The placement of the portraits may suggest the importance Edwards gave each person. In the center is Andrew Kingkade, the first Santa Fe agent at Norman station and Norman's first resident. Other prominent individuals include A.D. Acres (upper left), Norman's first hardware merchant; D.W. Marquart (upper right), Norman's first postmaster; T.R. Waggoner (bottom left), the town's first mayor; and D.L. Larsh (bottom right), Norman's first furniture dealer. The two women are Edith Burns (top row, second from left), Norman schoolteacher, and Lucy T. Kingkade. Following the key Edwards provided, the men of lesser importance are Deacon J.H. Miller (top row, second from right), who preached the first sermon in Norman; W.T. Mayfield (center row, right), the first druggist; and J.D. Grigsby (center row, second from left), the first attorney. Edwards (center row, second from right) added his own portrait to the collage. He is known today for the park named after him, which was later renamed James Garner Plaza. Edwards is a part of Legacy Trail. (CCHS.)

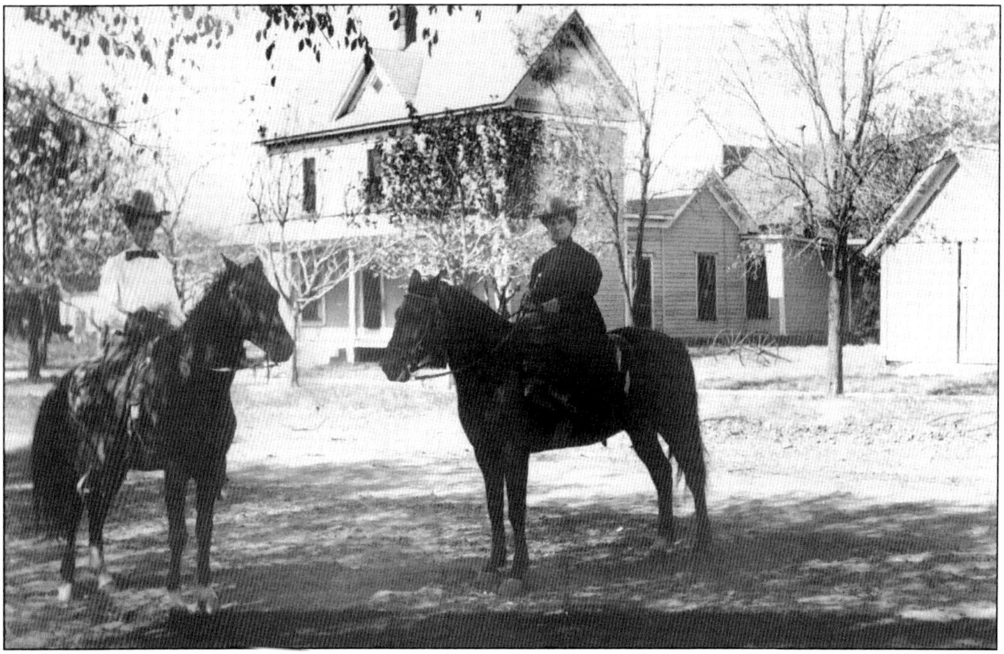

Martha Giles (right) is sitting on the saddle she used in the land run in 1889, now displayed at Moore-Lindsay Historical House. In the background is her residence. William Cary Renfrow, who was appointed territorial governor in 1892 by Pres. Grover Cleveland, built the house, at the corner of Crawford Avenue and Comanche Street, as his residence. Renfrow invested in Norman real estate and was president of Norman State Bank. The woman on the left is unidentified. (CCHS.)

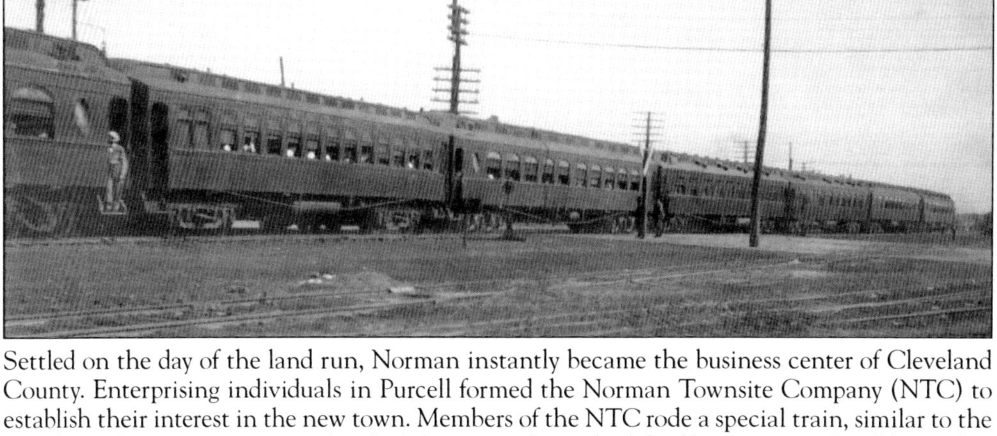

Settled on the day of the land run, Norman instantly became the business center of Cleveland County. Enterprising individuals in Purcell formed the Norman Townsite Company (NTC) to establish their interest in the new town. Members of the NTC rode a special train, similar to the one shown here, to Norman and staked their town lots, which had been surveyed and located in advance by employees of the Achison, Topeka & Santa Fe Railroad. (CCHS.)

Albert Rennie was a lawyer and prominent member of the Norman Townsite Company. He wrote the agreement establishing the company, which was signed by the members. It listed rules and obligations of those who sought townsites. The agreement became the governing covenant for the new town. Delbert L. Larsh, Santa Fe station agent in Purcell, organized the first meeting of the NTC in Purcell before the run on April 2. (CCHS.)

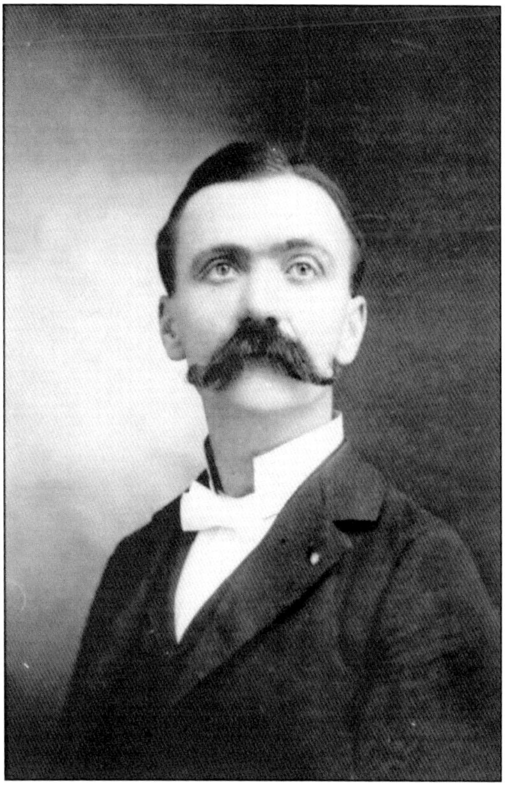

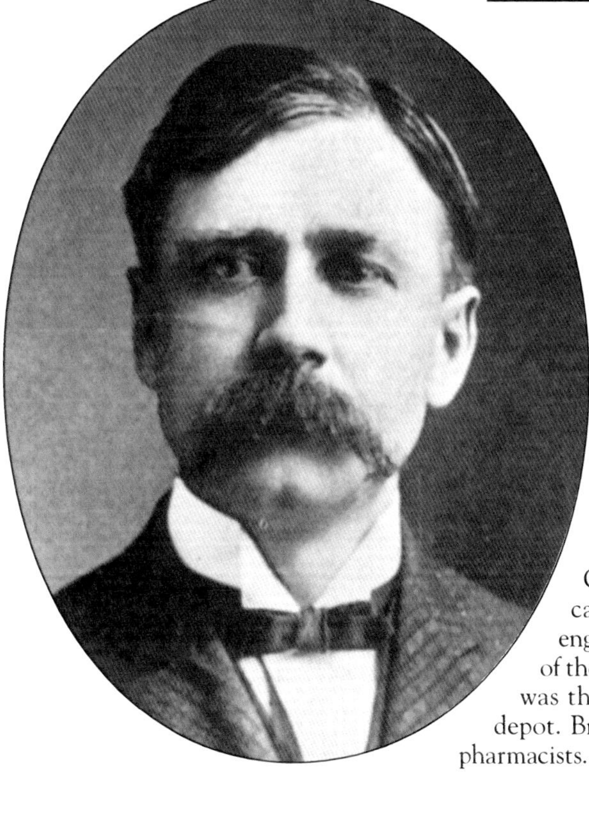

Along with Delbert Larsh, shown here, the men of the NTC came from varied backgrounds. Pryor Adkins and Charles T. Gorton were Chickasaw cattlemen. John Helvie was a Santa Fe engineer. Edward P. Ingle was the publisher of the *Purcell Register*. Thomas R. Waggoner was the chief clerk and cashier of Purcell's depot. Brothers Tyler and George Blake were pharmacists. (CCHS.)

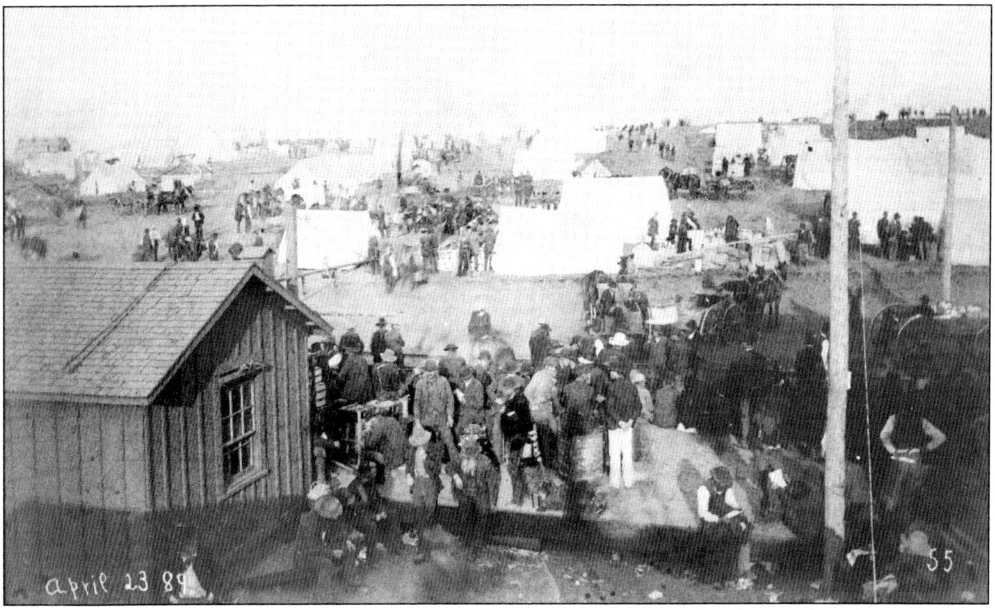


From the first day of settlement, those who acquired agricultural land and town lots demonstrated their initiative and tenacity in developing productive farms and successful businesses. Businessmen who claimed lots on Main Street sold goods from tents until lumber shipped on the Santa Fe could be bought and more permanent buildings established. (CCHS.)

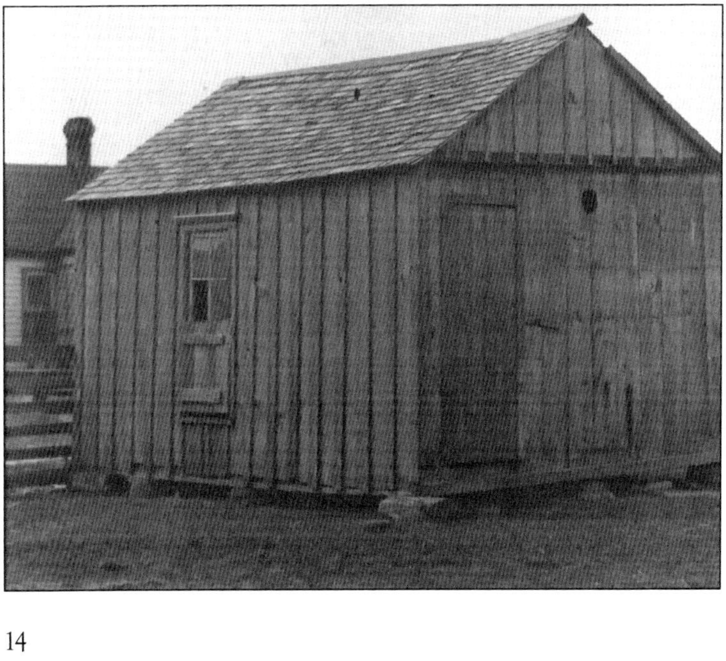

Charles T. Gorton, member of the Norman Townsite Company, had this small building constructed and stored on the south side of the Canadian River. On the day of the run, he moved the building north of the Canadian River into Norman, where he opened for business, selling general merchandise. Gorton's merchandise establishment was the first business in Norman. (CCHS.)

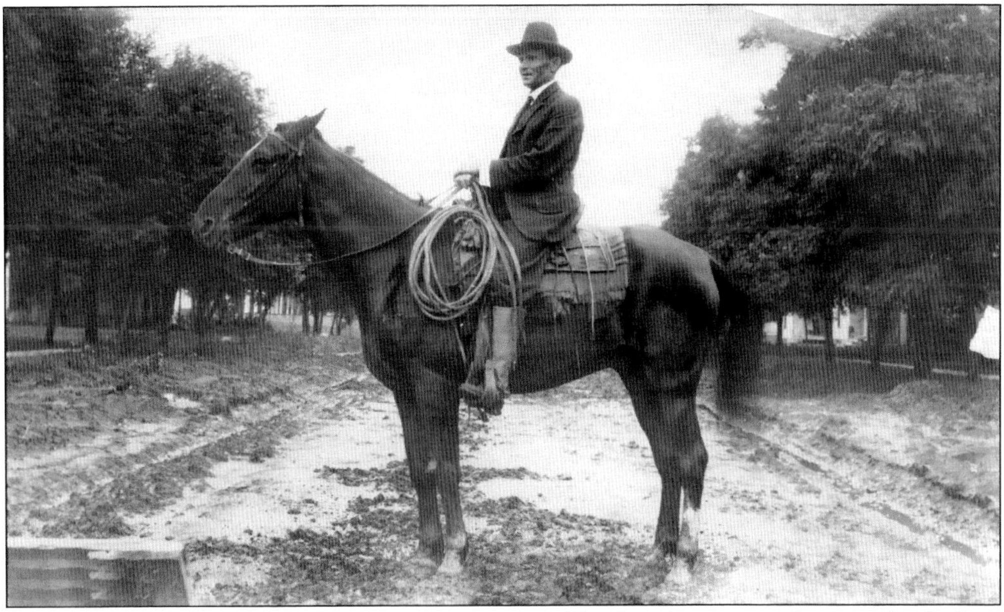

Charles Gorton, seen here, owned a quarter section of land at the corner of present-day Jenkins Avenue and Boyd Street. In 1890, the territorial legislature approved Norman as the site of a university. The site chosen was 20 acres of Gorton's cornfield, in return for which he accepted $2,000. Eventually, the university acquired all of Gorton's land. (CCHS.)

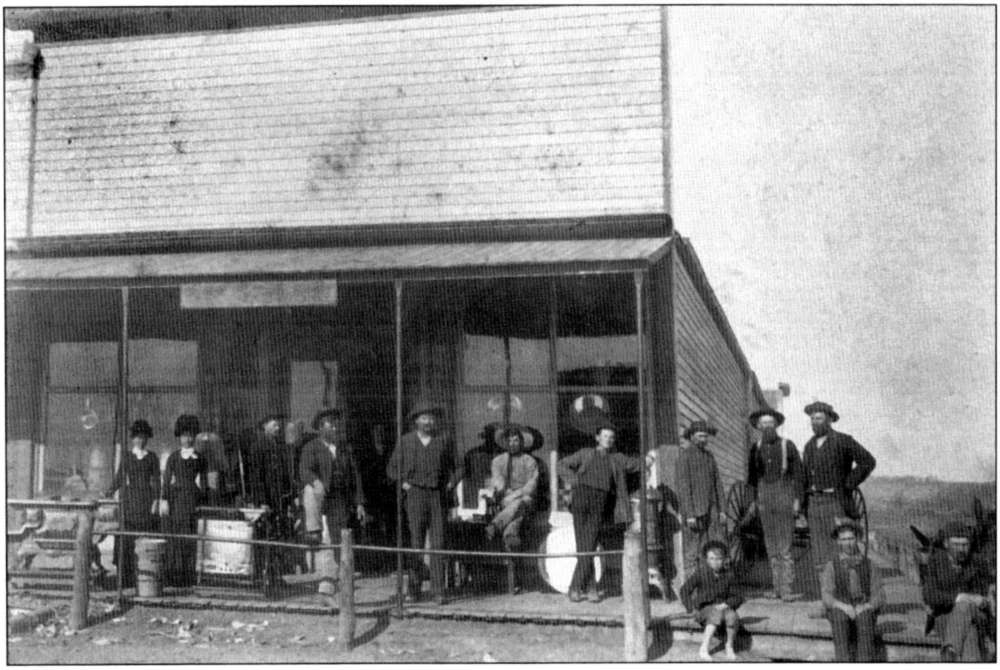

Visible past this hardware store are the wide-open plains beyond Main Street. The false-front building was typical of frame structures on the American frontier. One-story buildings with pitched roofs and false fronts were made to look like two-story buildings. Railroad towns in particular copied the general pattern of Eastern commercial storefronts. Tin ceilings, cast-iron fixtures, and large glass windows were easily transported by the railroad. (CCHS.)

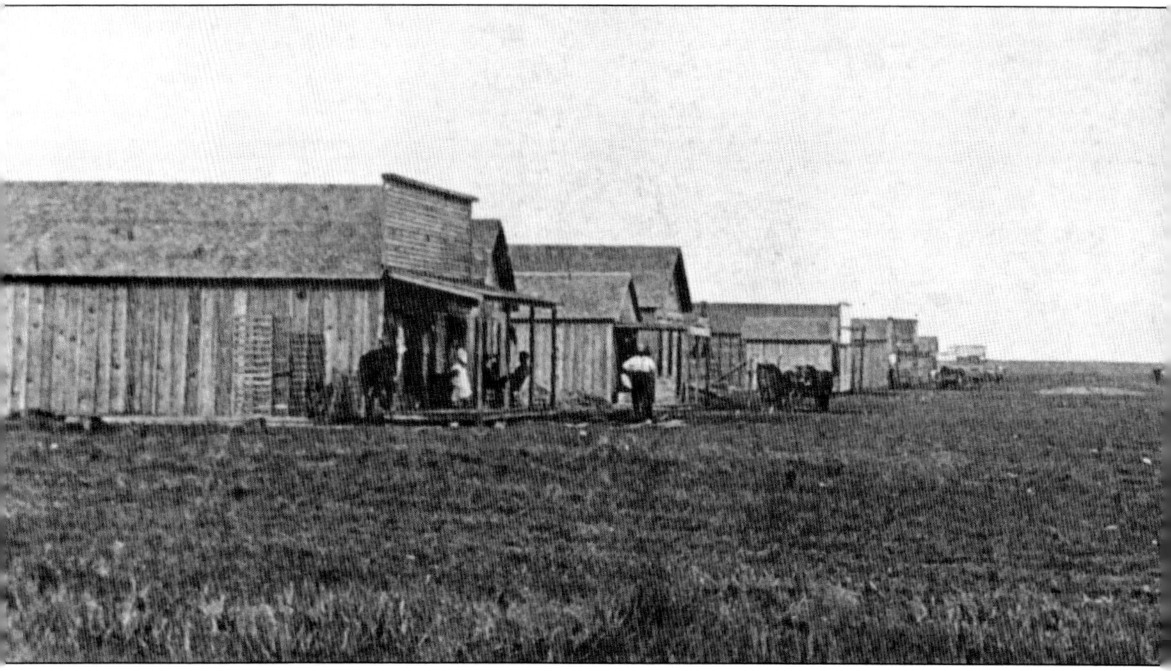

Only two months after the land run, Norman's Main Street was lined with wood-frame buildings. On the siding at the Norman Depot, flatcars of merchandise arrived daily for local merchants, who filled their shelves in anticipation of homesteaders' needs. New business establishments included drugstores, general merchandise stores, liveries and stables, hotels, saloons, eating establishments, and

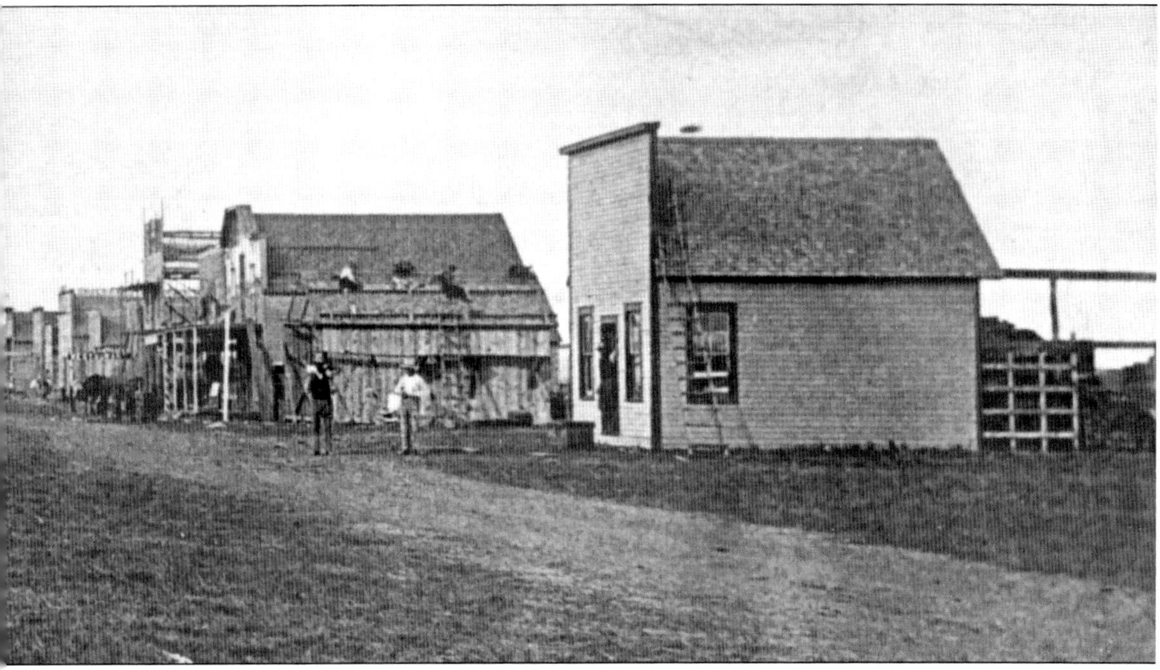

lumberyards. Many of the first wooden buildings were prefabricated structures, box-shaped, measuring 12 feet by 12 feet. The buildings were nailed together at the lumberyard and finished on the merchant's town lot. These structures provided the lot owner with a weatherproof business and enhanced his or her right to the lot, discouraging claim jumpers while claims were being finalized. (CCHS.)

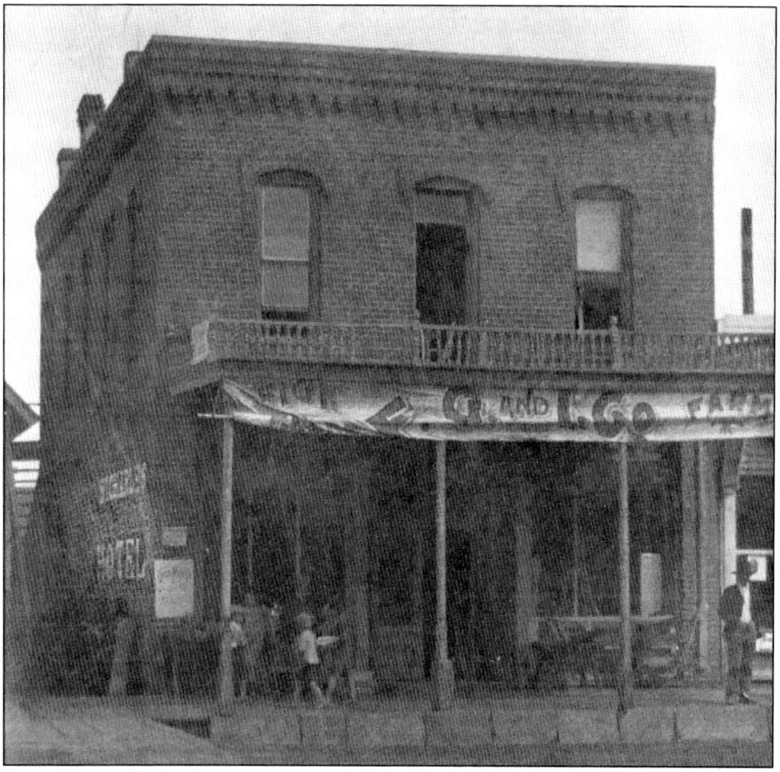

NTC member Pryor Adkins built the Planter's Hotel at 101 East Main Street in May 1889. The hotel was the first brick building in Norman. The brick came from a factory established in Noble, seven miles south of Norman. C.M. West, the first dentist in Norman, rented an office on the second floor. Today, 101 East Main is the site of the Sooner Theatre. (CCHS.)

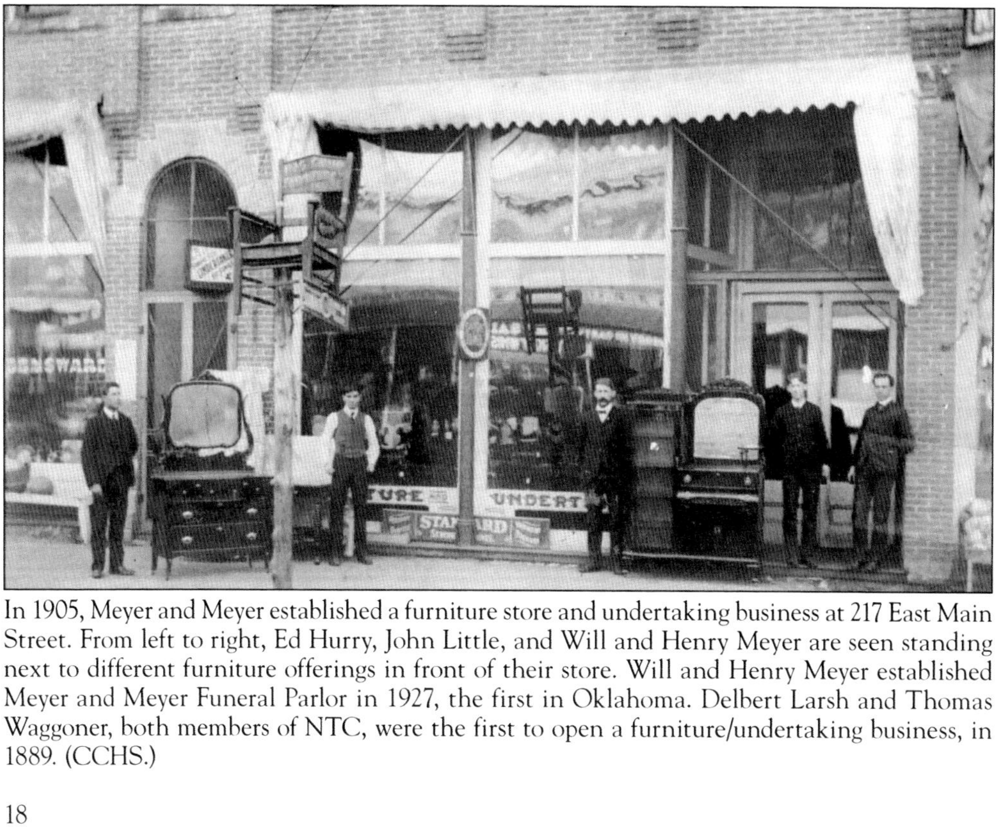

In 1905, Meyer and Meyer established a furniture store and undertaking business at 217 East Main Street. From left to right, Ed Hurry, John Little, and Will and Henry Meyer are seen standing next to different furniture offerings in front of their store. Will and Henry Meyer established Meyer and Meyer Funeral Parlor in 1927, the first in Oklahoma. Delbert Larsh and Thomas Waggoner, both members of NTC, were the first to open a furniture/undertaking business, in 1889. (CCHS.)

Warren T. Mayfield established Pioneer Drug in a tent on Main Street on the day of the run. He later erected the Mayfield Building at 205 East Main Street. Mayfield's oldest son, William, obtained a pharmacy degree in 1918 and joined his father in the business. The second son, Thomas, born in a tent behind the drugstore in September 1889, was the first child born in Norman. (CCHC.)

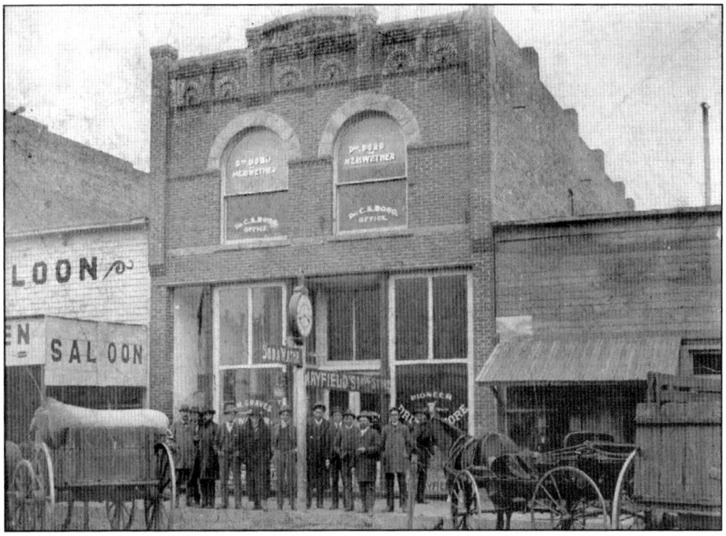


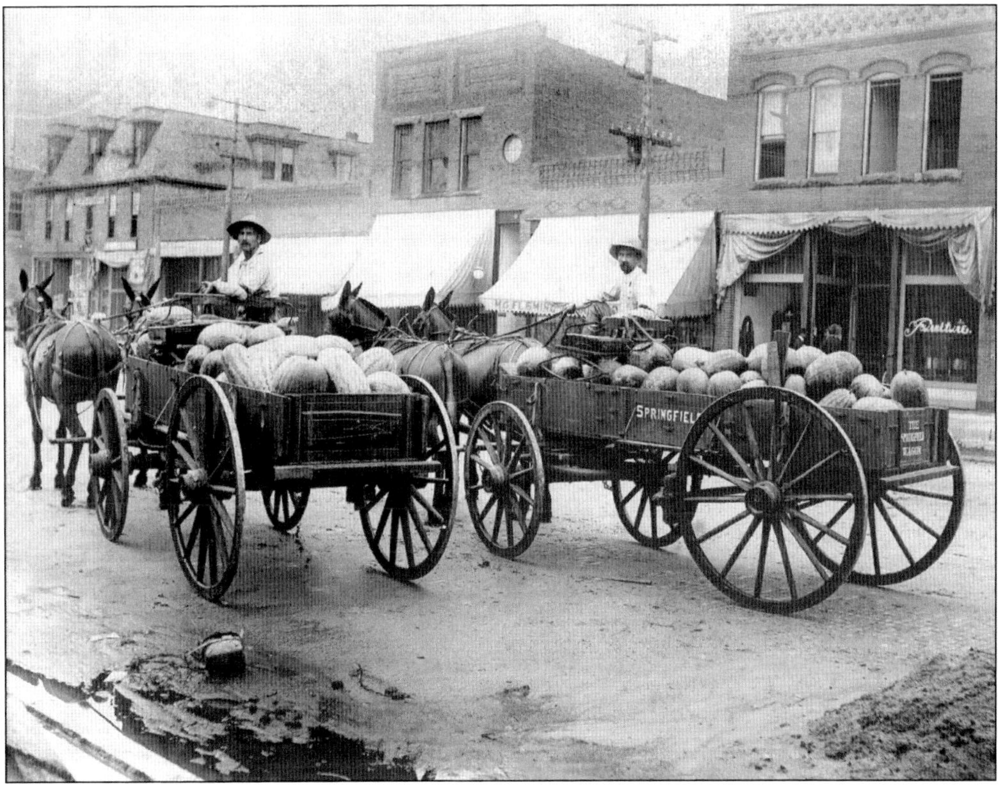


Norman farmers market their watermelons on Main Street. Farmers quickly learned what crops grew best in the red clay soil and semiarid climate of Cleveland County. There was sufficient rain during the first decades of settlement, and watermelons grew in abundance, but only a local market existed for the product. Locally grown strawberries, however, were shipped to markets outside the region. Fleming Grocery is visible in the background. (CCHS.)

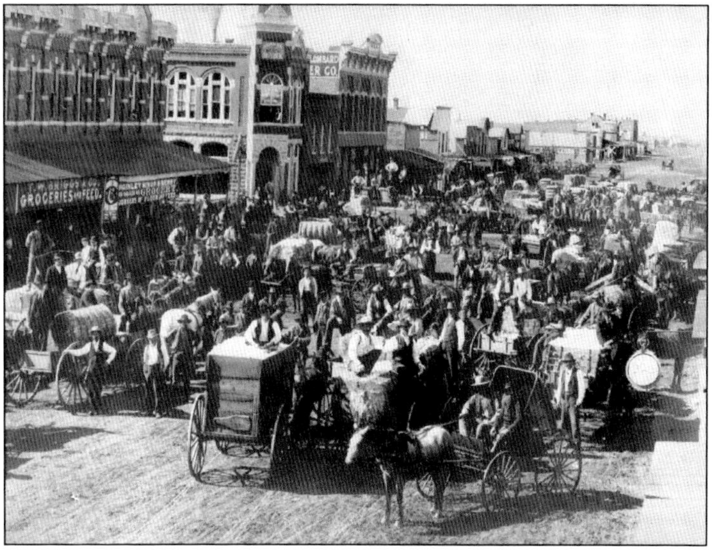

George Lee was the first Norman farmer to raise cotton, which was a very successful crop for local farmers. Because the town did not have a cotton gin, Lee hauled his product to Purcell for ginning. In 1890, J.E. Turner and Company shipped two train cars of cottonseed to Norman. That same year, W.R. Jennison established the town's first cotton gin, west of the Santa Fe tracks and depot. (CCHS.)

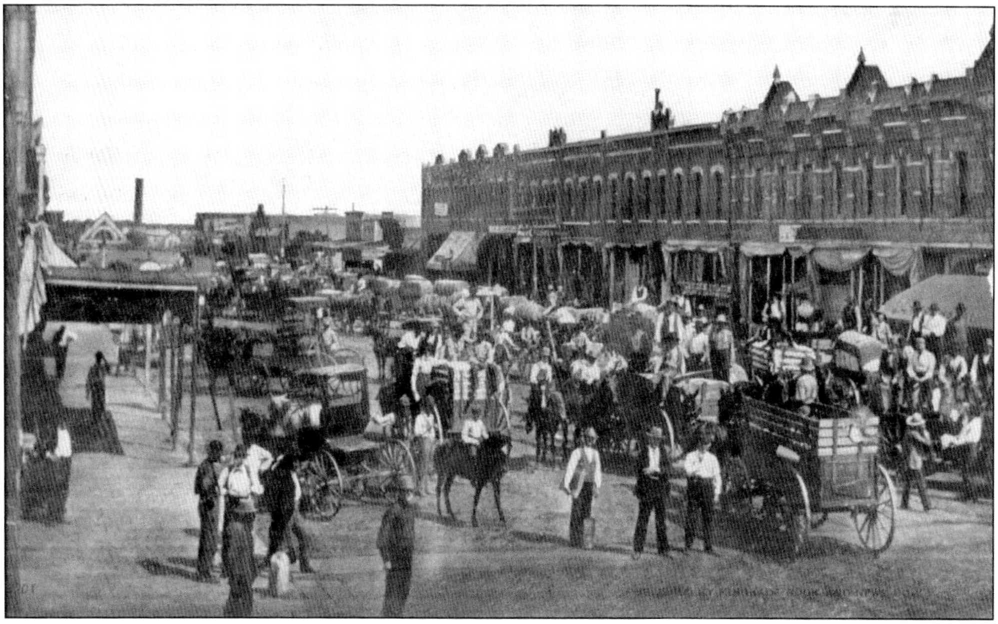

On Saturdays, farmers brought raw cotton to Norman to be ginned and baled. After ginning, owners drove their wagons of baled cotton to Main Street in search of a buyer. Prospective buyers analyzed the cotton's quality by cutting a plug from the bale, then feeling and tasting the product. If the cotton was satisfactory, a bid would be offered. (CCHS.)

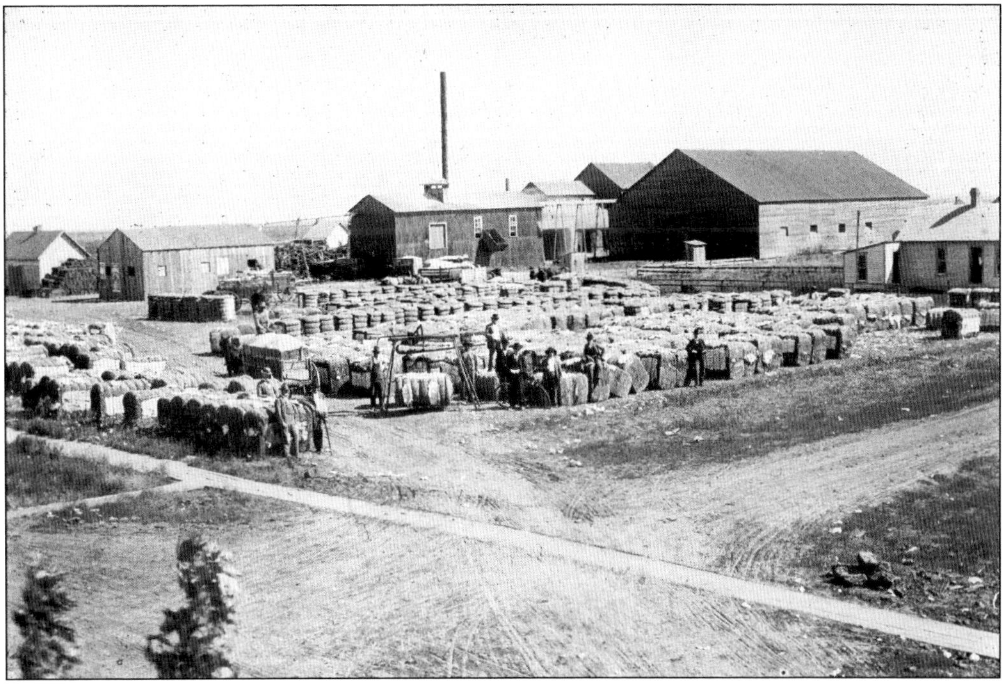

One of Norman's cotton gins was located on West Comanche Street, within a block of the Santa Fe tracks. In 1890, over 2,000 bales of cotton were processed and shipped on the Santa Fe railroad to St. Louis. By 1894, another gin, on East Tonhawa and Front Streets, was established. (CCHS.)

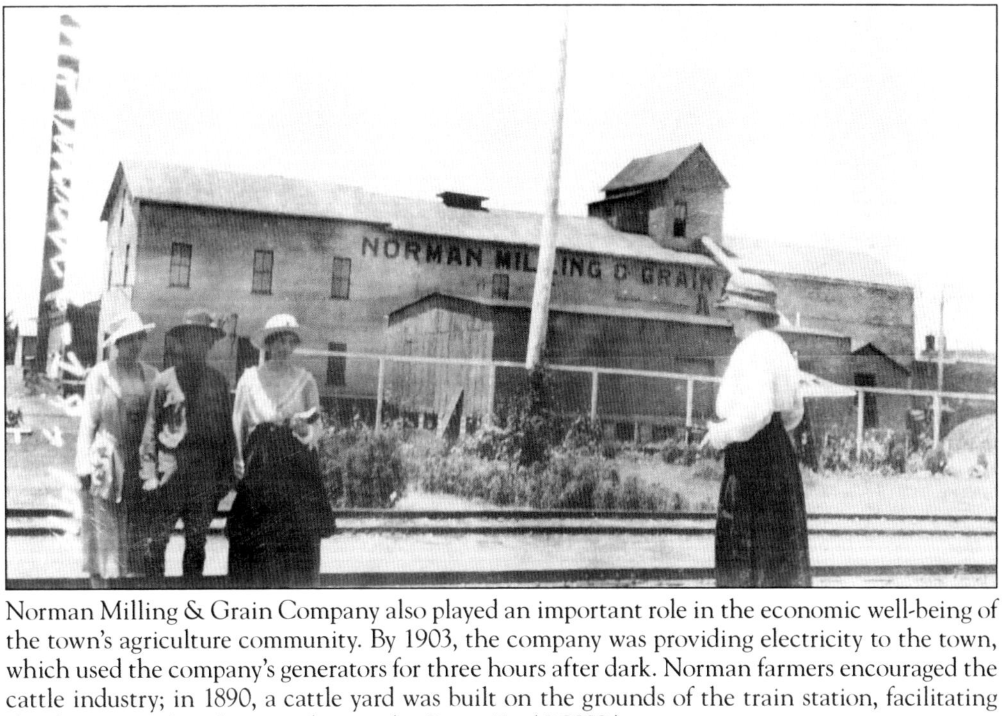


Norman Milling & Grain Company also played an important role in the economic well-being of the town's agriculture community. By 1903, the company was providing electricity to the town, which used the company's generators for three hours after dark. Norman farmers encouraged the cattle industry; in 1890, a cattle yard was built on the grounds of the train station, facilitating the shipment of cattle to market on the Santa Fe. (CCHS.)

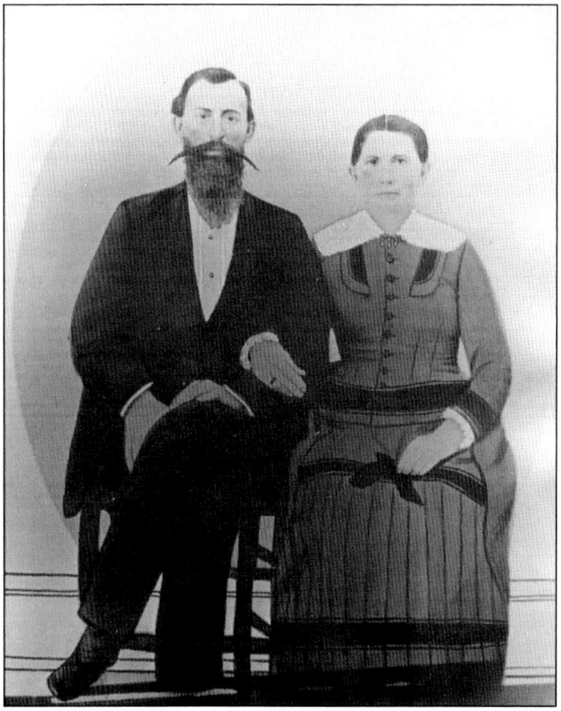

Mr. and Mrs. Levi Briggs exemplify the entrepreneurial spirit of those who settled Norman. Briggs arrived in 1891 and bought several town lots, erecting most of the buildings in the 200–300 block of East Main Street. Briggs and Crado Runyon ran general merchandizing establishments. Briggs, however, spent most of his time as a cotton buyer; he owned interests in gins in several Oklahoma towns. (CCHS.)

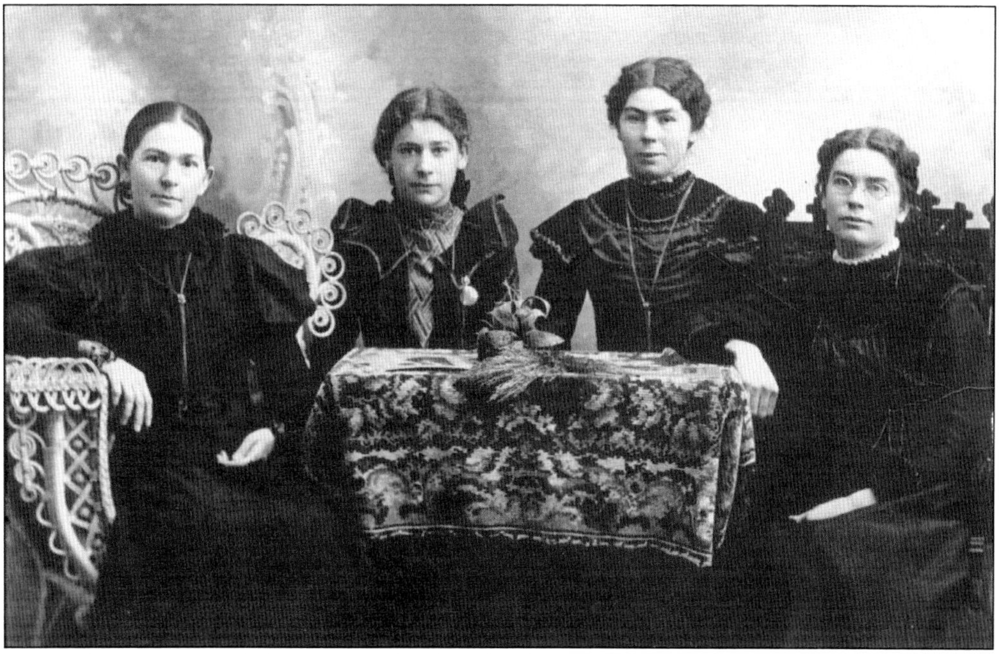

Shown here are, from left to right, the four daughters of Levi Briggs: Malinda, Ollie, Lydia, and Louella. All four women married into leading Norman families at the turn of the 20th century. Malinda married town doctor M.T.J. Capshaw; Ollie married R.E. Clement, financier and deputy Cleveland County treasurer; and Louella married Will Bumgarner. Their grandson, James Bumgarner, became television and movie actor James Garner. Levi Briggs was his great-grandfather. (CCHS.)

*Two*

# CENTER OF COMMERCE

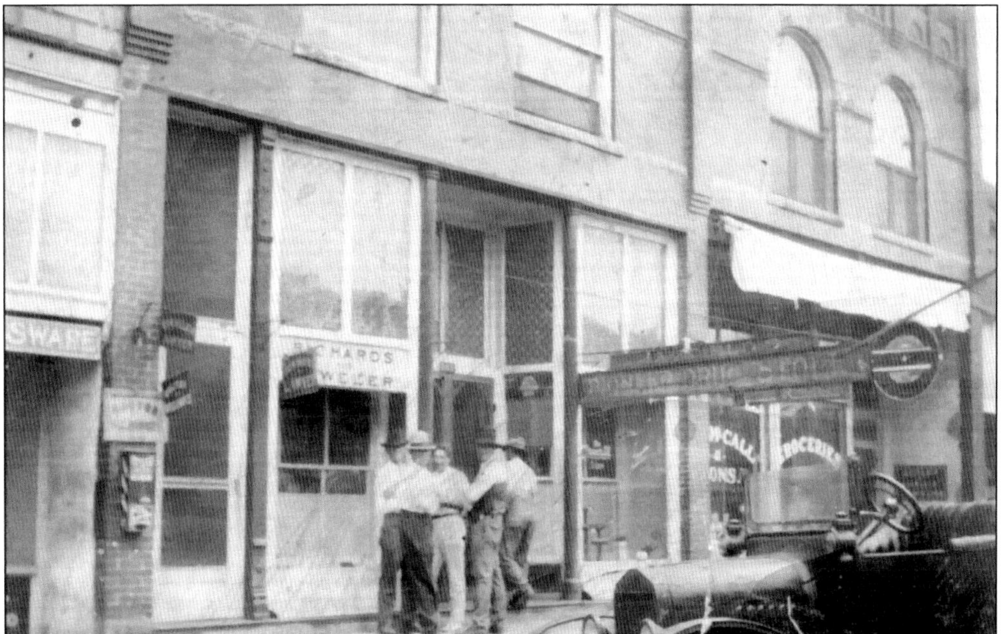

By 1920, Warren Mayfield's Pioneer Drug Store, previously sandwiched between two wooden structures on Main Street, had merged with other brick buildings as Norman matured. Mayfield helped organize the Oklahoma State Pharmaceutical Association and was active in civic affairs. He served on Norman's city council and was a member of the Norman Board of Education. He died in 1914, and the Mayfield building continued in the family until 1970. (CCHS.)

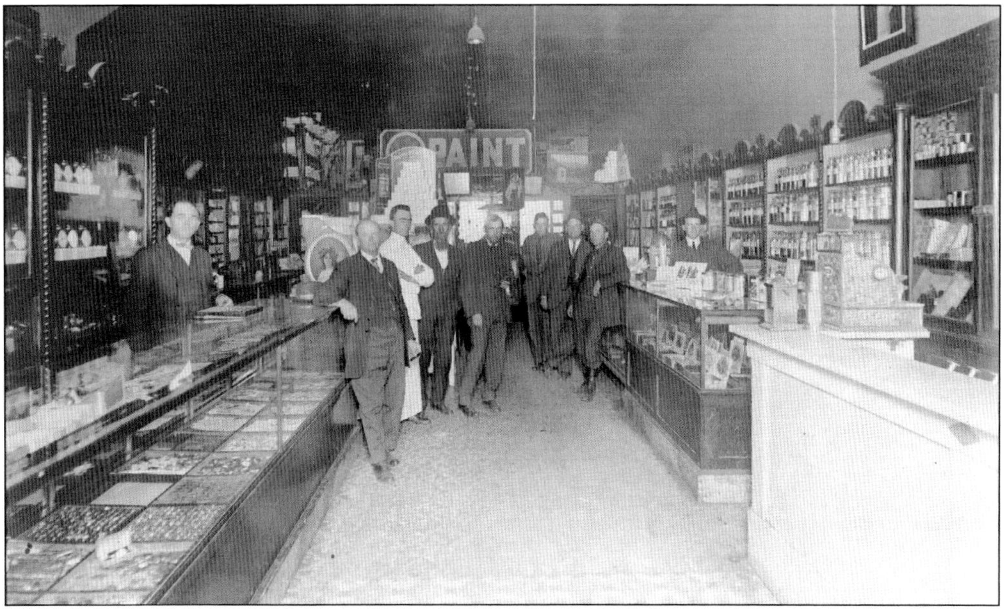


This interior photograph of Mayfield Drug reveals that, besides pharmaceuticals and toiletries, drugstores sold paint, wallpaper, ice, and liquor. The Organic Act, which established Oklahoma territorial government, stipulated that only drugstores could sell liquor, and only if it was used for medicinal and mechanical purposes. To control the use of liquor, the act permitted five drugstores per 1,000 inhabitants. This stipulation was enforced until county commissioners controlled liquor licenses. (CCHS.)

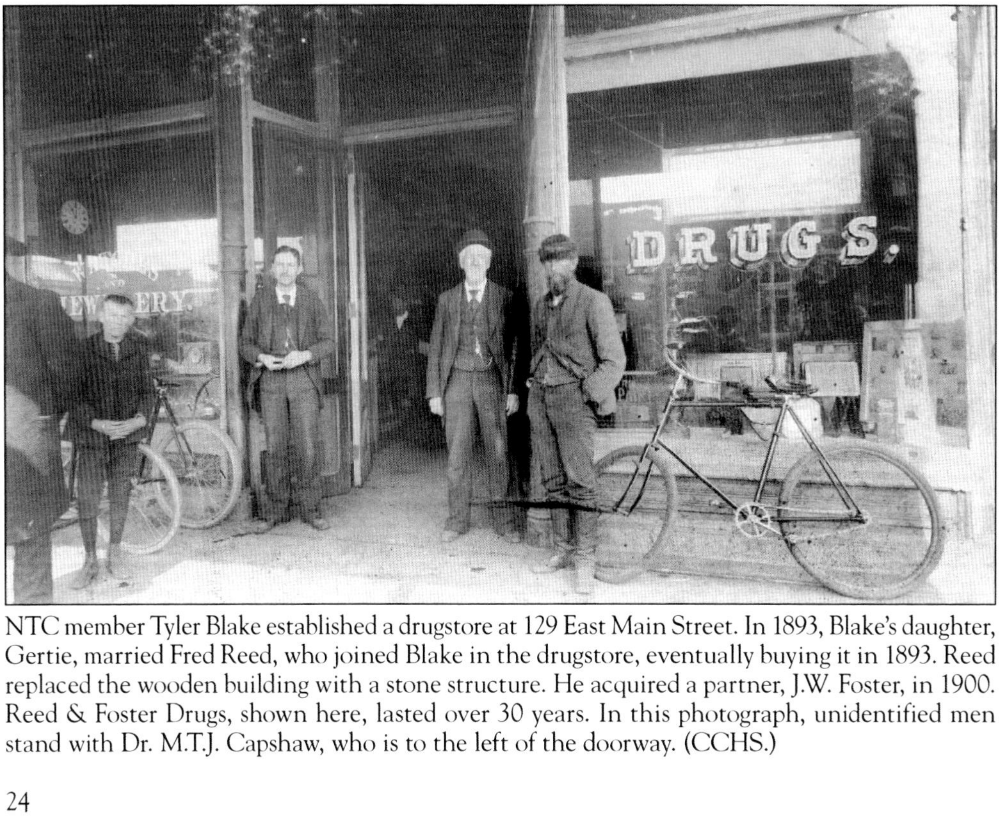


NTC member Tyler Blake established a drugstore at 129 East Main Street. In 1893, Blake's daughter, Gertie, married Fred Reed, who joined Blake in the drugstore, eventually buying it in 1893. Reed replaced the wooden building with a stone structure. He acquired a partner, J.W. Foster, in 1900. Reed & Foster Drugs, shown here, lasted over 30 years. In this photograph, unidentified men stand with Dr. M.T.J. Capshaw, who is to the left of the doorway. (CCHS.)

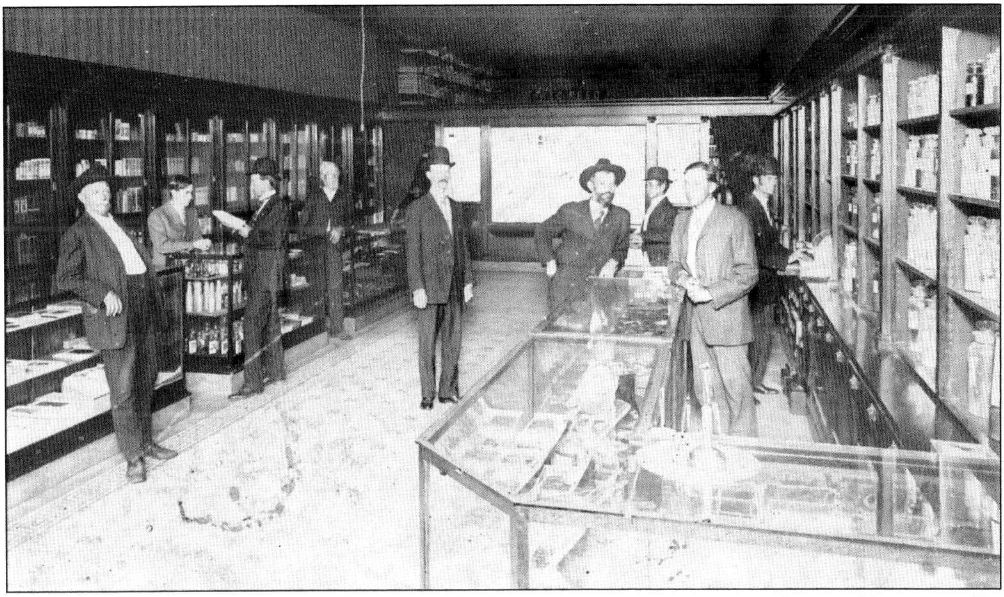

In 1895, Norman residents elected Fred Reed to be town treasurer, a position that paid $50 annually. Reed helped organize the Norman Cornet Band on January 29, 1890. On September 16, 1893, Reed participated in the land run into the Cherokee Outlet, as did many other Norman citizens. As veterans of the Norman land run, they knew the opportunity of a quick financial gain. Here, unidentified men stand in Reed's drugstore. (CCHS.)

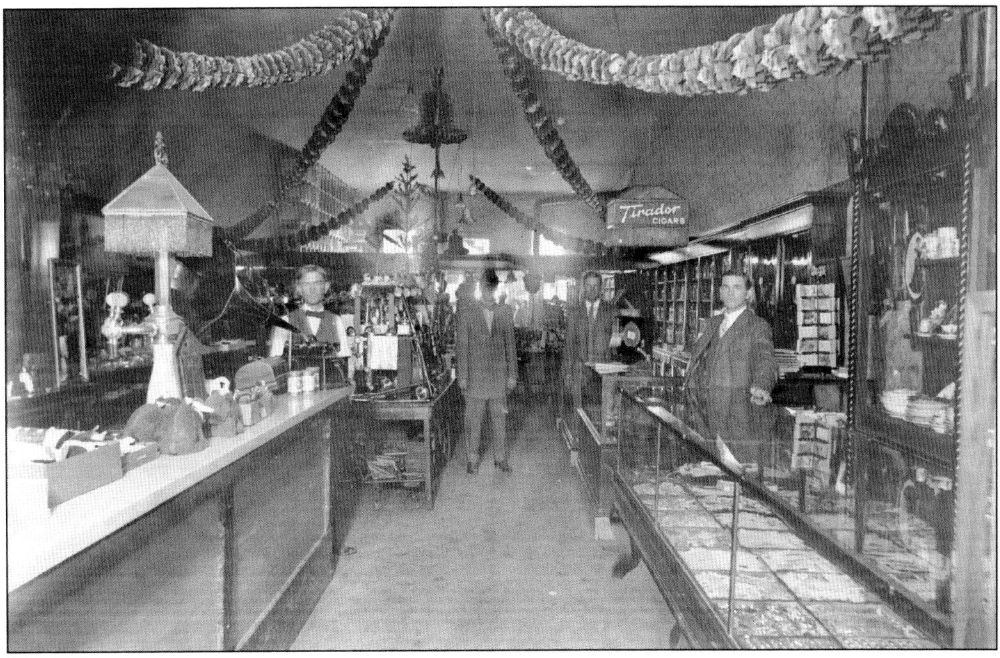


Rae Paese Lindsay (left) established Lindsay's Drug Store at 269 East Main Street in 1907. Lindsay was one of three brothers who moved to Norman in 1896 from St. Joseph, Missouri. The Rae Lindsay family lived on North Peters Avenue in "Silk Stocking Row." Rae's brother Harry Ginter Lindsay lived in what is now the Moore-Lindsay Historical House, at 508 North Peters Avenue. All three brothers were active in business and civic affairs. (CCHS.)

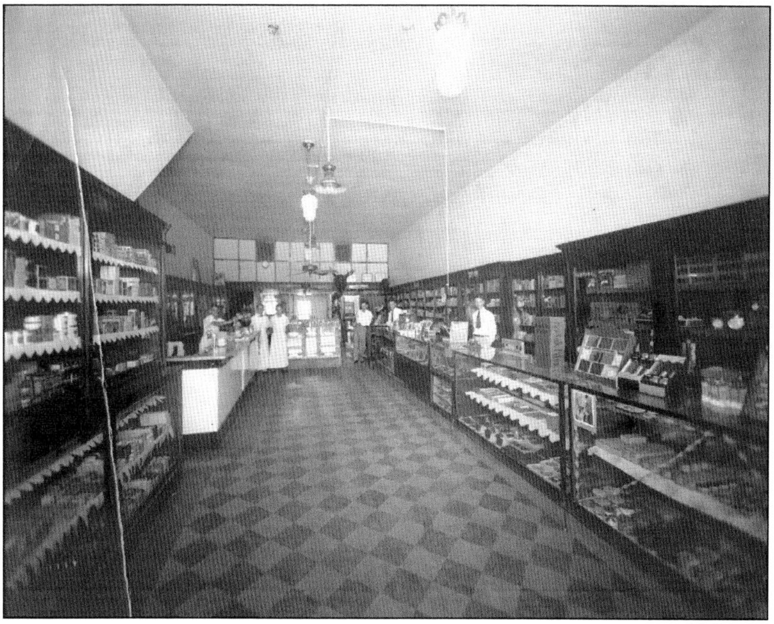

Many of the first Norman businesses survived for over 30 years. Rae Lindsay maintained his drugstore on Main Street until 1926, when he sold it to James S. Downing, seen here standing under the moose head at the rear of the store. Downing's partner in the drugstore was Miller Thompson (right). (CCHS.)

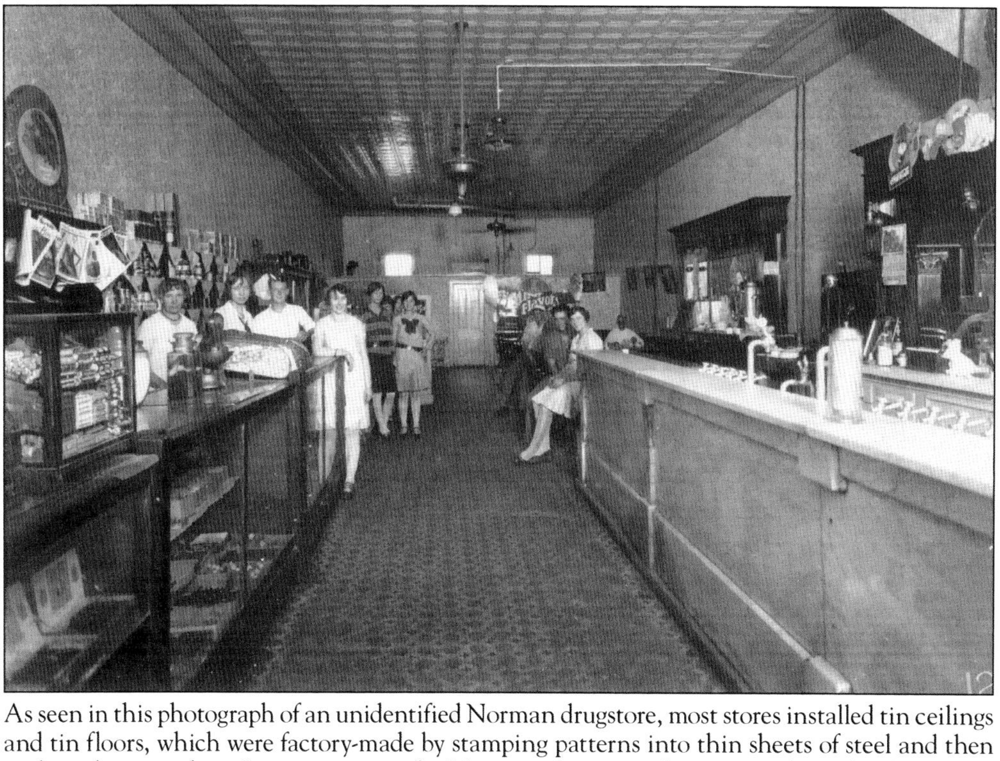

As seen in this photograph of an unidentified Norman drugstore, most stores installed tin ceilings and tin floors, which were factory-made by stamping patterns into thin sheets of steel and then nailing them in place. It was common for Victorian homes to have tin ceilings for decoration and to cover cracked plaster. There were several tin shops in Norman, and McGuire's Hardware employed a tinsmith. (CCHS.)

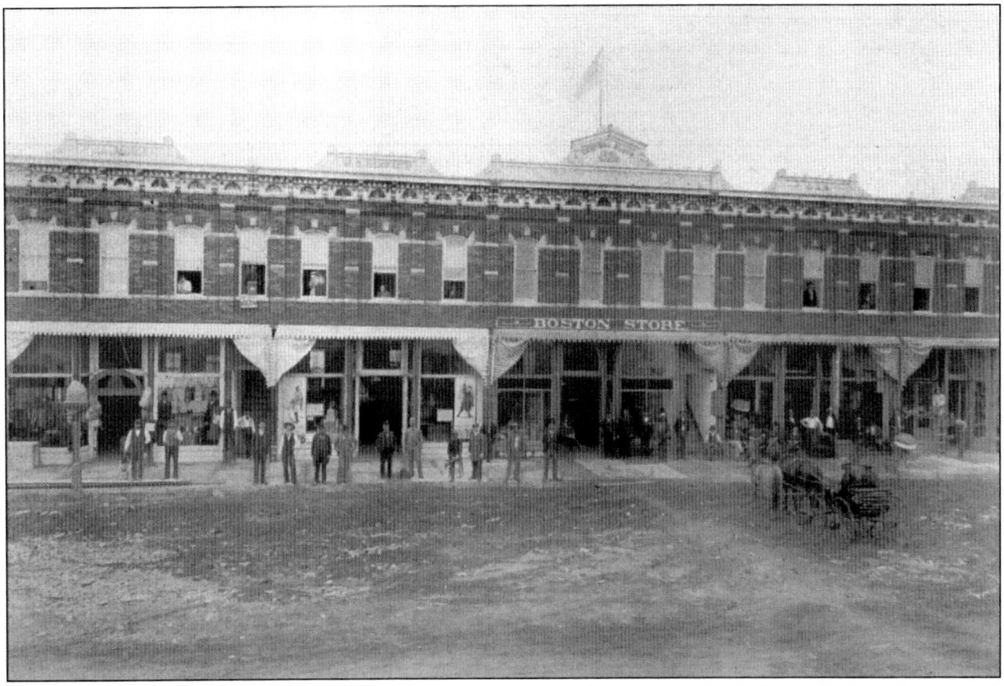


In 1900, The Boston Store occupied a space in what was known as the "Central Block," from 219 to 227 East Main Street on the thoroughfare's north side. The Boston Store was a dry-goods store that had its headquarters in Milwaukee, Wisconsin. One of the first retailers to offer departments, the store displayed dry goods, shoes, ready-to-wear clothes, and furniture. The Boston Store also carried a catalog for mail-order business. (CCHS.)

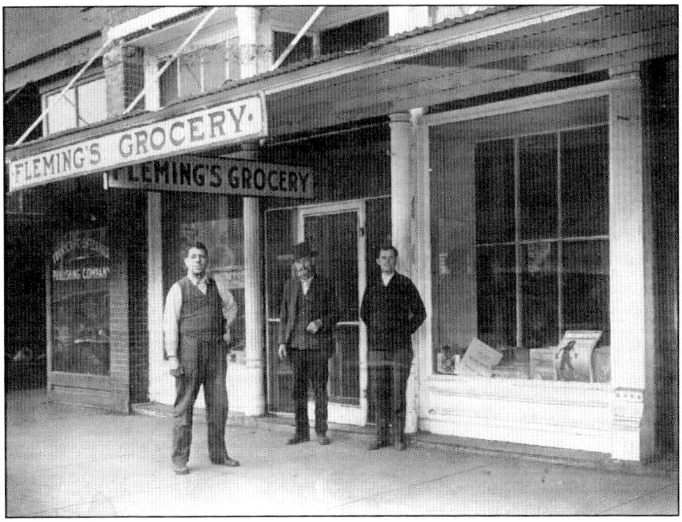


Ben Fleming (right) stands with unidentified men in front of Fleming's Grocery, next to the Transcript Enterprise Publishing Company. Edward P. Ingle, NTC member, published the first issue of the *Norman Transcript* in July 1889, two days after the *Norman Advance*'s debut. Ingle was born in Staffordshire, England, in 1858. A farmer by trade, he moved his family to Purcell in 1888 and started the *Purcell Register*. (CCHS.)

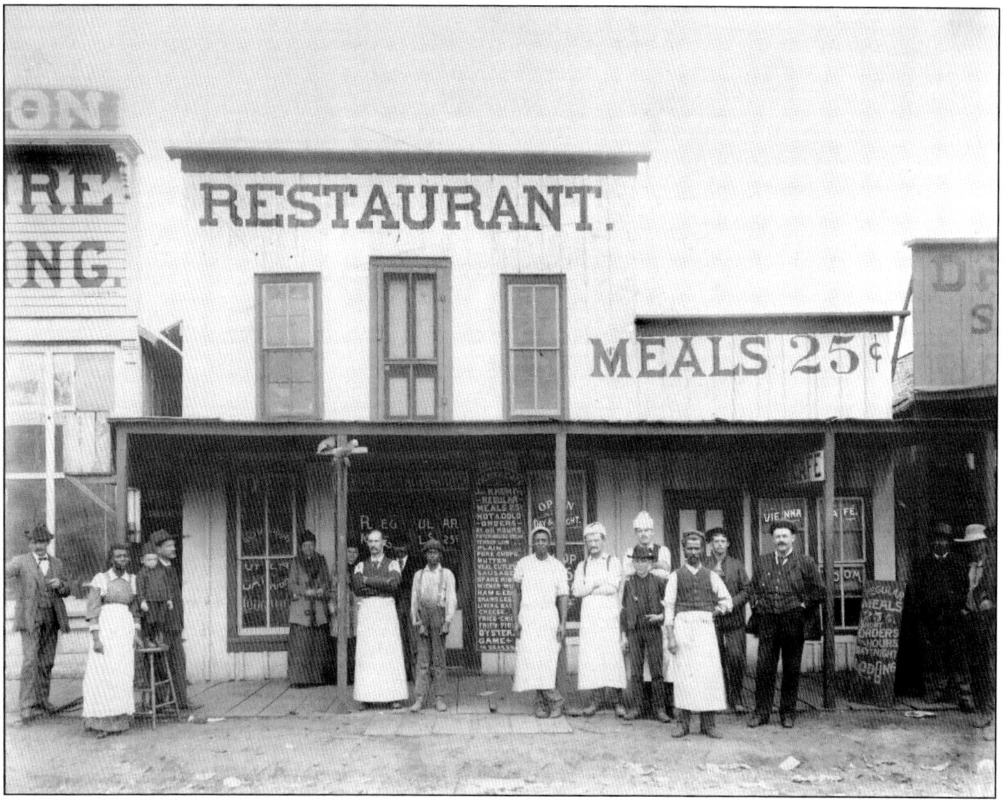


Joe E. Heim (center, arms crossed) owned the Vienna Café. The restaurant/rooming house offered room and board and was open 24 hours a day. The café's menu offered a wide variety of meals for 25¢, hot or cold. The meals featured porterhouse steak, tenderloin, pork chops, mutton, veal, ham, cheese, fried chicken, cheese and oysters, and in-season game. (CCHS.)

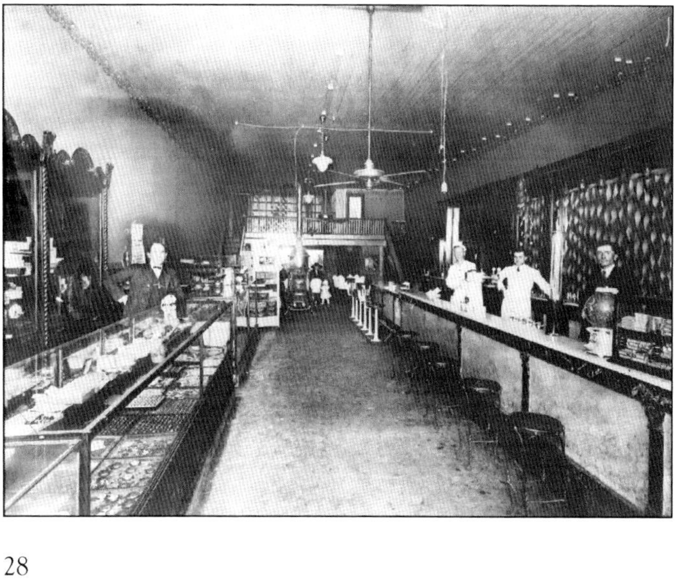

Davis Confectionery and Soda Fountain, which was available for dances and receptions, was known as the "student resort." In 1767, Joseph Priestly of Leeds, England, learned how to create an effervescence of mineral water by infusing carbon dioxide into water. By the 20th century, innovation in pumping devices to carbonate water made soda drinks a popular addition to pharmacies, restaurants, and candy stores. (CCHS.)

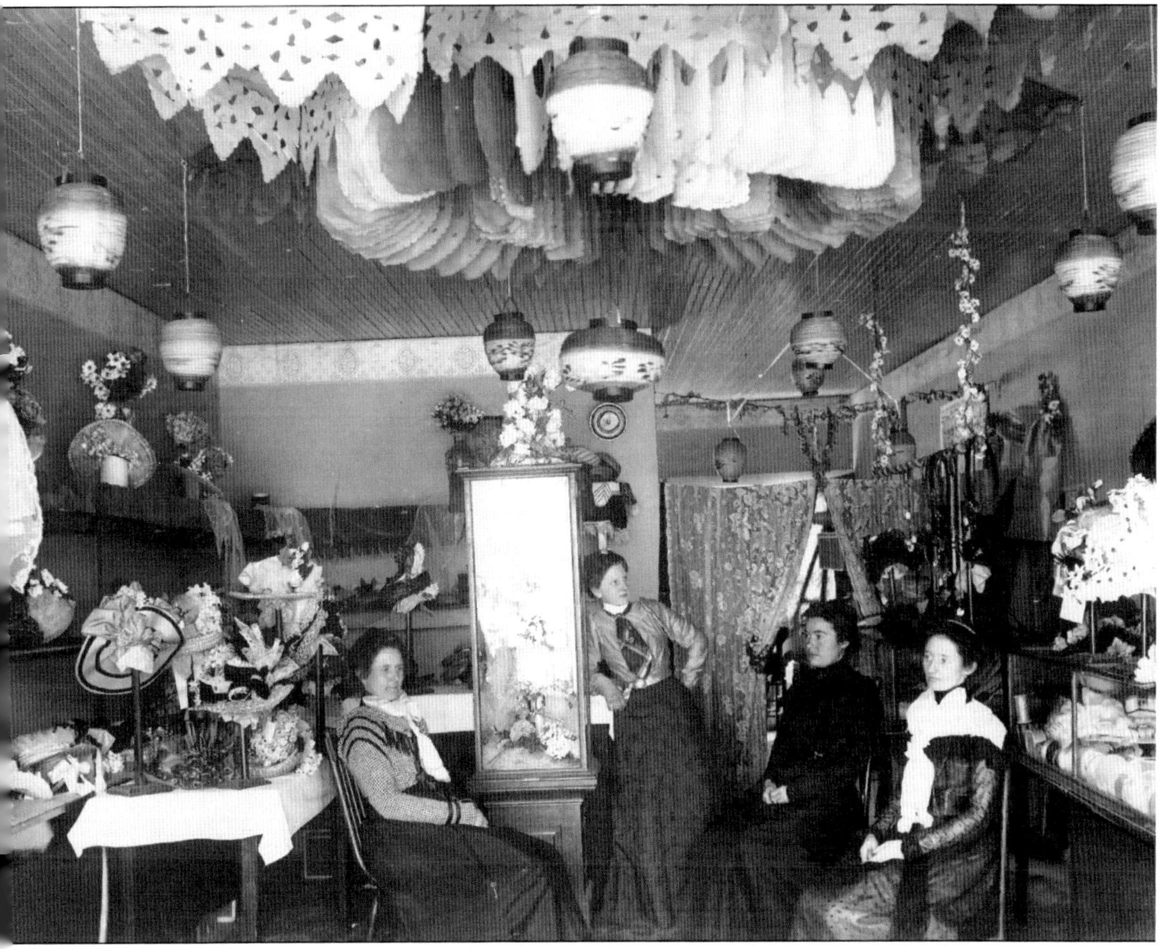

Callie Graham (center, hand on hip) was one of several successful businesswomen in Norman. Her brother, Isaac Graham, moved to the Chickasaw Nation from Chillicothe, Missouri, in 1878 and worked on a ranch as a cowboy. Upon hearing his favorable reports of the area, his father, Robert Graham, moved the entire family, including Isaac's sisters, Callie, Hattie, and Mollie, to Indian Territory. During the land run of 1889, Robert and his sisters staked claims to four-quarter sections. A house was built at the intersection of the four sections, with one room on each respective corner. Mollie married Edward Johnson, the son of Chickasaw cattleman Montford T. Johnson. Callie and Hattie opened Graham's Millinery Shop at 224 East Main Street. Edward Johnson bought the Victoria Hotel, renamed it the Arline Hotel, and asked Callie to manage it. She successfully ran the business and chaperoned female university students who lived at the hotel. Hattie fell ill, and Callie quit and moved her sister to Arizona, where Callie taught in a Native American school. The sisters never returned to Norman. (CCHS.)

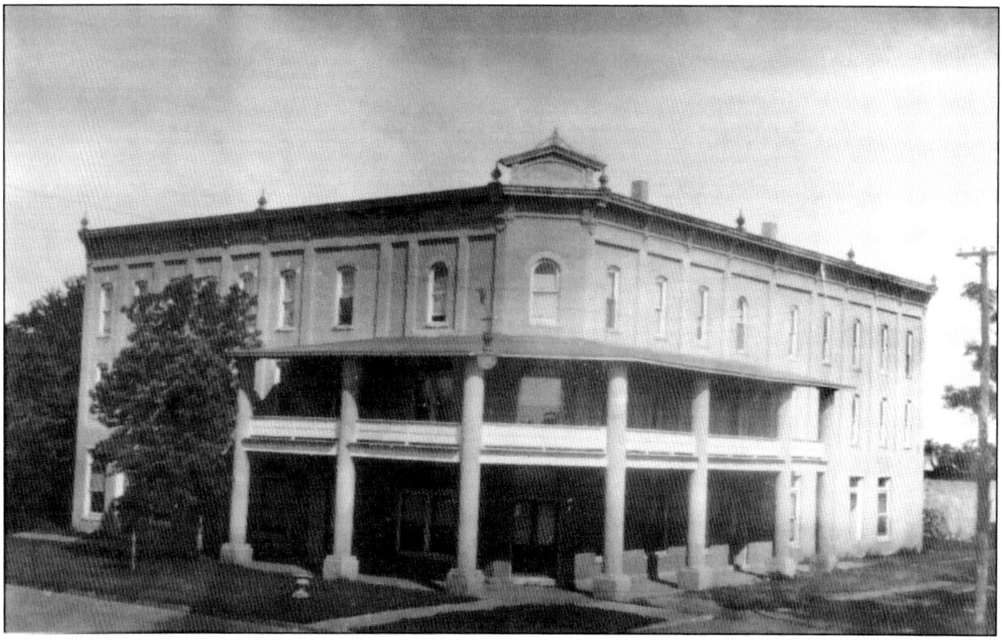

Edward Johnson bought the Victoria Hotel, on the corner of West Main Street and Webster Avenue, in 1894. He renamed the hotel Arline House, after his daughter. The hotel was within walking distance of the University of Oklahoma. The first floor housed offices, a restaurant kitchen, and a dining hall. In 1914, the hotel became the First Christian Church, which lasted until 1928. (CCHS.)

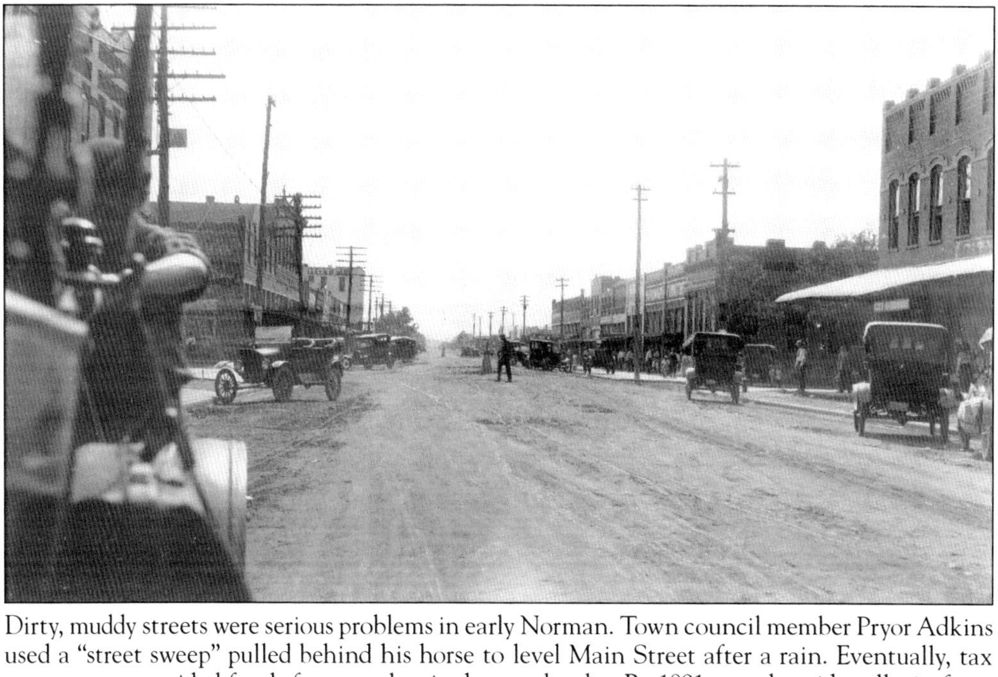

Dirty, muddy streets were serious problems in early Norman. Town council member Pryor Adkins used a "street sweep" pulled behind his horse to level Main Street after a rain. Eventually, tax assessments provided funds for a mechanized street leveler. By 1891, wooden sidewalks in front of all businesses on Main Street were mandatory. By 1913, the city council contracted for paving Main Street, Boyd Street, and Muskogee Boulevard. (CCHS.)

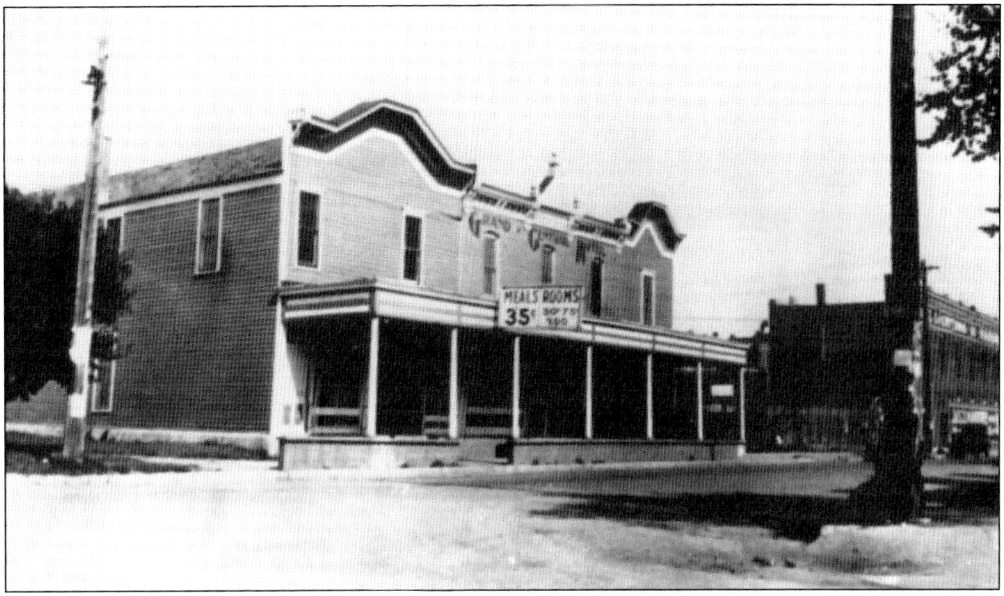


The Grand Central Hotel, built around 1893, stood on the southeast corner of Gray Street and Peters Avenue, two blocks from the Santa Fe depot. In the Great Depression of the 1930s, Norman authorities took over the abandoned hotel, using it to provide shelter for homeless families, many of whom had arrived in Norman looking for work. A heating stove provided warmth, and mattresses were placed on the floor for sleeping. (CCHS.)

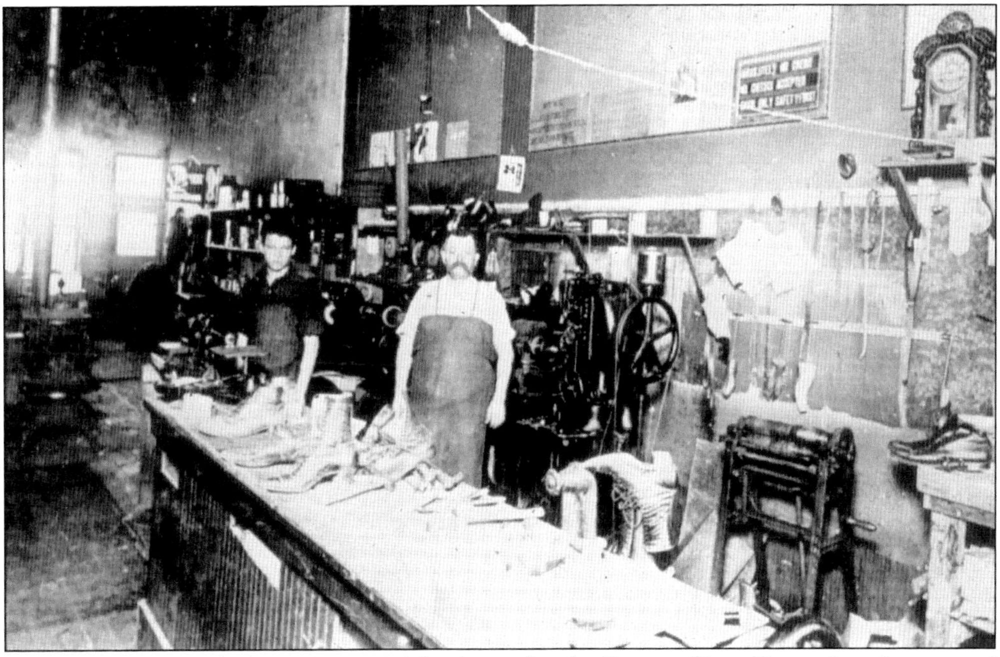

This 1909 photograph shows August Miller (center) in his Pioneer Shoe Shop, where he repaired and made shoes for citizens of Norman and Cleveland County. In 1889, shoemakers found a ready market in Norman. However, with the advance of technology in the early 20th century, the once essential profession of shoemaker quickly became a lost art as ready-made shoes flooded the market. (CCHS.)

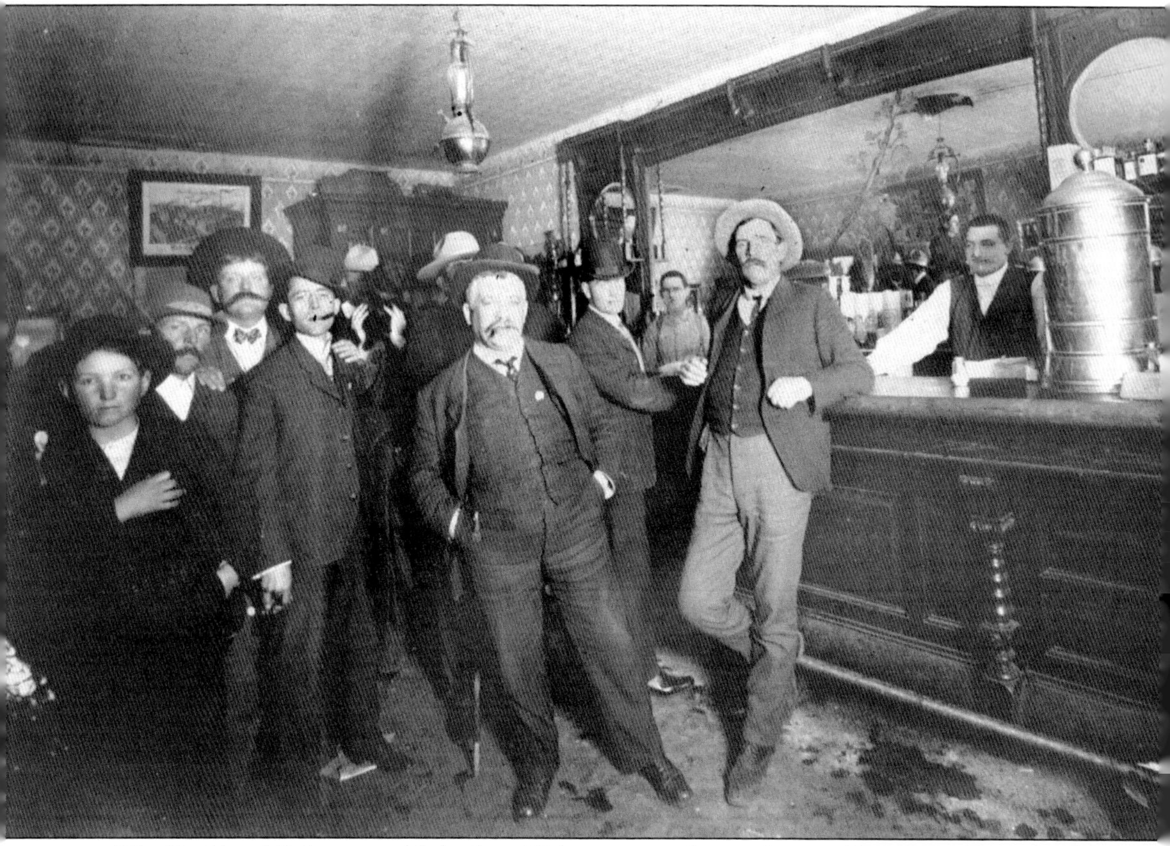

The Buckhead Saloon, established in 1901, was one of many bars in Norman. When the first president of the University of Oklahoma, David Ross Boyd, stepped down from the coach of the Santa Fe train in Norman in 1893, he looked southwest across an open field of prairie grass, to a location where the new university would be built. All he saw was a well-trodden cowboy trail, which he later learned led to a ranch headquarters near the Canadian River. Thirsty cowboys working in the dry Chickasaw Nation often traveled to Norman to buy liquor. Boyd wrote that cowboys enjoyed drinking at any one of 15 saloons in town. After the territorial legislature authorized county commissioners to grant liquor licenses to anyone with a good character and $200, saloons took the place of drugstores in dispensing liquor. Since liquor was not allowed in any of the Indian Nations, Norman did a booming business until dry statehood, when Progressive politicians in 1907 outlawed the manufacture and sale of alcohol in the state constitution. (CCHS.)

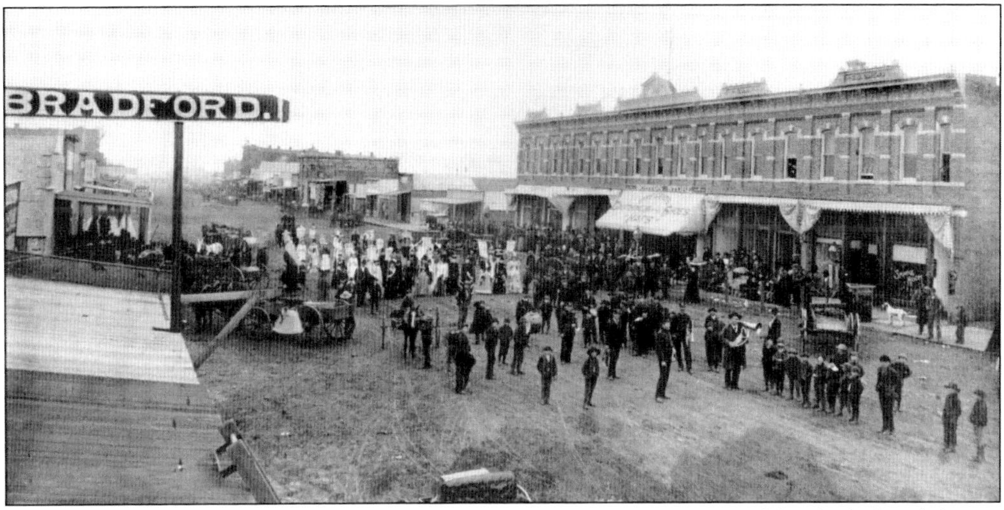


In 1888, the Women's Christian Temperance Union (WCTU) campaigned for alcohol prohibition in Indian Territory. By 1900, the WCTU was in most towns in Oklahoma Territory. The WCTU parade on Main Street in downtown Norman, shown here, indicates prohibition activity in Cleveland County. Carry Nation, prohibition advocate known for her propensity to use a hatchet to destroy saloons, was in Oklahoma when this photograph was taken. It may be her leading this parade. (CCHS.)

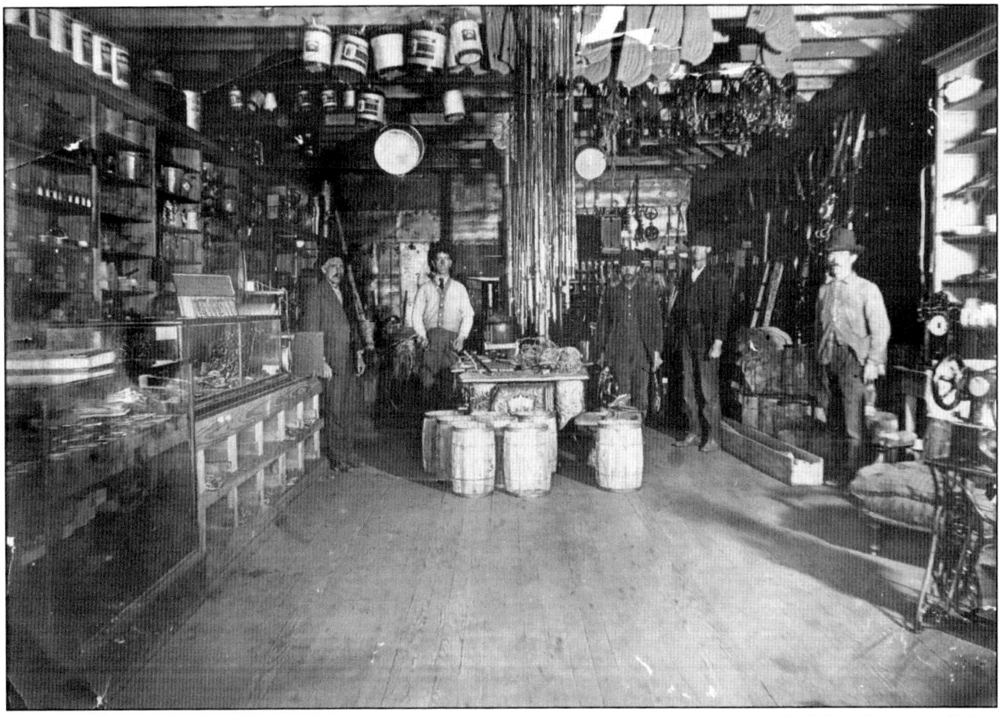

There were probably as many harness shops as drugstores in Norman in 1900. Until automobiles completely replaced horses, wagons and buggies were the primary modes of transportation. Most travel before 1920 required harness shops. The stores also provided cattle feed, barrels of nails, cooking and heating stoves, coffee pots and pans, buckets, washtubs, buggy harnesses, cowboy tack, bridles, and farm implements. (CCHS.)

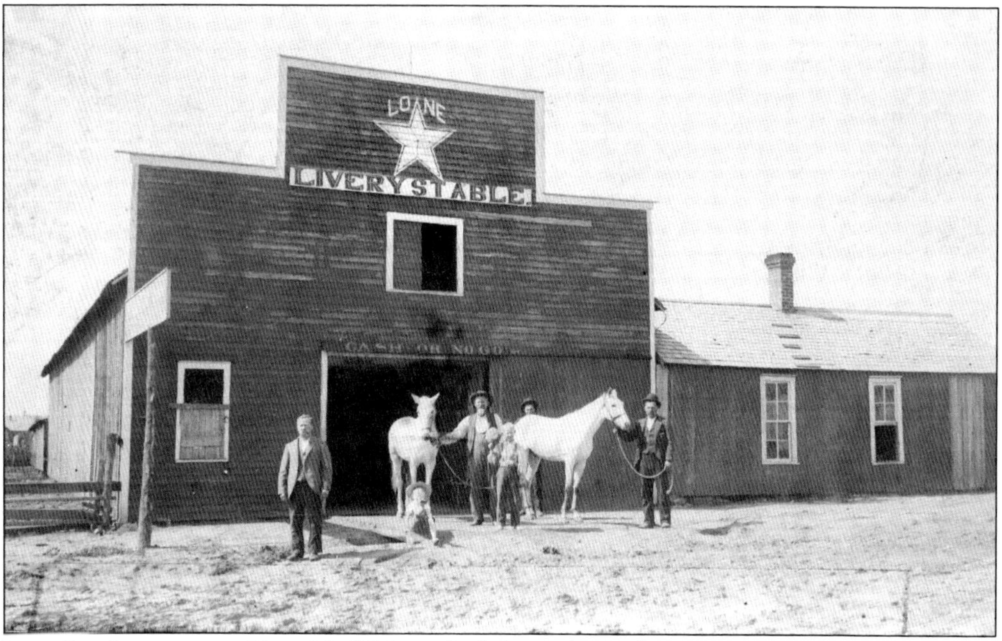


Lone Star Livery, owned by a Mr. Webster (right), was located on Gray Street, just east of Peters Avenue. Livery stables boarded horses for guests staying at one of the hotels and rented horses and buggies to locals. The sign above the door of Mr. Webster's livery indicated his attitude toward financial transactions: "Cash, or No Go." There were at least four livery stables in Norman in 1894. (CCHS.)

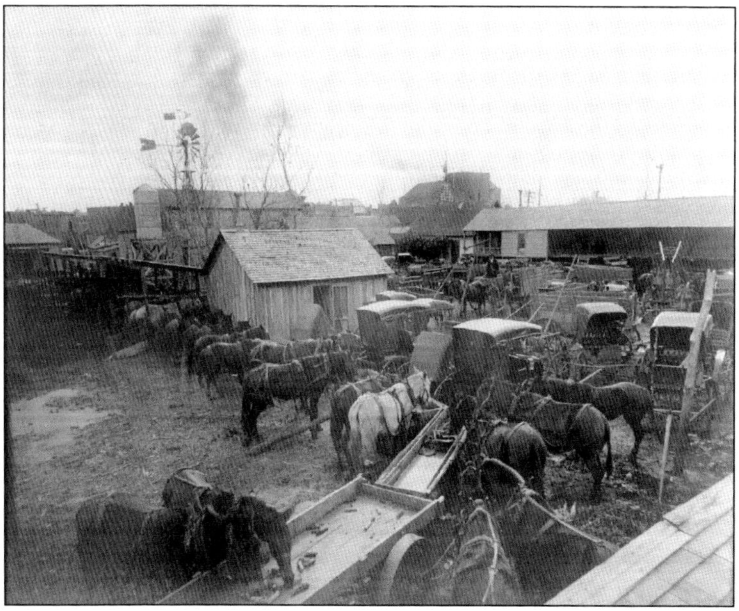

Norman's wagon yards were the parking lots and garages of their day. Most were located on either side of Main Street, one block north or south, and several were located within walking distance to downtown shopping. Emma Coleman, who took many of the photographs of early Norman, had a studio on Crawford Avenue, next to this wagon yard. (CCHS.)

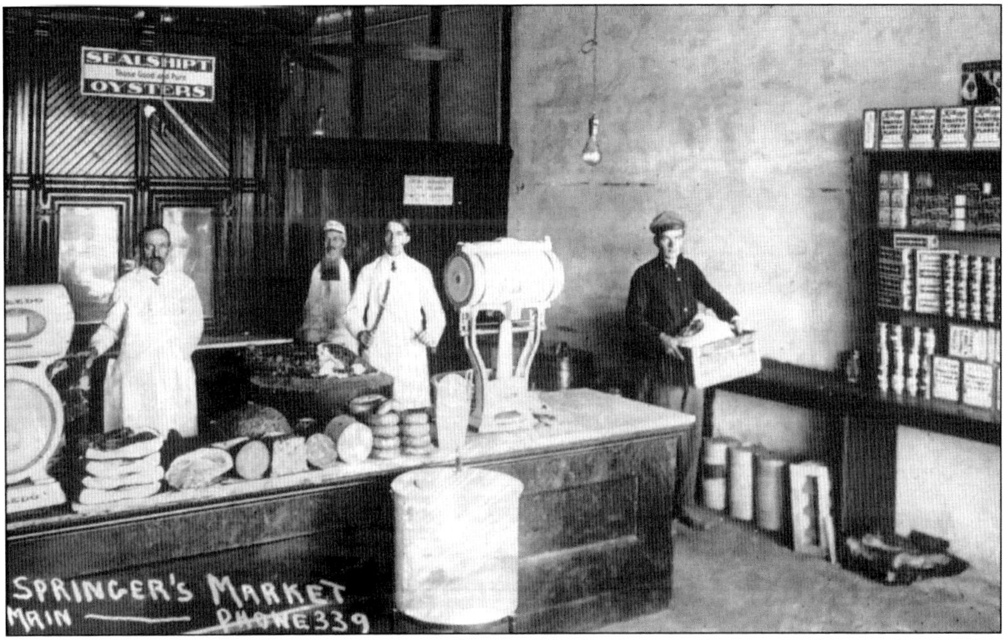

Springer's Market provided meat and manufactured food items. As the sign indicates, the market also sold oysters, as did other grocers in town. Oysters were one of the most popular foods in the 19th century and were prepared in a variety of ways: creamed, frizzled, deviled, in the shell, oyster cocktail, kabobs, and on toast. (CCHS.)

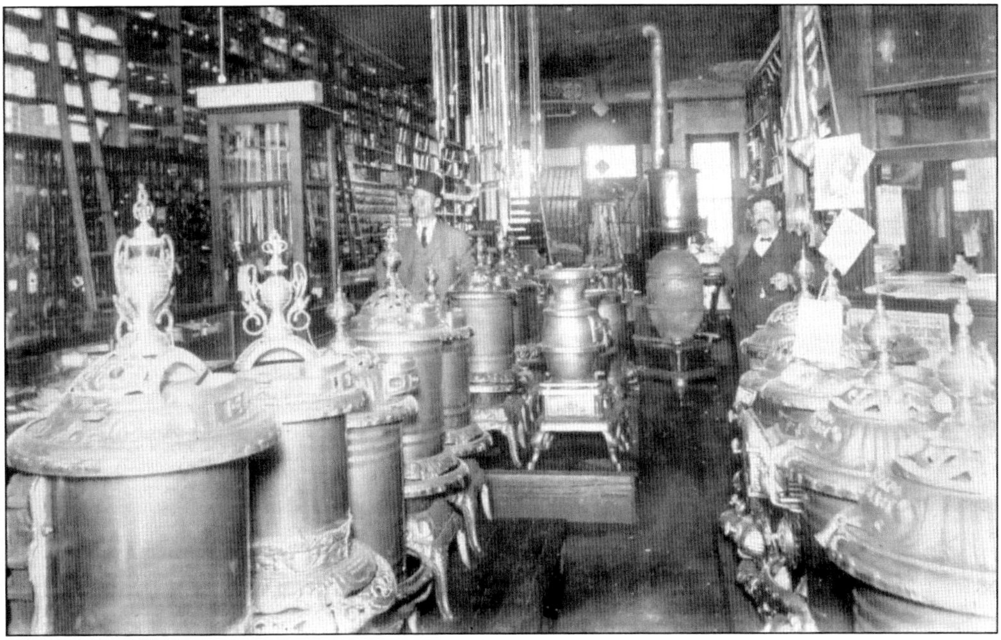
Nolan-Martin Hardware specialized in home heating stoves. Anthony Nolan had established a store in Purcell, but moved to the 100 block of West Main Street in Norman after the land run. He eventually sold his store and went to work for McGuire Hardware. In 1909, along with his brother-in-law, Owen J. Martin, he purchased Carry-Lombard Hardware and changed the name to Nolan-Martin. In 1898, Nolan served as city clerk. (CCHS.)

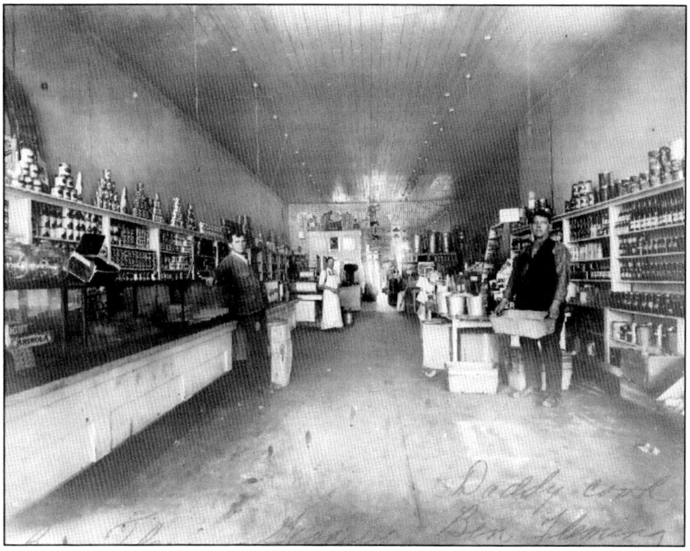

Ben Fleming (right) and "Dad" Cook pose in Fleming's Grocery. Early-20th-century Norman grocery stores took advantage of commercial canning and bottling. Food items that were once shipped in 200-pound barrels were now more readily available in cans, boxes, and bottles. Fleming's Grocery reflects this technological advance. The modern store had a meat department and displayed seasonal vegetables and locally grown fruits. (CCHS.)

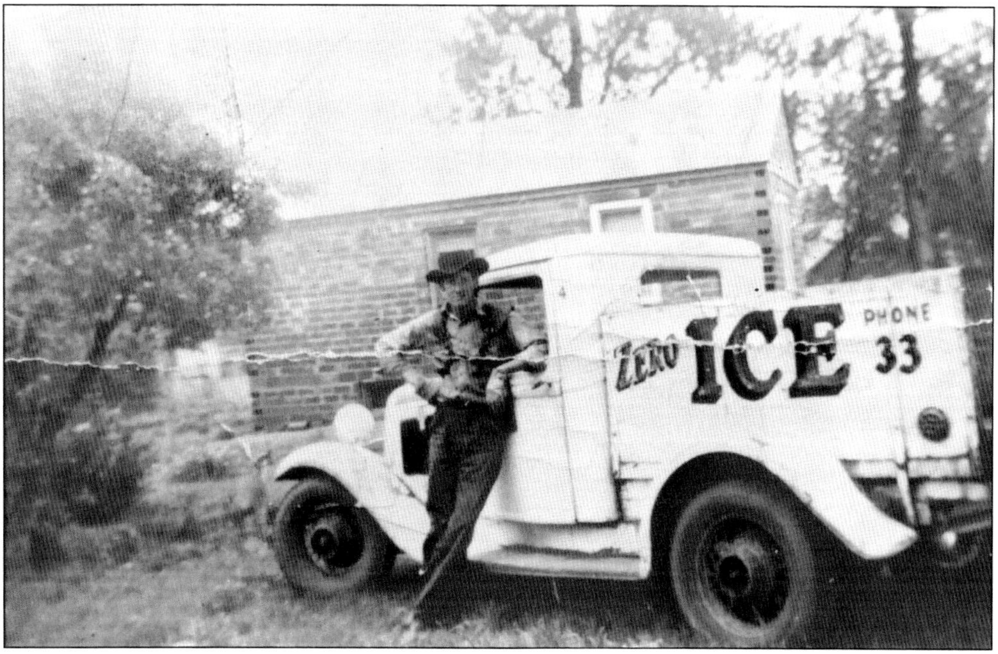


In the 1940s, Ray Kier, pictured here, delivered ice door to door in Norman. In 1920, Norman Milling & Grain expanded into the ice business when part-owner Delbert Larsh added an ice plant to the milling company. The firm's ice delivery service grew to nine trucks and offered residents routine home service. Ice was also available at drugstores. (CCHS.)

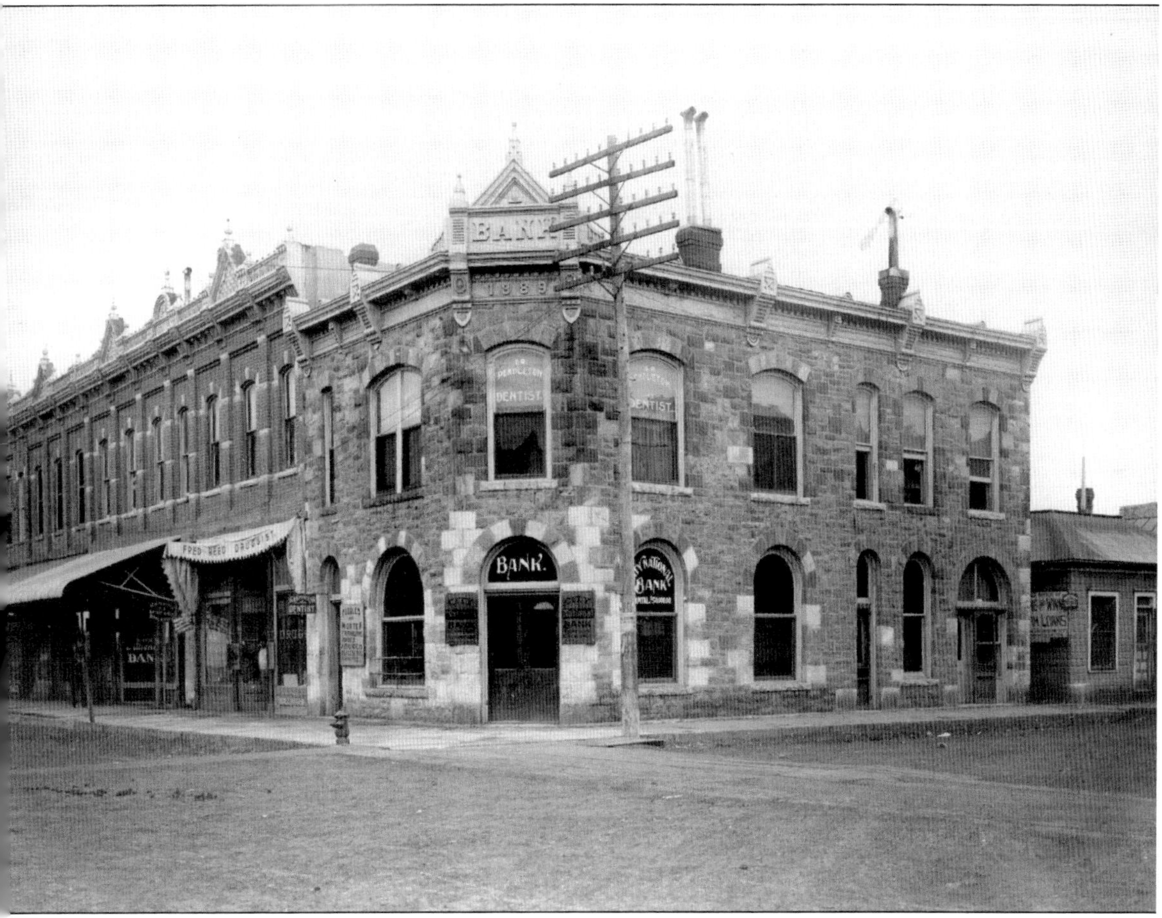


The first Norman bank was the 1889 Commercial Bank, seen here, on the northwest corner of Main Street and Peters Avenue. The bank, a branch of the Commercial Bank of Newton, Kansas, lasted eight months, closing when the Newton Commercial Bank failed. After the institution went out of business, a group of Norman businessmen, understanding the need for capital, organized Citizens Bank. (CCHS.)

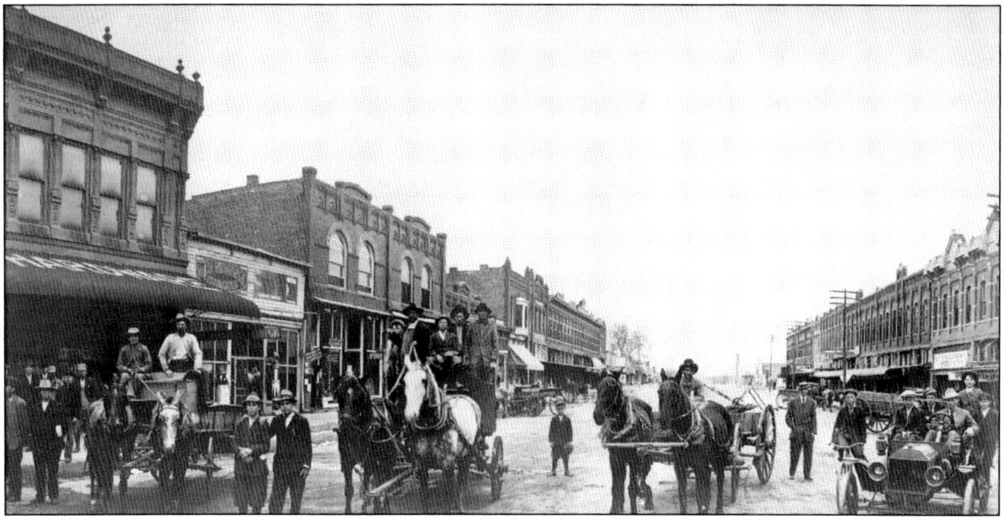

Photographer M.M. Marables came to Norman from Pilot Point, Texas, around 1910. He set up his panorama camera in the middle of Peters Avenue and Main Street and, from this vantage point, captured the "cityscape" of Norman. Marables's panoramas testify to the prosperity of Norman in the early 20th century. This image, and the following four photographs, were taken from that single panorama view. (CCHS.)

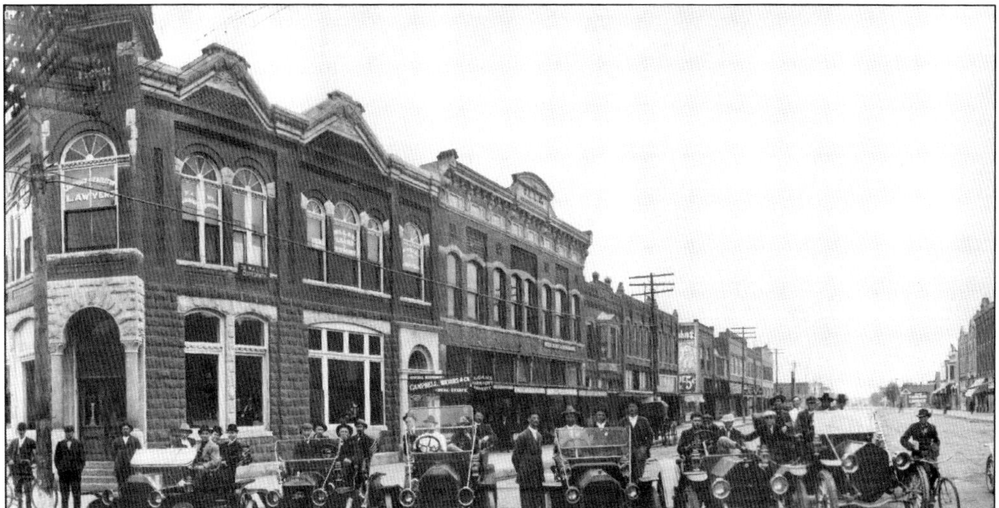

Norman State Bank, on the corner, was founded in 1890 in temporary quarters at 101 East Main Street in the Pryor V. Adkins building. In 1891, the bank moved into offices next door, at 103 East Main. The following year, it moved into a newly constructed bank building on the southwest corner of Main Street and Peters Avenue. The Norman State Bank was a branch of the First National Bank of Oklahoma City. (CCHS.)

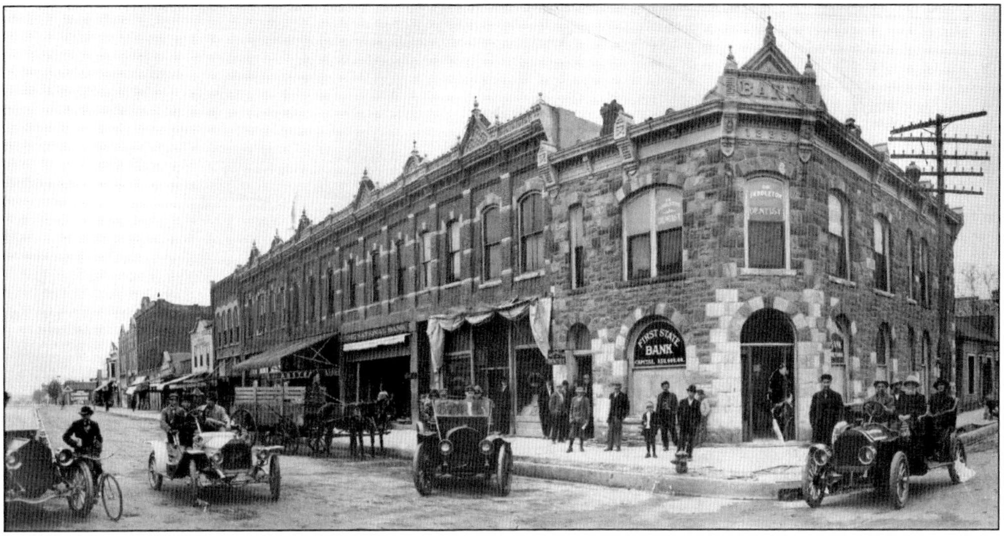


In 1910, the First State Bank occupied the building on the northwest corner of Main Street and Peters Avenue. Fred Reed's Drug Store was next door, to the west on Main Street. The Vienna Bakery was next to the drugstore. Above the First State Bank was the dental office of Dr. Pendleton. In the middle of the block was The National Bank and, just visible in the distance, Cox Lumber Yard. (CCHS.)

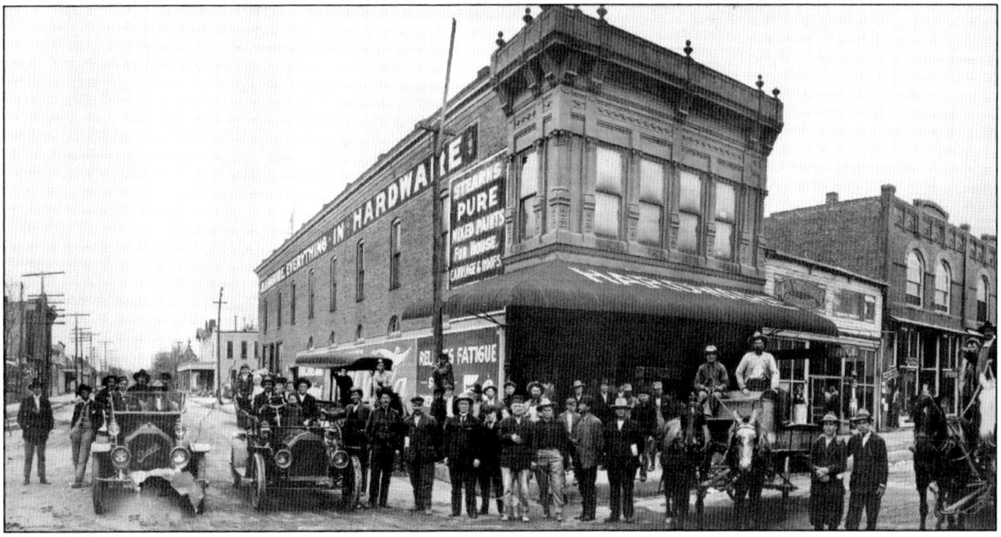


On the northeast corner of Peters Avenue and Main Street was J.D. McGuire's Hardware Store. James Douglas McGuire was born in Ireland in 1855 and arrived in Norman on the Santa Fe a few days after the land run of April 22, 1889. He immediately established his hardware store, which became well known for its tin shop and building cornices. Most buildings within a 50-mile radius of Norman had tin cornices from McGuire's Hardware. J.D. McGuire was active in building the infrastructure of the new town. He served on committees that established waterworks, churches, and schools. He also helped to promote Norman as a desirable place for a university. He raised $10,000 and donated personal funds toward land for the school, and served as a University of Oklahoma regent from 1895 to 1899. McGuire was active in the Republican Party and was considered for territorial governor, but declined the offer. In 1901, McGuire married Grace King, the first director of the School of Music at the University of Oklahoma. (CCHS.)

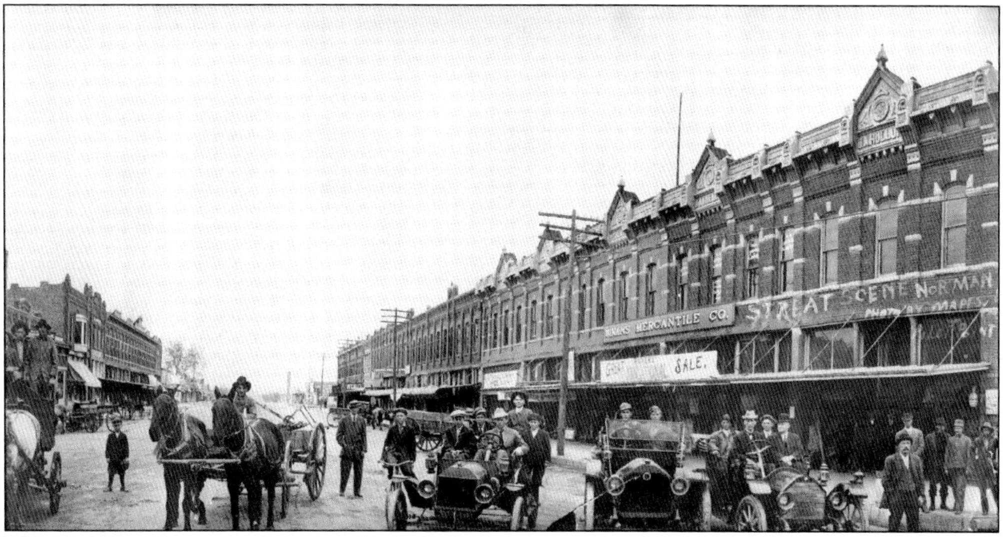

This is part of the panoramic view, looking east on Main Street from the intersection of Main and Peters Avenue. In the distance is the smokestack of Central State Hospital. On the south (right) side is Winan's Mercantile Company. Also on the south side, in the 200 block, is S.K. McCall's Dry Goods Store. McCall's was one of the largest mercantile businesses in Norman. (CCHS.)

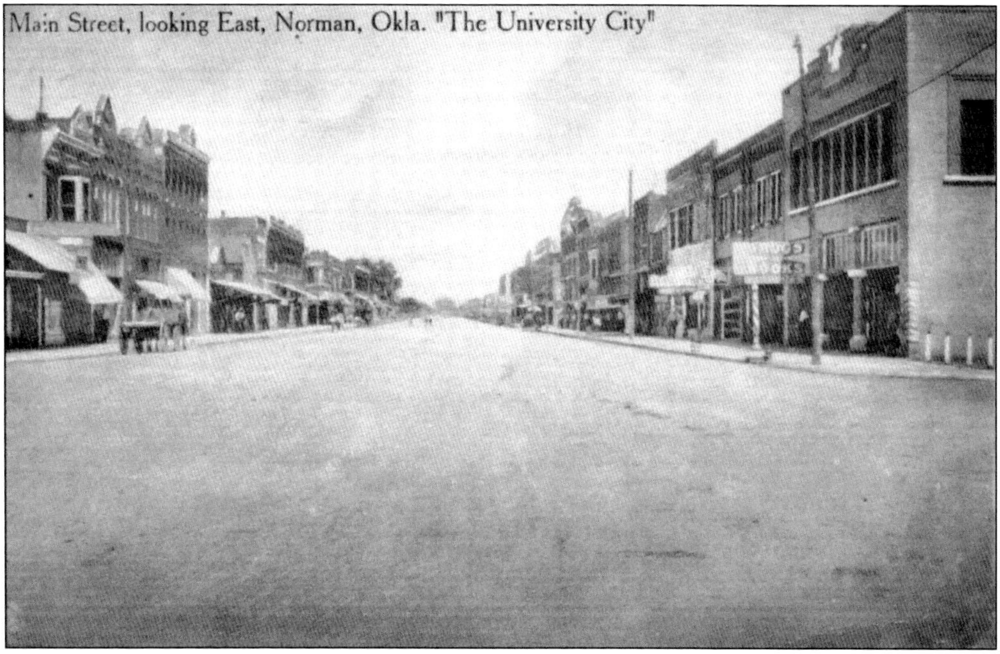


This photograph shows Norman around 1912. By the second decade of the 20th century, the settlers of Norman had established successful businesses and were part of a thriving farming community. The founding families had a stake not only in the financial community, but developed the town infrastructure so that the community would continue to grow along with the progressive nature of early-20th-century America. (CCHS.)

# *Three*

# Organizing a Community

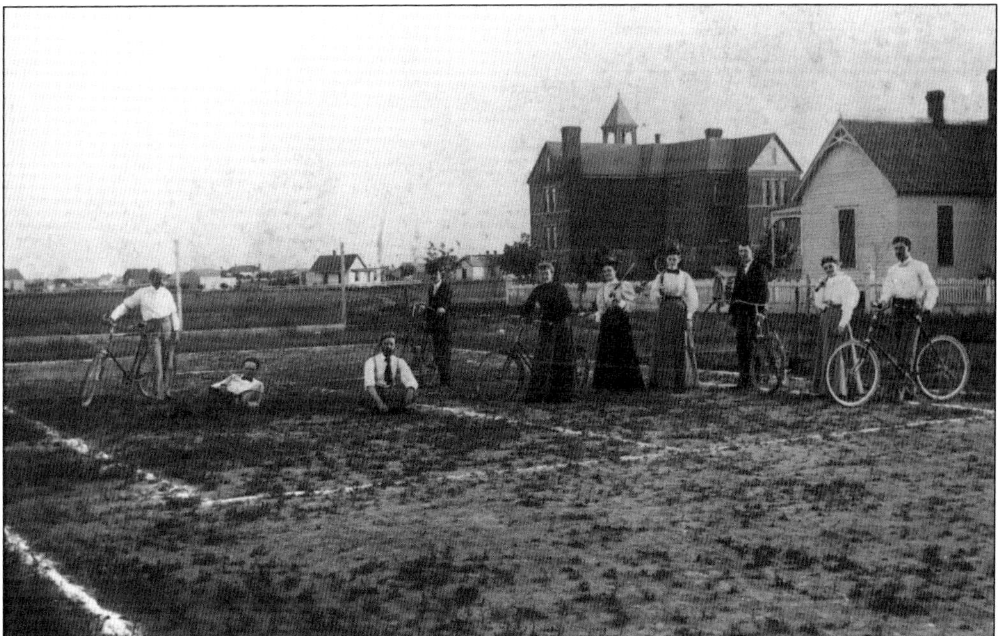

Men and women who settled Norman worked hard to prosper economically and to build a community that included a civic body, police, and fire protection. Citizens also came together to organize churches, schools, entertainment venues, and clubs. Residents sought to develop in Norman the same community organization of the towns and cities they left behind. In this photograph, high school students organize a badminton court. Eastside School is in the background. (CCHS.)

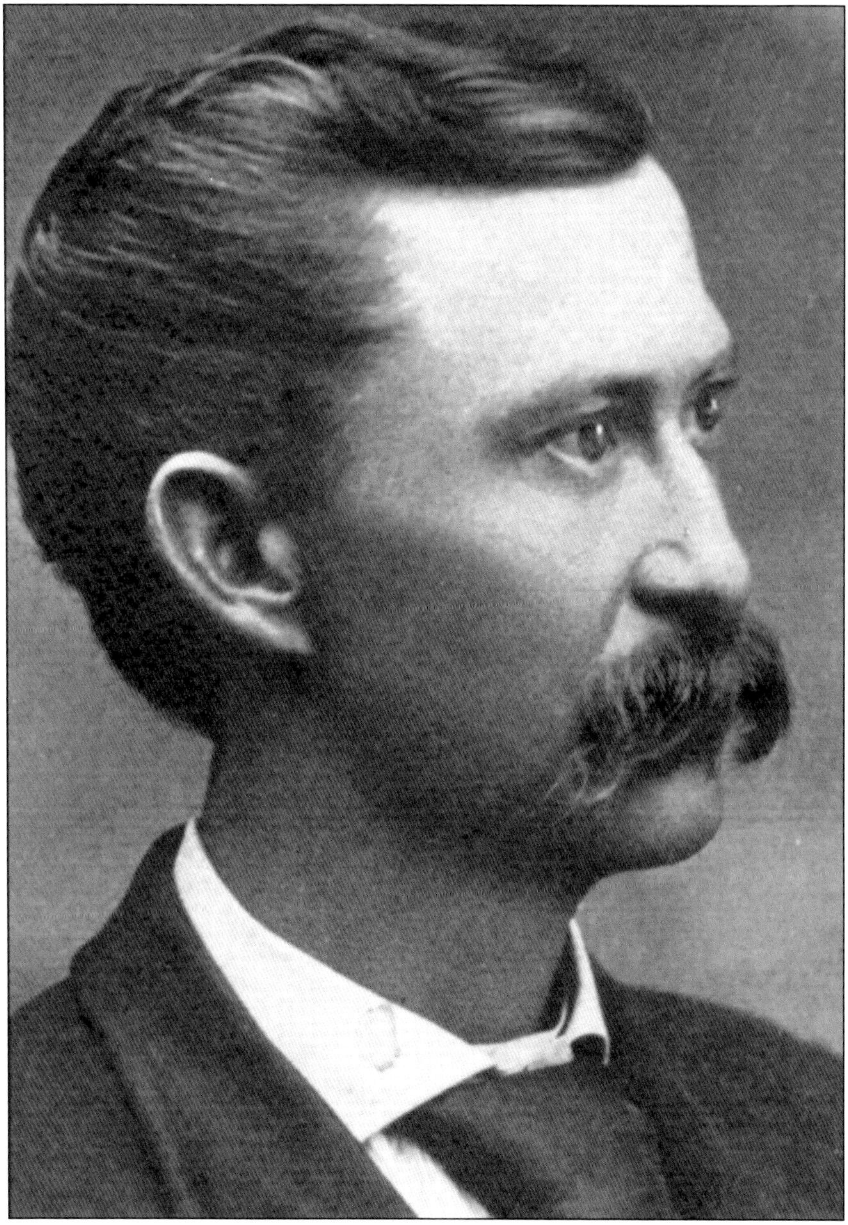

The Norman Townsite Company's governing council was quickly organized on May 14, 1889, after B.F. Smith tried to claim the entire western half of the townsite. Pryor Adkins called a meeting in Edwards Park, at Main Street and the railroad tracks. From the back of a wagon, Adkins conducted the business of electing city officials. Thomas R. Waggoner, shown here, was elected mayor; George Blake was elected clerk and recorder; and four councilmen were chosen: Pryor Adkins, E.C. Hall, Andrew Kingkade, and Delbert L. Larsh. On May 27, the new town council met and officially adopted the entire townsite plat, thereby overriding Smith's claim to the western half. The council passed laws directed toward health, sanitation, and morality. For example, each residence was required to carry dead animals out of the city, and privies had to be dug to a depth of at least three feet and cleaned out regularly. A "village scavenger" was hired to inspect and clean out the public privies. One law stated that stallions and mares could not breed in public view. (CCHS.)

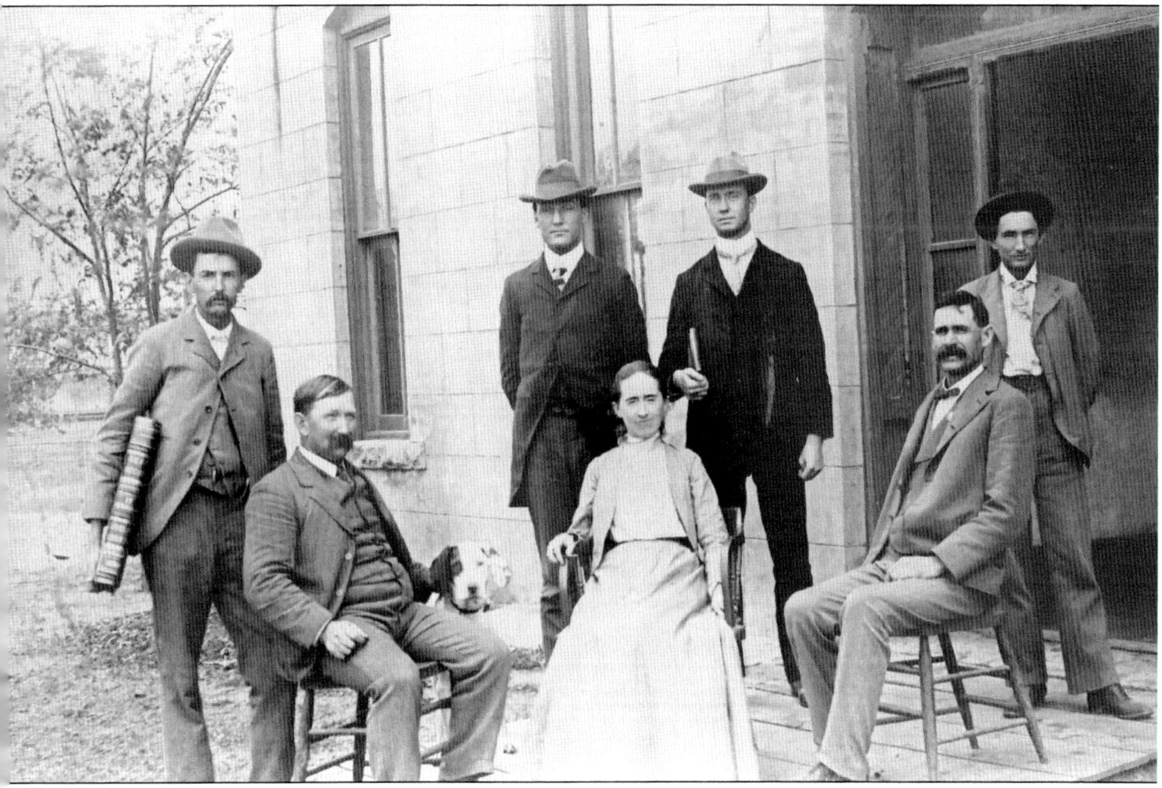

The Cleveland County Courthouse, shown here around 1910, was a gathering place for citizens of Norman. The Organic Act, which established Oklahoma Territory in 1890, provided for the selection of executive and county offices. Citizen sentiment regarding the location of the courthouse was divided geographically, the railroad being the dividing line. The division was also a political and economic one. The west side tended to be Republican, while the east side was Democratic. The east side won the debate, and the county courthouse was built at "Courthouse Square," the corner of Ponca Avenue and Tonhawa Street, in 1893. The site of the courthouse was not satisfactory to either factions, and the building was condemned in 1899. Mysteriously, the building was destroyed by fire sometime between 1899 and 1910. In 1906, the county built another courthouse and jail, in central Norman, on the southwest corner of Comanche Street and Peters Avenue. This courthouse was demolished after the present courthouse, built with federal funds, opened in 1938. The east side/west side rivalry also influenced the location of Norman schools. (CCHS.)

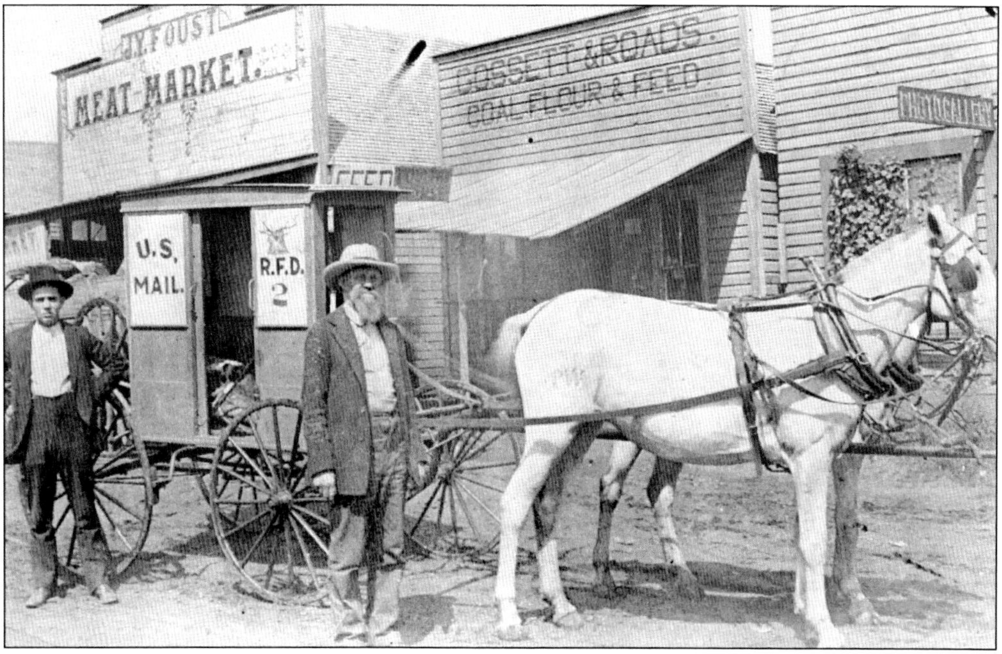


After the land run, US mail was dropped off at the AT&SF Norman depot. The agent piled the mail in a box on the floor for individuals to sort through. D.W. Marquart, the first postmaster, arrived in May 1889 and established the first US Post Office, on his own lot at 115 East Main Street. It took five weeks to establish the post office. (CCHS.)

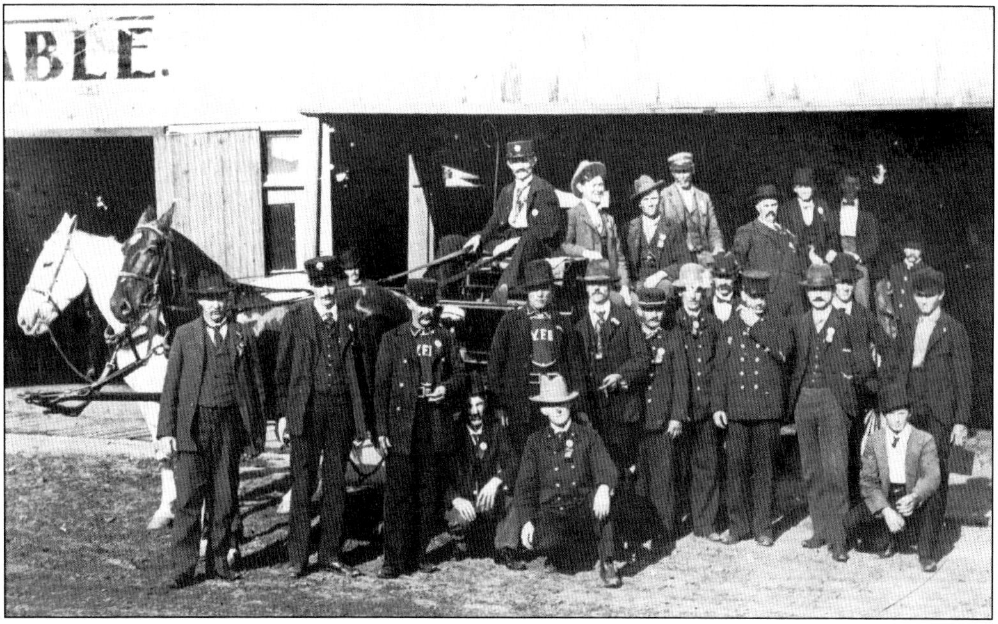

A Norman ordinance passed in 1893 required that every business have a water barrel for fighting fires. Two major fires that year had a sobering effect on the town. T.J. Wiggins's house and a brothel in the 400 block of East Comanche Street burned down. Brothel occupants were at the Territorial Fair in Oklahoma City. By 1894, the town established a volunteer fire department and acquired a hose cart and ladder wagon. (CCHS.)

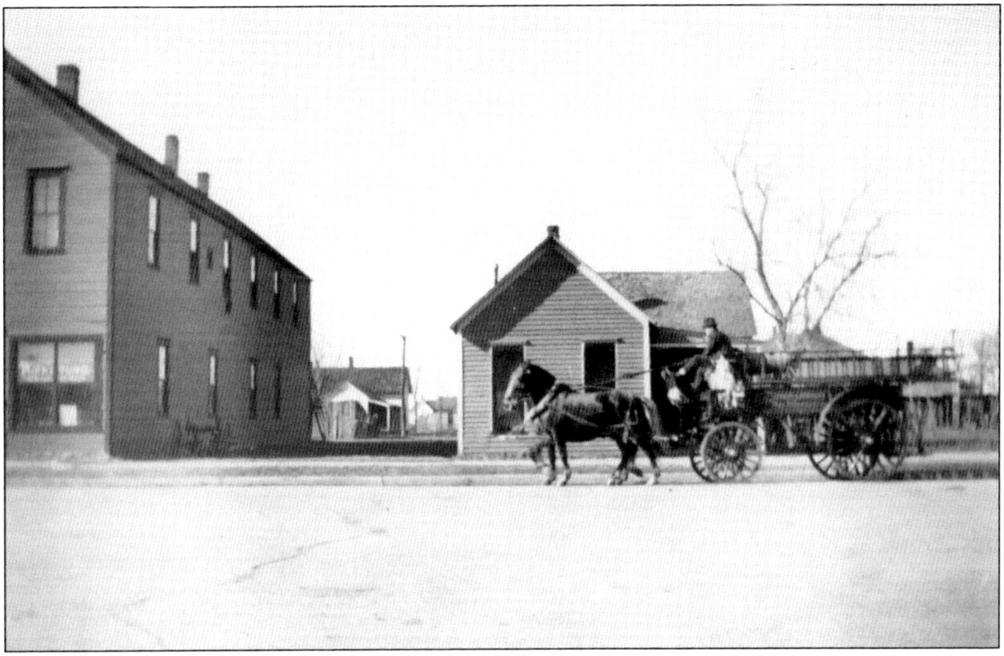

Anheuser-Busch Brewing Company, located along Front Street and the railroad, donated money to the City of Norman to purchase the ladder wagon. The firehouse was initially a sheet-iron structure located on the north side of Main Street near Jones Avenue. In 1895, G.W. Tackett was hired as fire chief. Pictured here is the fire wagon in front of a more substantial firehouse. (CCHS.)

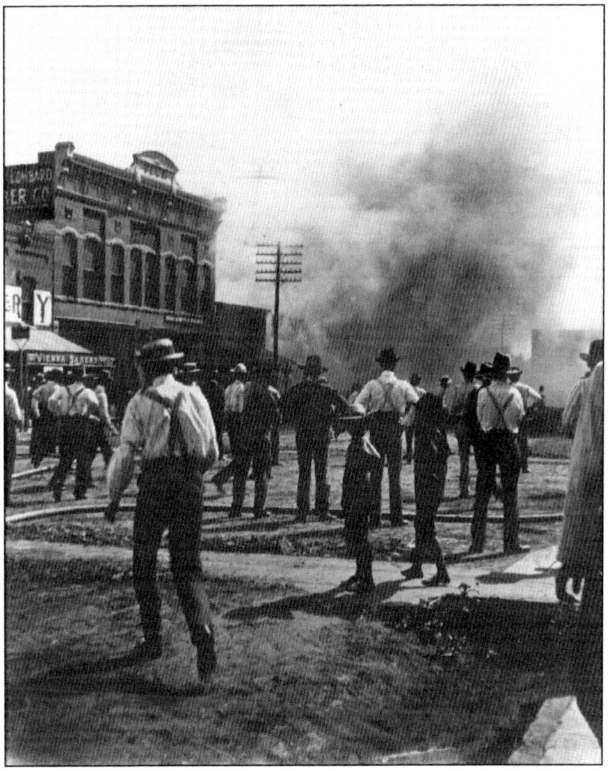

In 1902, a fire destroyed most of the south side of the 100 block of Main Street, between Peters Avenue and the railroad. The buildings that did not burn—Norman State Bank and Carey Lumber Company—were of brick construction. The destroyed structures, including a barbershop, cobbler shop, grocery, and drugstore, were frame buildings. (CCHS.)

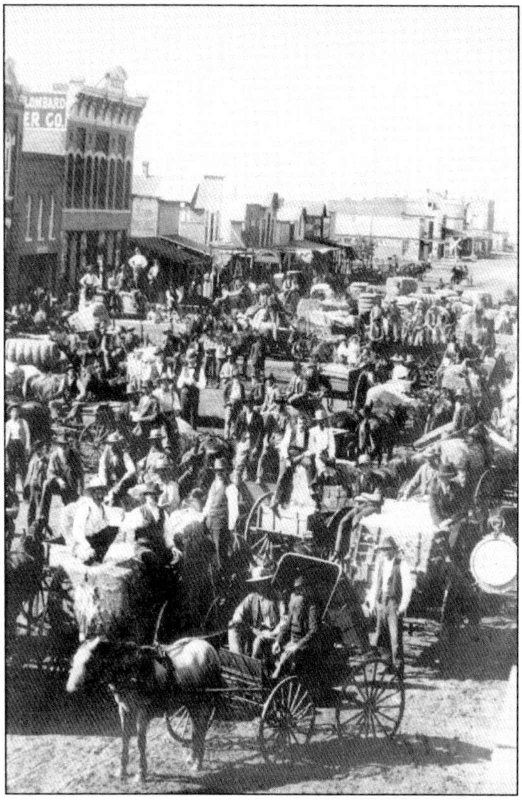

Wood frame buildings on the south side of the 100 block of East Main Street can be seen in this photograph taken before the 1920 fire. The wooden buildings were destroyed in the fire. The blaze was believed to have started in Holland's restaurant or "Pedro Ramos' chili joint." (CCHS.)

After the 1902 fire, the owners of Wheeler's Barber Shop and Barbour Drugs rebuilt their businesses in the same block. The new buildings were constructed with fire-resistant brick facades. As seen in this photograph, Ira Wheeler created an elegant interior, with mirrored walls and marble counters. Citizens expressed relief that no injuries resulted from the blaze. Those first buildings, considered shacks, had been erected quickly and had served their purpose. (CCHS.)

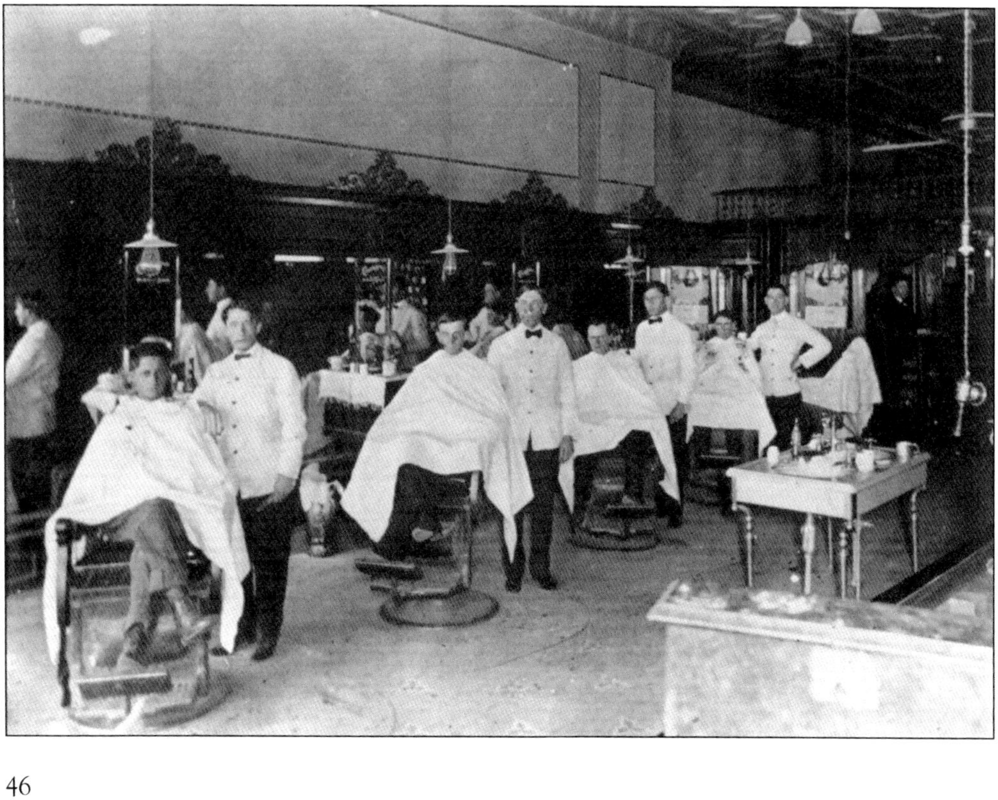

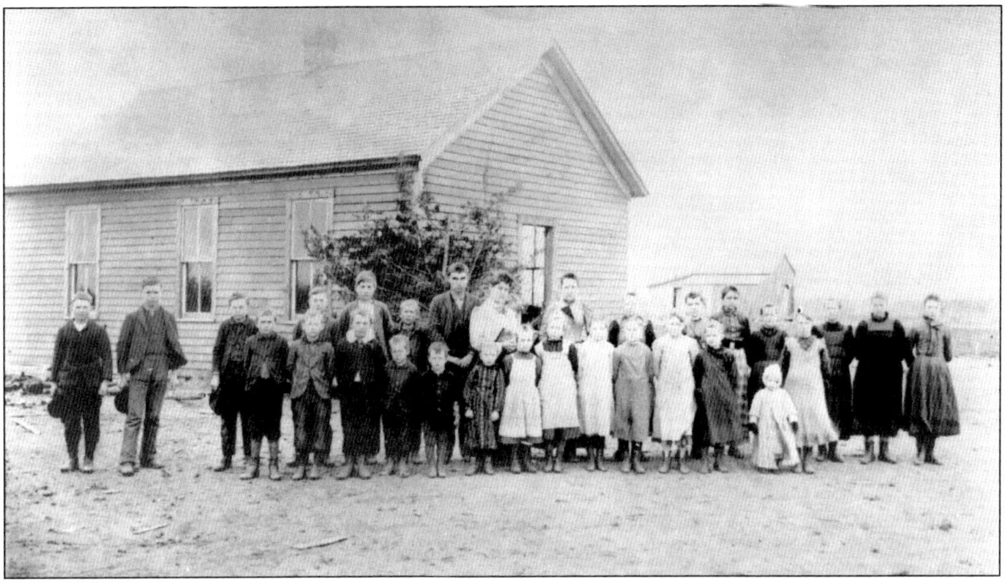

The first school in Norman, established in November 1889, was a subscription institution in the Methodist Episcopal Church, South. The Land Ordinance of 1785 established townships and section lines, stipulating a section in each township for schools. Valley View School, shown here, was established in 1894 on today's South Berry Road. The Norman town plat did not provide for public schools. Town officials eventually set aside seven town lots near today's Norman Public Library. (CCHS.)

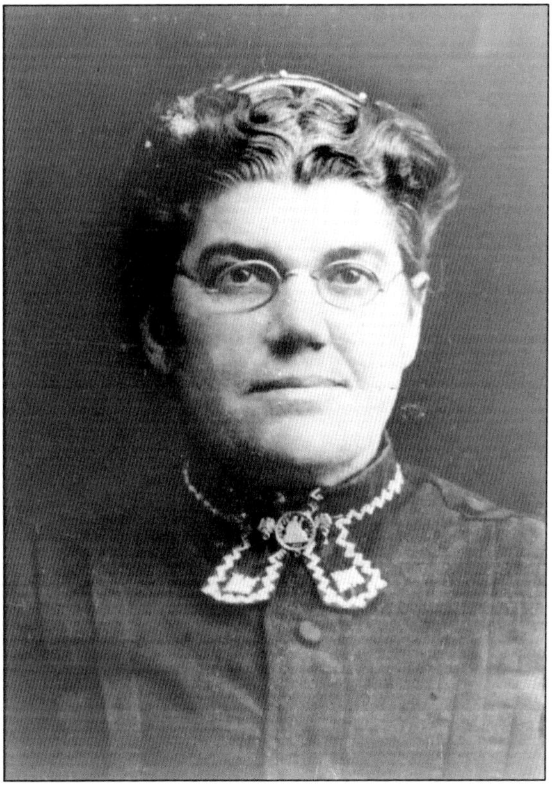

Mattie Dollarhide was the teacher at the subscription school at the M.E. Church, South. In her November 2, 1889, school ledger, she recorded 68 students under her instruction. Mattie and her husband moved to Norman from Dennison, Texas, in the spring of 1889, after the deaths of her two small children. The family bought land at "Johnson's Corner," which was at the intersection of Twelfth Avenue Northeast and Robinson Street. (CCHS.)

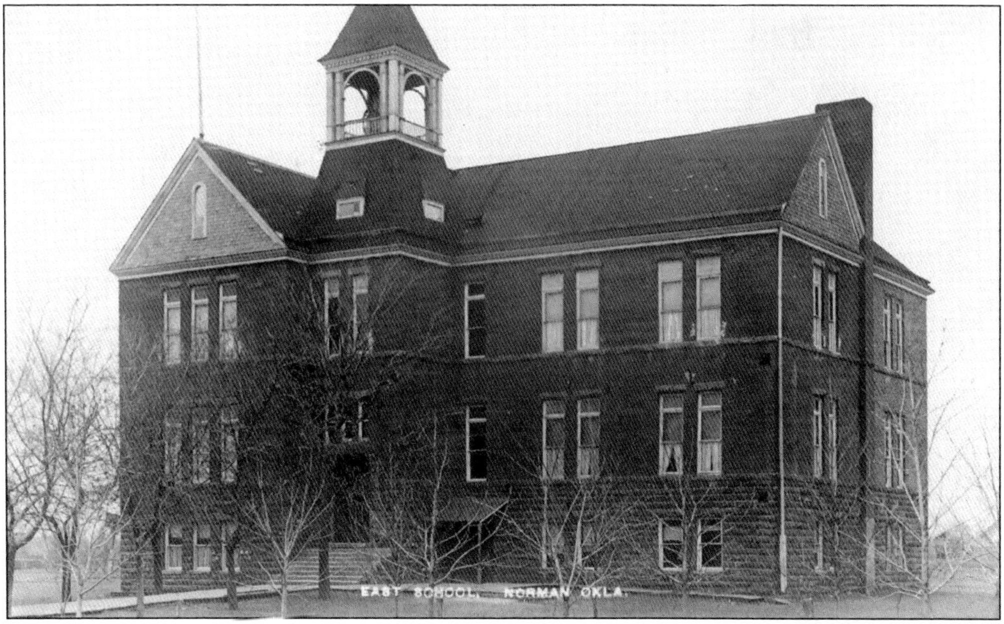


A one-room frame public schoolhouse was built on the new school lot, but it was not adequate to see to the educational needs of Norman's children. Until a substantial school building could be constructed, classes were held in various businesses in Norman. The eastside and westside factions once again argued, this time over the new school building's location. As with the courthouse, the east side won, and the school was built where Jefferson school is today. (CCHS.)

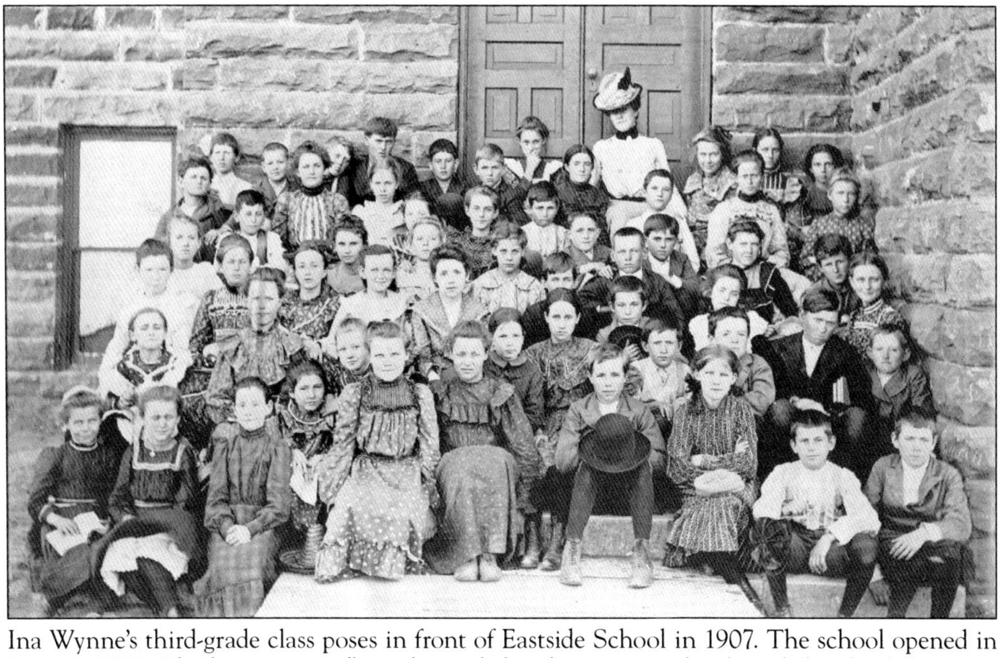

Ina Wynne's third-grade class poses in front of Eastside School in 1907. The school opened in January 1894. The bottom two floors housed the elementary school, and the third floor was occupied by high school students. After the building was condemned in 1916, the sandstone rock on the bottom third of the building, quarried from Rock Creek, was used in the construction of a house at Ponca Avenue and East Gray Street. (CCHS.)

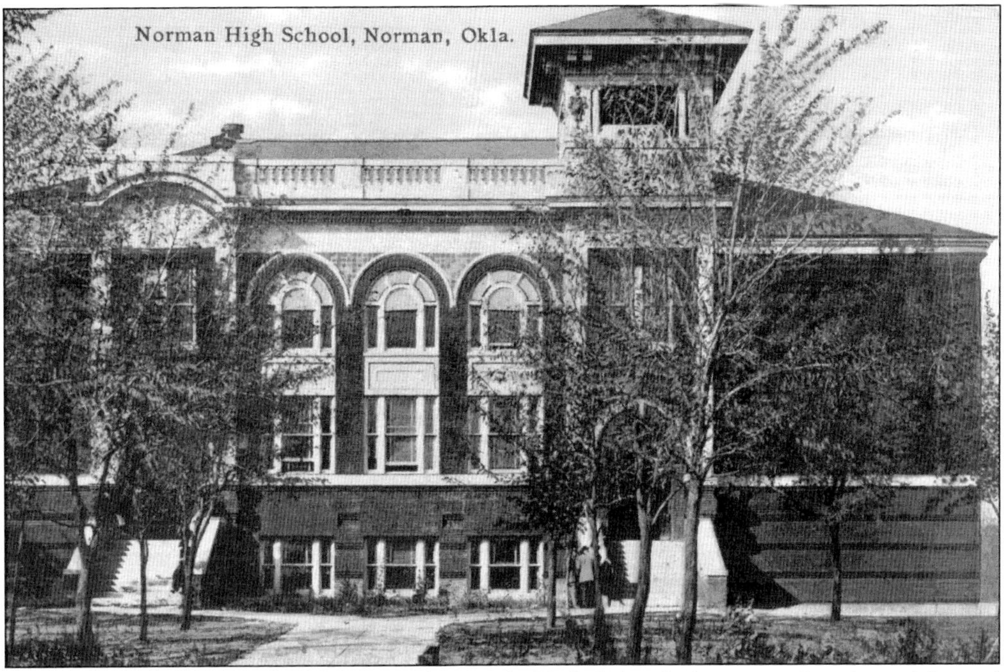


Following the completion of the second Eastside High School, the west side split and formed school district No. 64. The Westside School, or Jefferson School, was located where Norman school district's instruction center is on North Flood, south of Main Street. By 1900, there were 200 students enrolled at the Westside School, 400 less than attended Eastside High. (CCHS.)

In 1909, the Westside School was condemned. Norman voters passed a bond issue to expand and remodel the building, and the school was renamed Washington School. In 1917, the building was destroyed by fire. Another bond issued, passed in 1918, allocated $22,000 to build the current Washington school. The building was later converted into an instructional center for the district. (CCHS.)

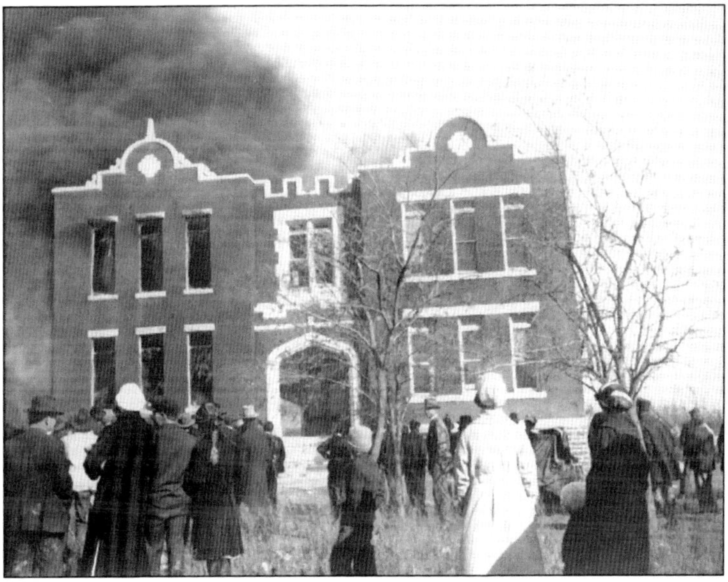

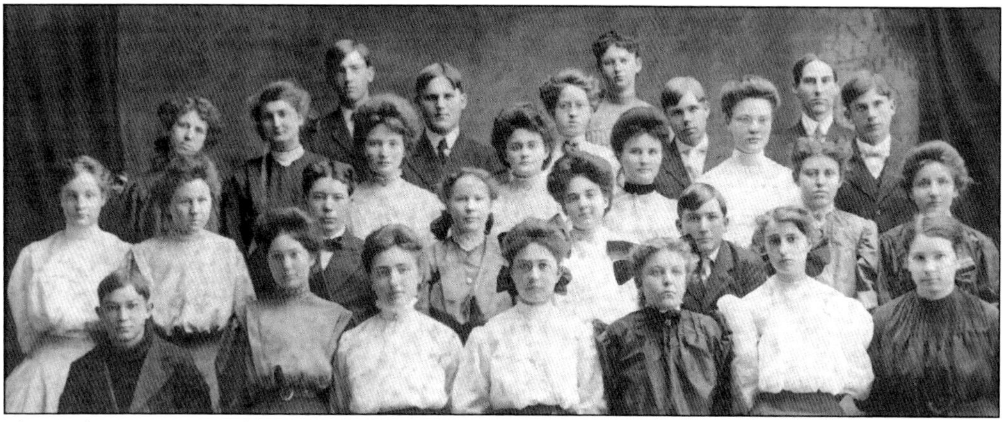

Shown here are 28 graduates of Norman High School's class of 1910. The students are members of the founding families of Norman, and some of their names will be familiar to residents in 2013, including Anna Pickard (Pickard Avenue), Alpha and Charlie Berry (Berry Road), Eloda Wheeler (Wheeler's Barbara Shop), and Bernice McGuire (McGuire's Hardware). (CCHS.)

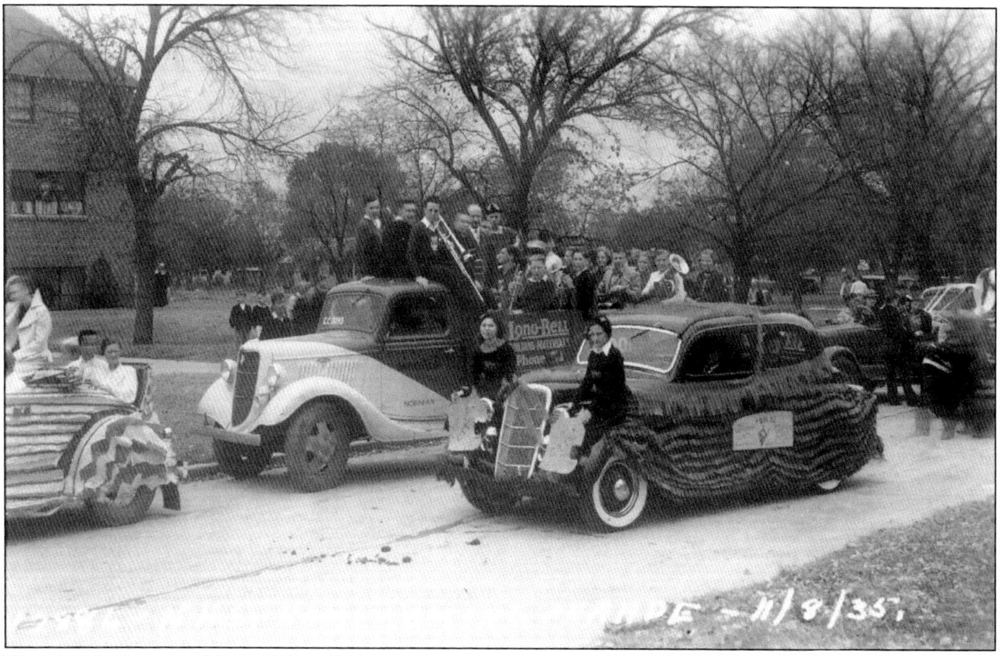


The 1935 Norman High School homecoming parade celebrated the school's football team, the Tigers. Jack Mckinney, class of 1935, later wrote that he remembered the Tigers players as being shorter in stature than the players on most school teams in the region. Regardless, in 1935, the Tigers played against the Texas champions in Amarillo and beat them 26-7. The Norman Tigers finished the season undefeated. (CCHS.)

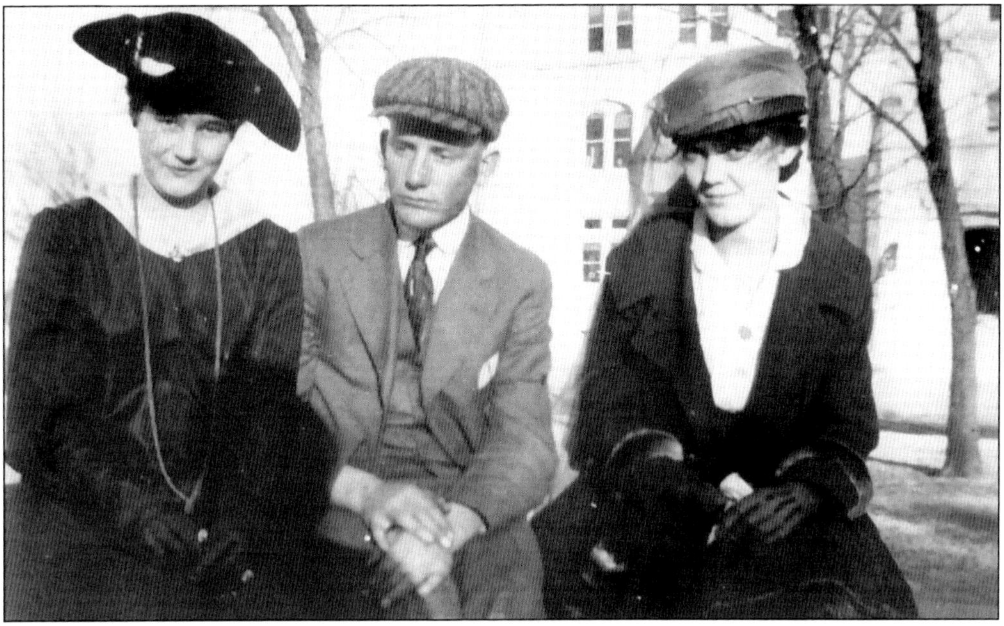

From left to right, Edith Bloomer, Milt Phillips, and Ruth Foster attended Norman High School in 1915. The Phillips family homesteaded outside of Norman shortly after the land run. Milt was a paperboy for the Norman newspaper, *Democrat-Topic*, and was freshman class president at Norman High School. He later attended the University of Oklahoma. In all, the Phillips family sent five generations of young men and women to the University of Oklahoma. (CCHS.)

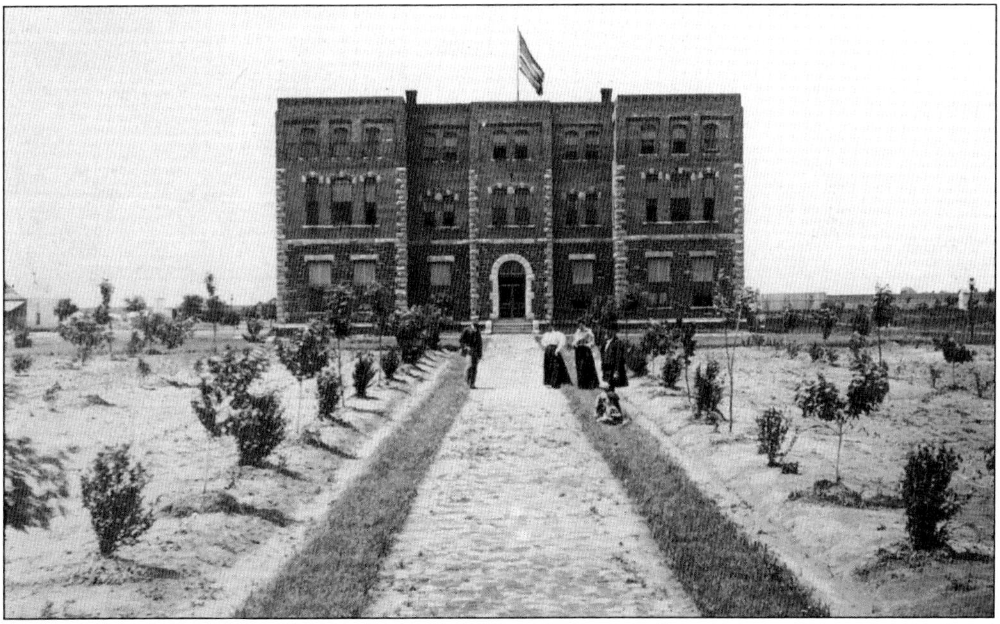

Methodist Episcopal Church, South established High Gate College in 1890. The school offered elementary, high school, and college instruction. The college was located on 10 acres at the end of Main Street. The new campus opened in 1893. Competition from Norman Business School, Nobel Academy, and the University of Oklahoma forced the school to close in December 1894. The Methodists sold the property to the Oklahoma Sanitarium Company. (CCHS.)

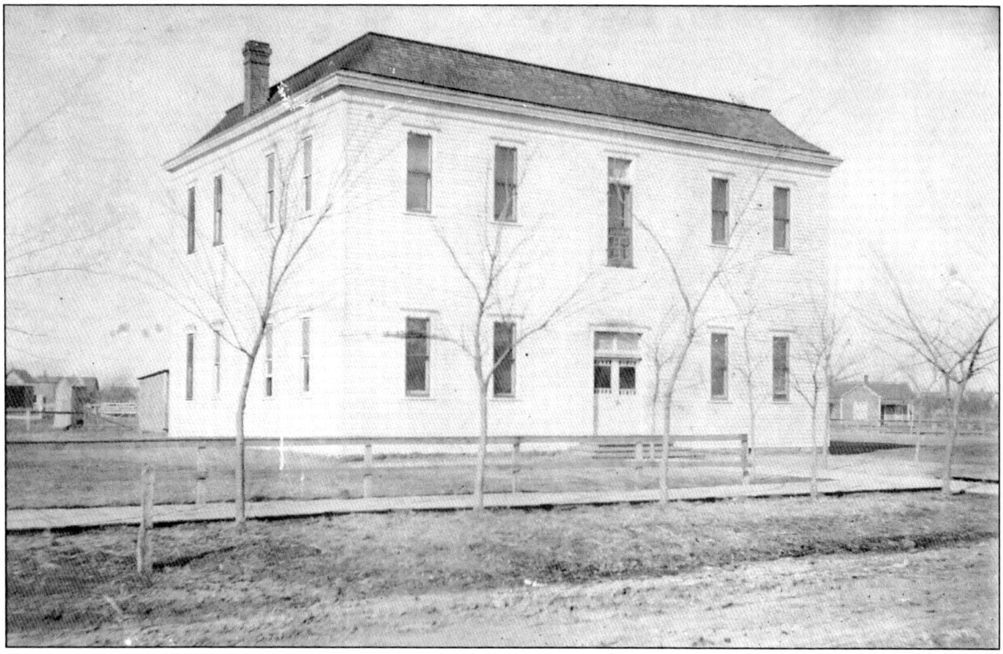

The first Catholic mass in Norman was conducted in Aniol's store in 1889. Con B. McGinley donated land in the 400 block of East Tonhawa Street for a Catholic church, seen here. Catholic officials dedicated the church to St. Patrick in March 1898. Most church members, however, favored the name St. Joseph, and today this is the commonly used name. (CCHS.)

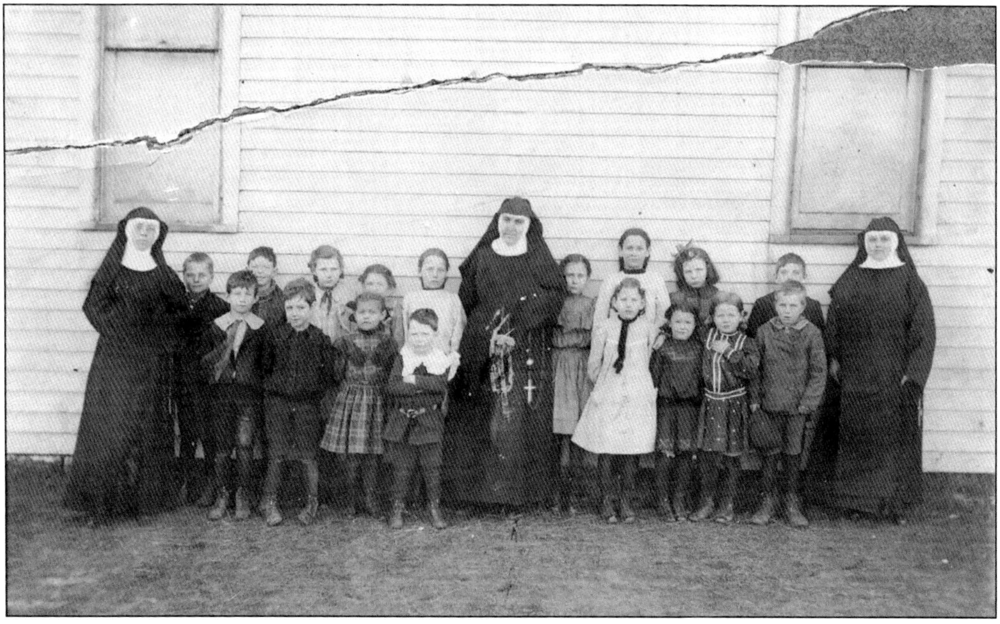

In 1899, Bishop Meerscheart of Oklahoma City dedicated the new school and convent located next to St Patrick's. A tornado struck Cleveland County on April 25, 1893, and killed many members of the parish near Forty-eighth Avenue Northwest and Franklin Road. Three members of the Maroney family, eight members of the O'Connor family, H.O. Clements, and Owen Rooney were killed. (CCHS.)

The First Presbyterian Church was established in 1889 at Gray Street and Crawford Avenue. Andrew Kingkade, Norman's first Santa Fe Railroad agent, is on the far left. Fourth from the right is Dr. David Ross Boyd, the first president of the University of Oklahoma. Behind the church, on the corner of Crawford and Tonhawa Street, is the Methodist Episcopal Church, South. (CCHS.)

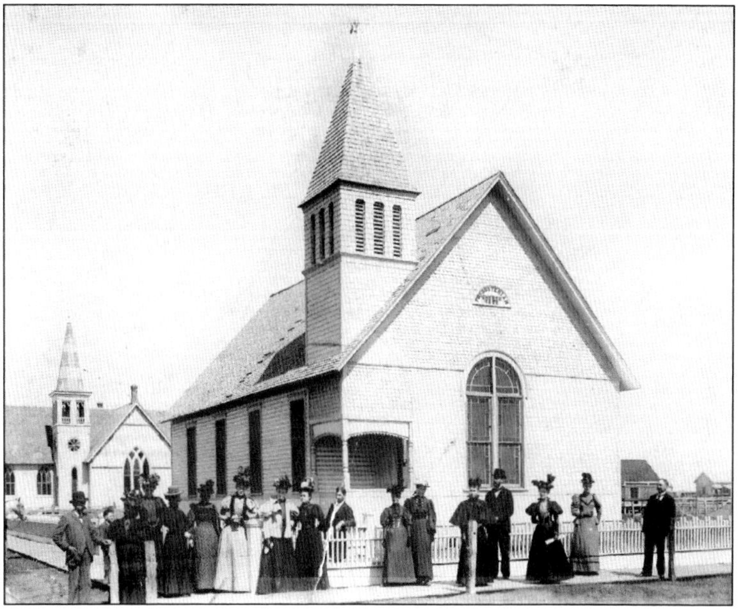

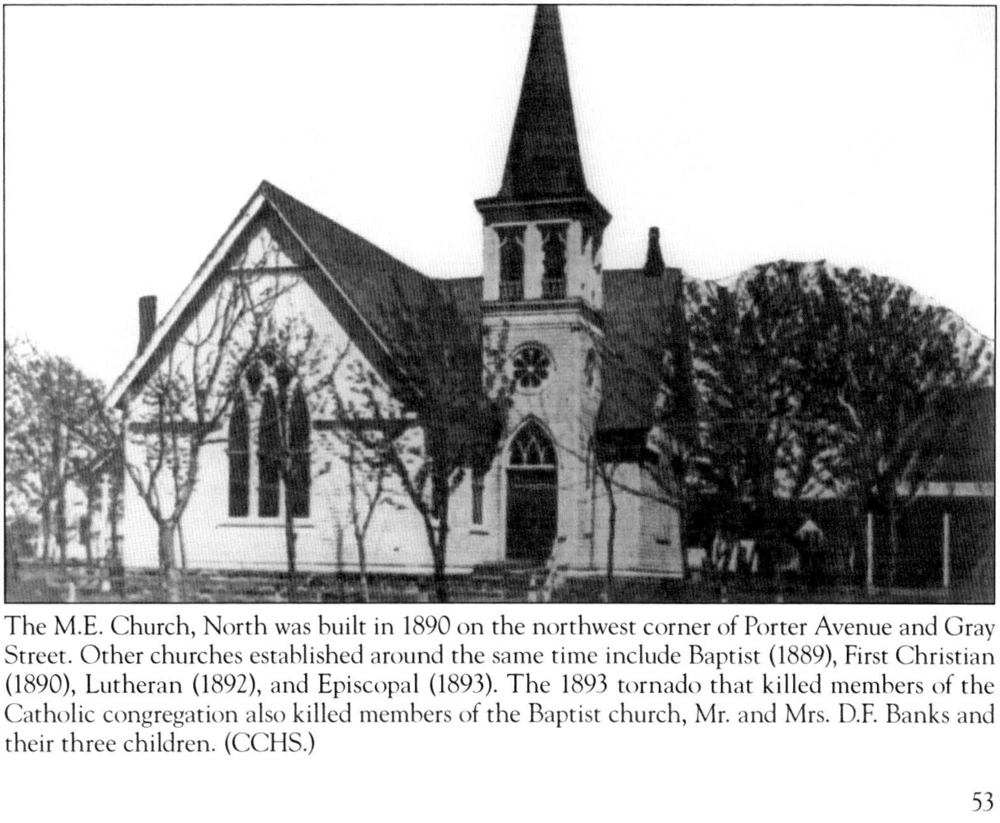

The M.E. Church, North was built in 1890 on the northwest corner of Porter Avenue and Gray Street. Other churches established around the same time include Baptist (1889), First Christian (1890), Lutheran (1892), and Episcopal (1893). The 1893 tornado that killed members of the Catholic congregation also killed members of the Baptist church, Mr. and Mrs. D.F. Banks and their three children. (CCHS.)

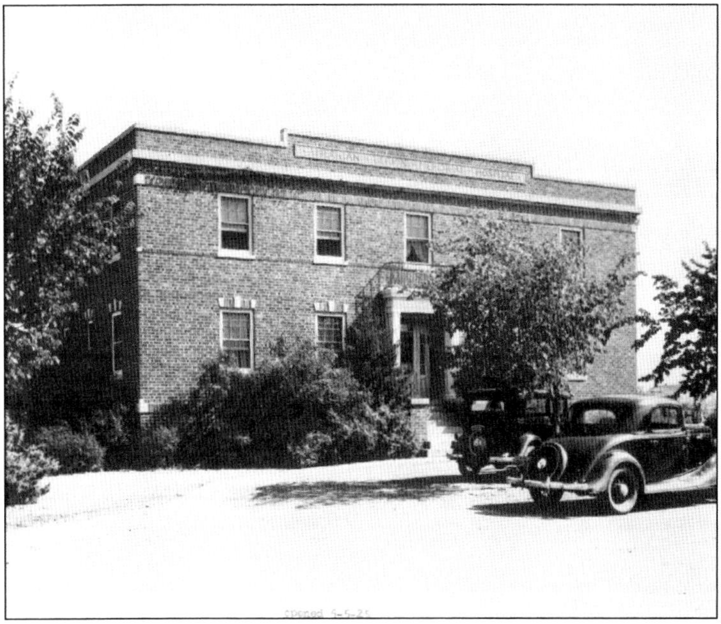

Norman's first hospital was built after World War I, when Dr. John L. Day approached the American Legion to see if it was interested in establishing a hospital. The legion agreed and purchased property at the corner of Johnson Street and North Ponca Avenue. The two-story, brick hospital opened on April 5, 1925. The Cleveland County Memorial Hospital was dedicated to 16 Cleveland County men who lost their lives in World War I. (CCHS.)

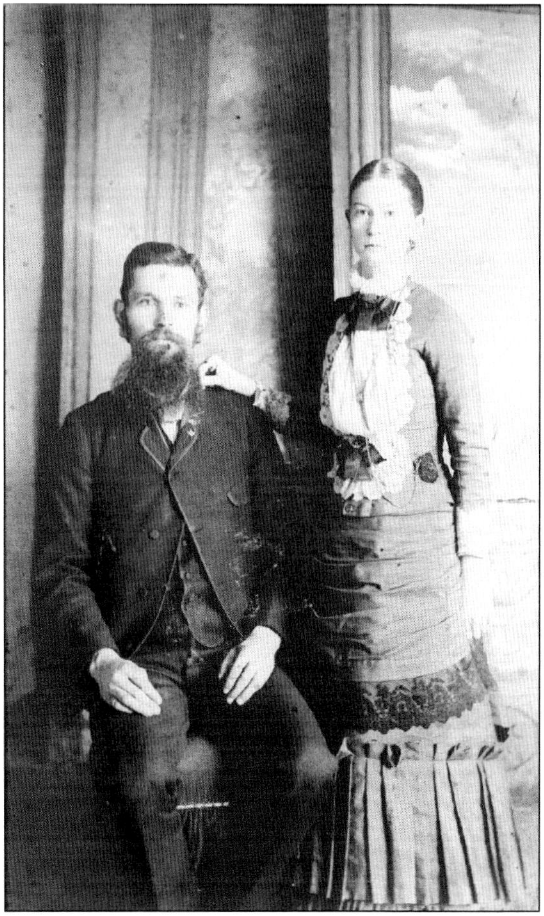

Newly married Dr. M.T.J. and Rebecca Capshaw settled in west Norman in 1891. Dr. Capshaw's first medical emergency was to tend to the 100 injured in the 1893 tornado. In all, 22 people were killed. Capshaw used a house in the vicinity of the tornado as an emergency hospital. A major threat to life in Norman was typhoid. In 1912, Rebecca was stricken and died of the fever. (CCHS.)

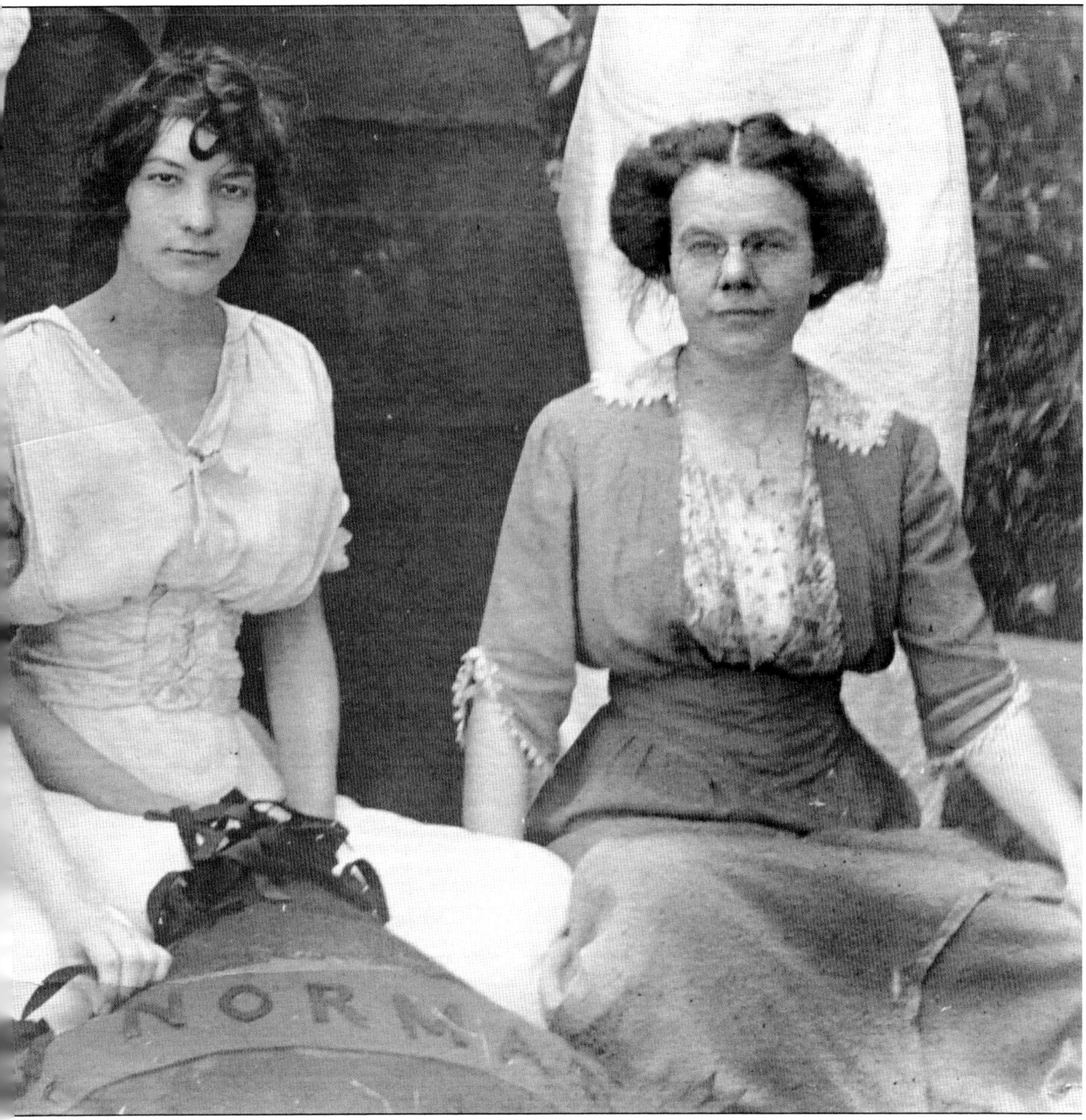


Typhoid was not the only disease that caused families to lose loved ones. In November 1922, a jewelry salesman made his pitch to potential customers at sororities and fraternities situated around the University of Oklahoma campus. He reported feeling ill and, five days later, died of smallpox. Before Thanksgiving break, 10 students were in the OU infirmary, and five of them died. University president Stratton Brooks issued a statement to the students, home for Thanksgiving break, requiring them to get a smallpox vaccination before they returned. The disease, however, had not been contained, and it spread into the greater Norman community. Nola Helms Rector (right), 37, contracted the illness and died within 10 days. At their doctor's insistence, Nola's 60-year-old mother, Mary Helms, received the vaccination because of her exposure to her daughter's illness. When she contracted the disease, the doctor thought her illness would be minor, but she also died within days. Smallpox continued to be a threat to Oklahomans into the 1930s, sometimes in epidemic proportions. (CCHS.)

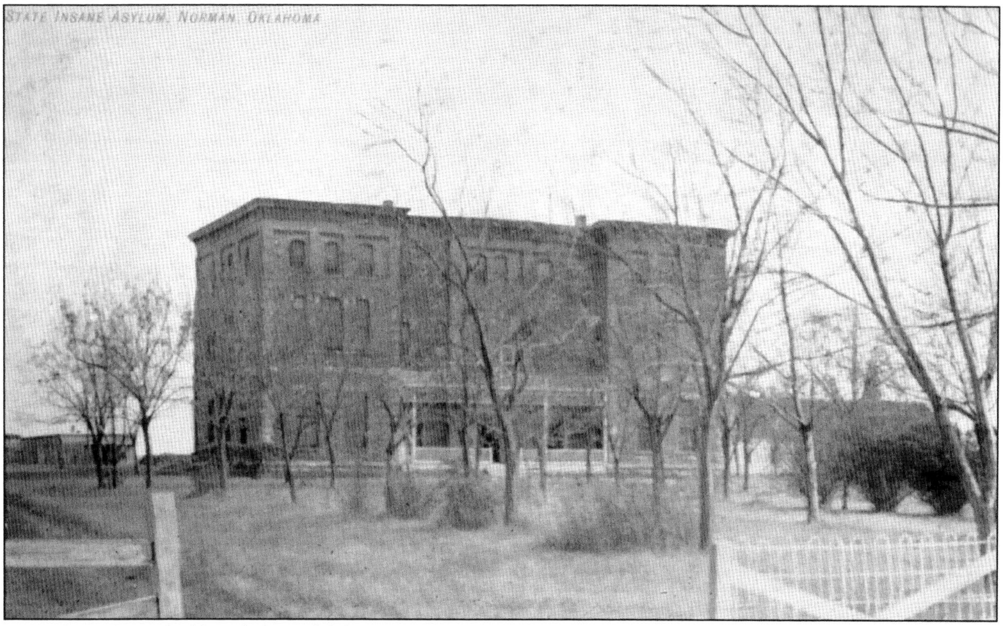


Dr. John Threadgill and the Oklahoma Sanitarium Company bought High Gate College in 1895. The first patients were transported in special railway cars from Illinois. Dr. David W. Griffin was hired in 1899 to run the sanitarium. When he arrived, he was astonished at the condition of the patients and their environment. He instituted a more humane treatment and sought psychiatric cures instead of restraints. (CCHS.)

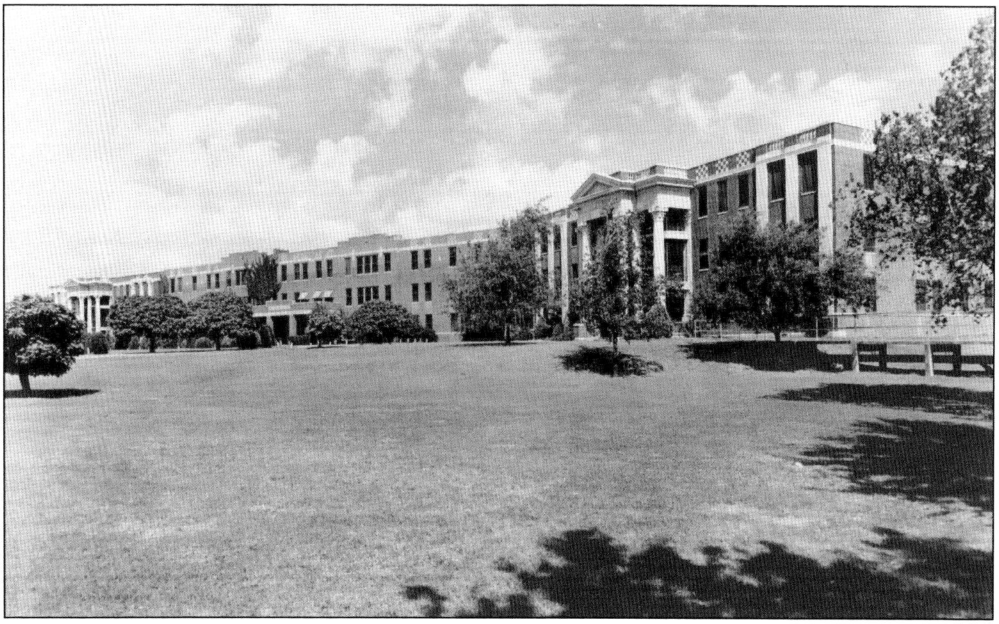

Dr. Griffin believed that the asylum would function better as a state institution than as a private facility. He appealed to the territorial legislature to appropriate money for the purchase of the hospital. Finally, in 1915, the state approved. Dr. Griffin became superintendent, a position he held until his retirement in 1950. Griffin was successful in changing the name from Central State Hospital for the Insane to Central State Hospital. (CCHS.)

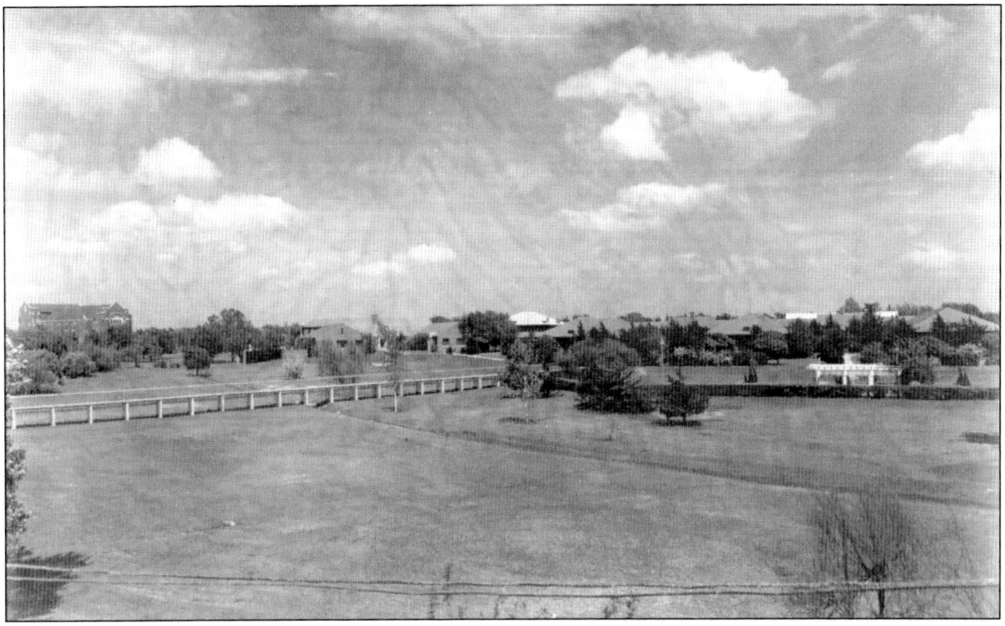

By 1930, Central State Hospital was a self-sufficient farm. Behind the gates were chicken houses, a hog farm, a laundry and ice plant, a power plant, an orchard, and a vineyard. Acres of vegetables grew in the field south of the grounds. Patients worked in the fields, milked in the dairy, and tended to the cannery and gardens. By 1950, there were 3,000 patients seeking treatment at the hospital. (CCHS.)

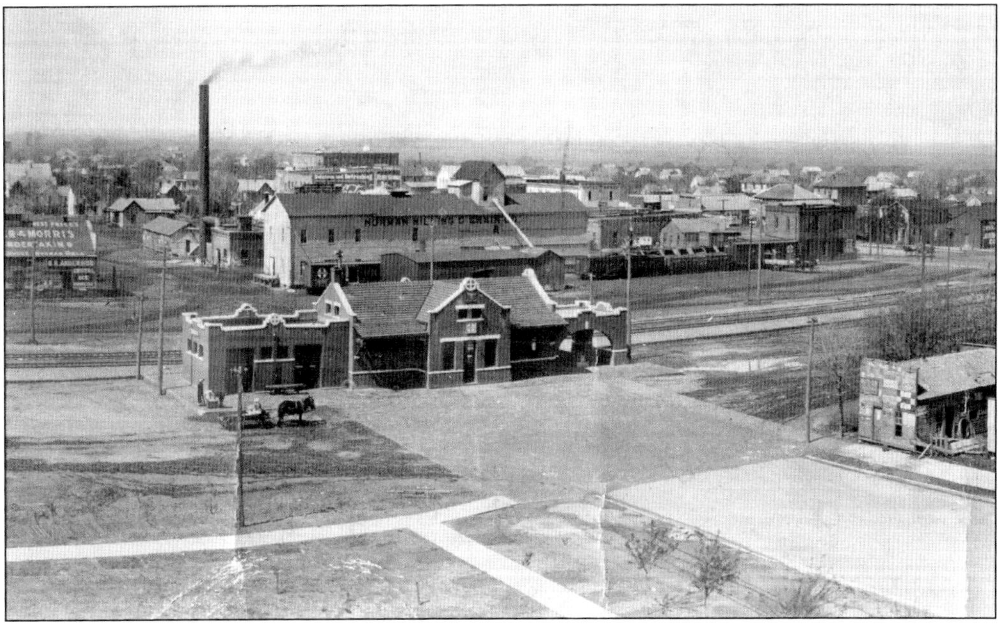

M.M. Marables's second panorama of Norman, conducted around 1910, appears to have been taken from the roof of the new, three-story Cleveland County Courthouse, at the corner of Comanche Street and Peters Avenue. As Marables pointed his camera west, he captured the agricultural processing and bulk commodities center of Norman. In the foreground is the newly completed Santa Fe Railroad station. Across the railroad tracks is the Norman Milling and Grain facility. (CCHS.)

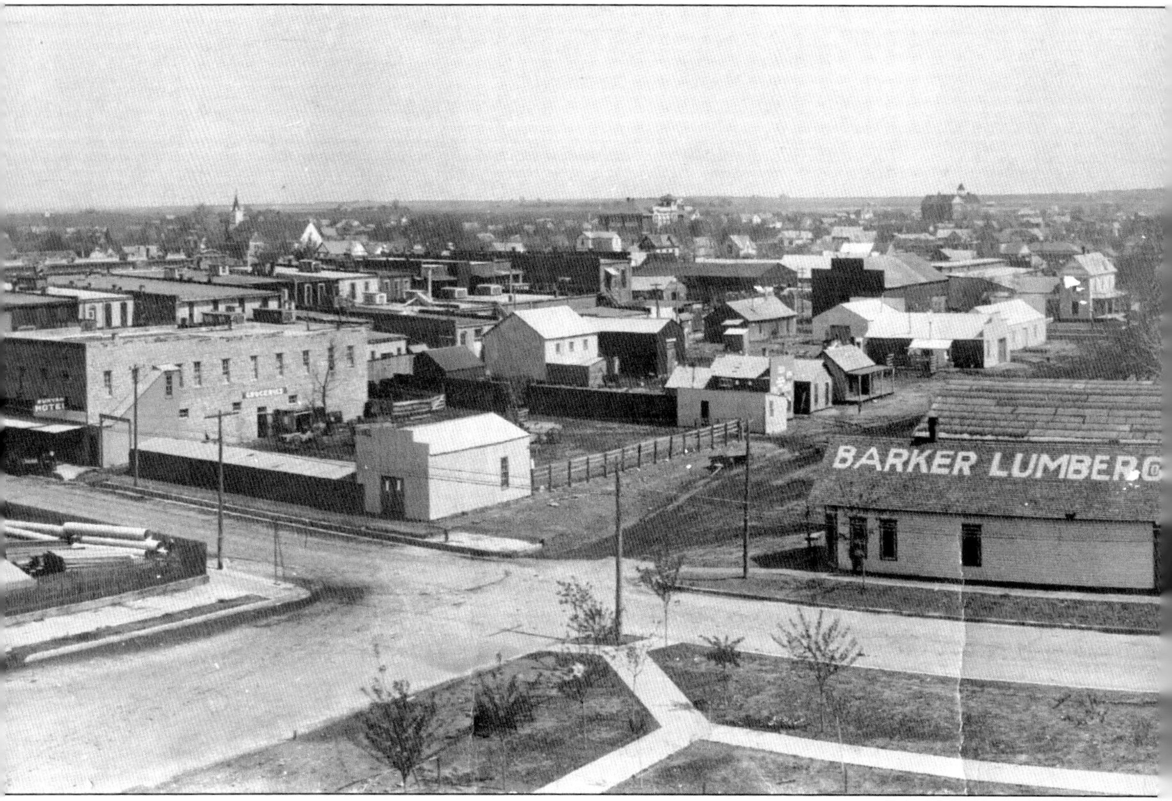


Marables pointed his camera east for the first shot. He then panned to the north with a sweep that took in the back of the buildings on the south side of Main Street. The photographer then panned to the railroad tracks, continuing from west to southwest, just short of capturing a 360-degree view. This photograph is looking to the northeast. In the foreground can be seen the courthouse lawn and sidewalks at the corner of Peters Avenue and Comanche Street. Across Peters is Barker Lumber, owned by Harry and Daisy Lindsay, who lived in the present-day Moore-Lindsay Historical House, 508 North Peters Avenue. Visible in the background on the left is the new Eastside High School, which was built on the old courthouse square. Also visible is the old Eastside School, which was condemned in 1916. This photograph was taken around 1910.

# *Four*

# CHANGING SOCIETY

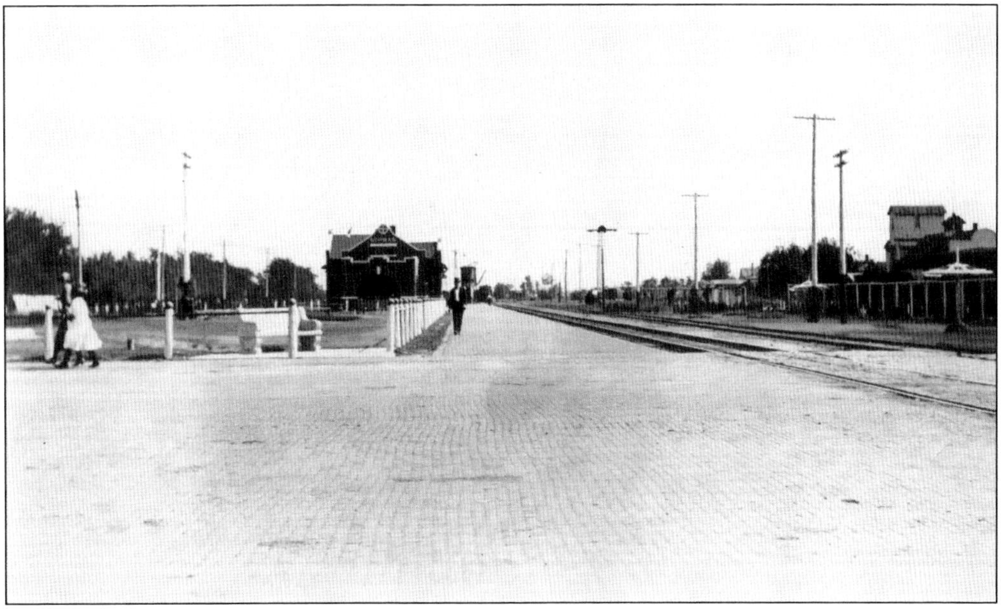

At settlement in 1889, the Santa Fe built the 16-square-foot wooden Norman Depot west of the tracks on the north side of Eufaula Street. *Norman Transcript* editor Ed Ingle campaigned for a new building in 1890. The new construction was a boost for workers in economically difficult times. The wooden structure's bay windows looked out at the tracks and a wooden stock pen. (CCHS.)

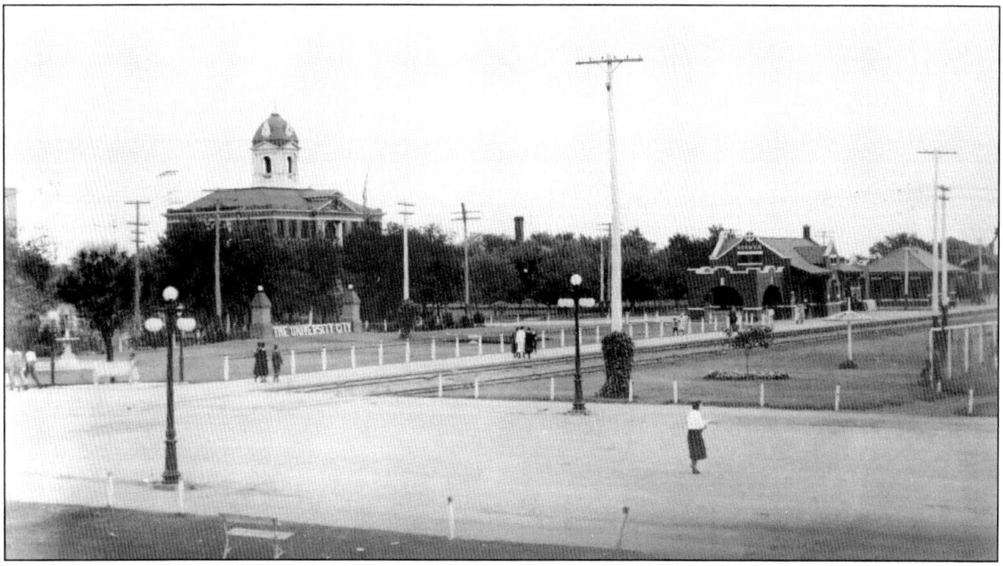


In 1905, Ed Ingle, along with Norman's mayor and city council members, campaigned for an even larger depot. In 1909, a $15,000 depot was finished. The new station included a 16-foot brick platform and a brick sidewalk to Courthouse Square. The courthouse, finished in 1906, can be seen in the background of this photograph. (CCHS.)

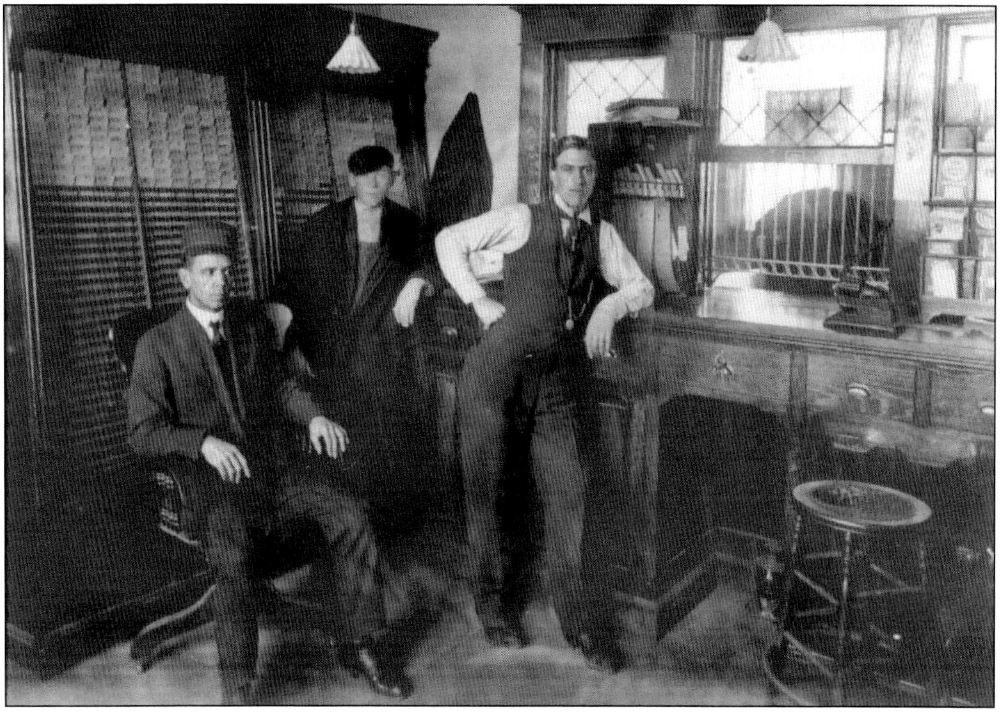

After the Norman Depot was finished in 1909, a 25-foot-by-56-foot Wells Fargo Express building was erected next door on the south. Freight agent John J. Baker (left) is seen in this photograph. The Norman freight station was a very busy one in 1915. From the settlement of Norman in 1889, the Achison, Topeka & Santa Fe Railroad played an important role in the economic and physical development of the town. (CCHS.)

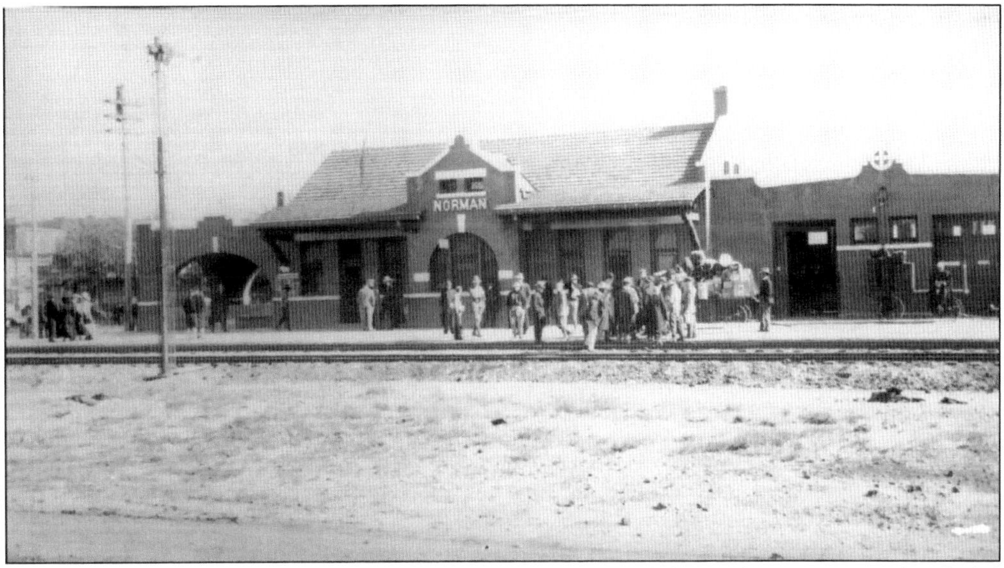


The design of the Norman Depot was a scaled-down version of the Guthrie station and included provisions for the latest Jim Crow laws—separate waiting rooms and bathroom facilities for African Americans. The site was on the east side of the tracks, at the end of Comanche Street. Over time, the south portico was enclosed, and the African American waiting room and bathroom were converted to office and storage space. (CCHS.)

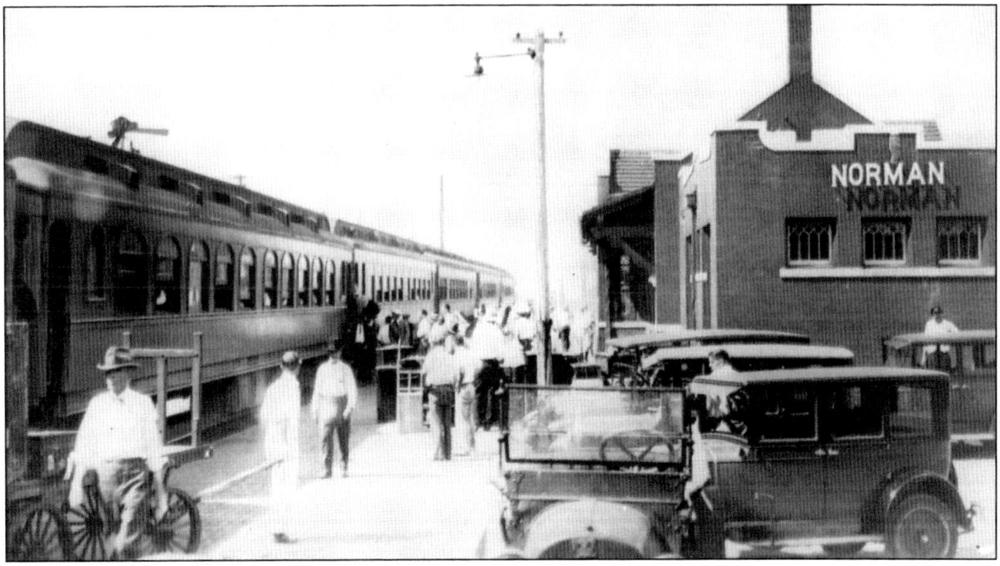


The Norman Depot was a busy place until passenger service was discontinued by the AT&SF in 1979. During the peak of railway travel, students attending the University of Oklahoma crowded the depot at the start and end of semesters. The platforms were especially crowded during home football games. Today, the Norman Depot is a historic landmark and is used for Norman art venues. (CCHS.)

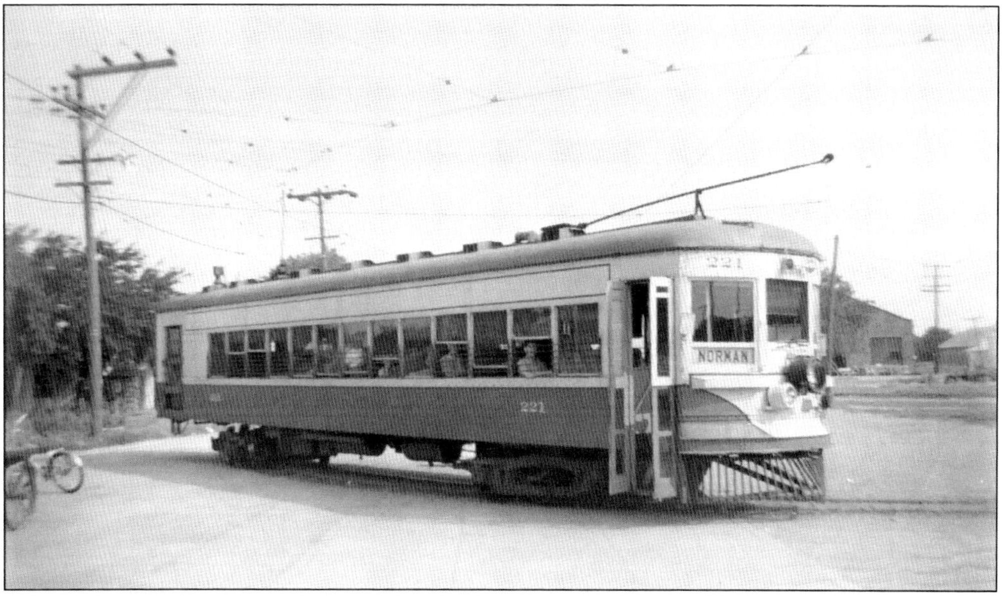


From 1900 to 1940, the interurban electric rail system was popular in most cities across America. The Oklahoma Railroad Company operated out of Oklahoma City beginning in 1904. By 1913, the line reached Norman. The interurban ran on light-rail tracks, receiving electric power from overhead lines. In adherence to Jim Crow laws, the cars were segregated by the use of two doors. African Americans entered through the rear door. (CCHS.)

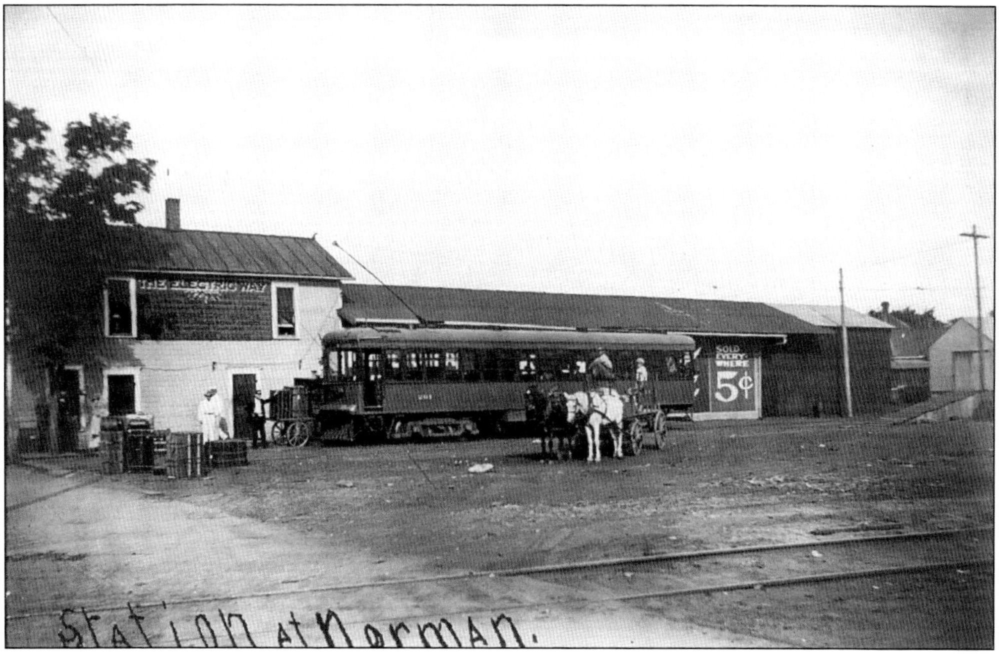


Many University of Oklahoma students commuting from Oklahoma City used the Norman interurban line. During World War II, when Norman had two Naval bases, traffic increased again. After the war, with the end of rationing, more Oklahomans could afford automobiles and gasoline, which quickly rendered the interurban obsolete. The interurban depot in Norman was on the north side of Main Street, just west of the Santa Fe tracks. (OHS.)

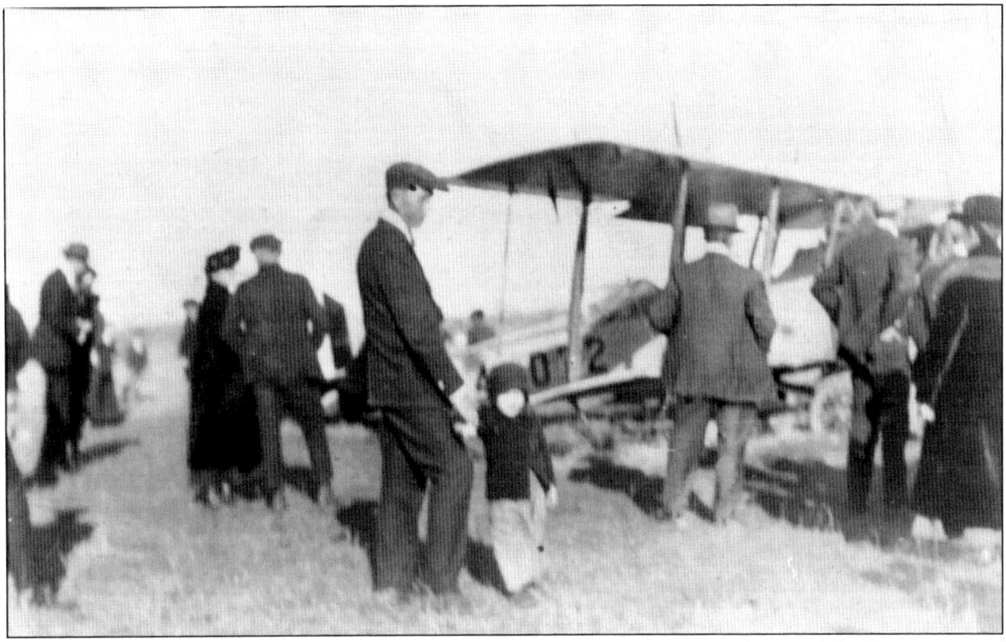

On December 6, 1919, 1st Lt. Charles Price of Waco, Texas, a 1918 graduate of the University of Oklahoma, flew an Army airplane over Norman, en route to his parents' home in Shawnee. He swooped down on the football field, brushed treetops, and landed west of campus. Price visited friends for a couple of hours and then continued his flight. This was the first airplane to land in Norman. (CCHS.)

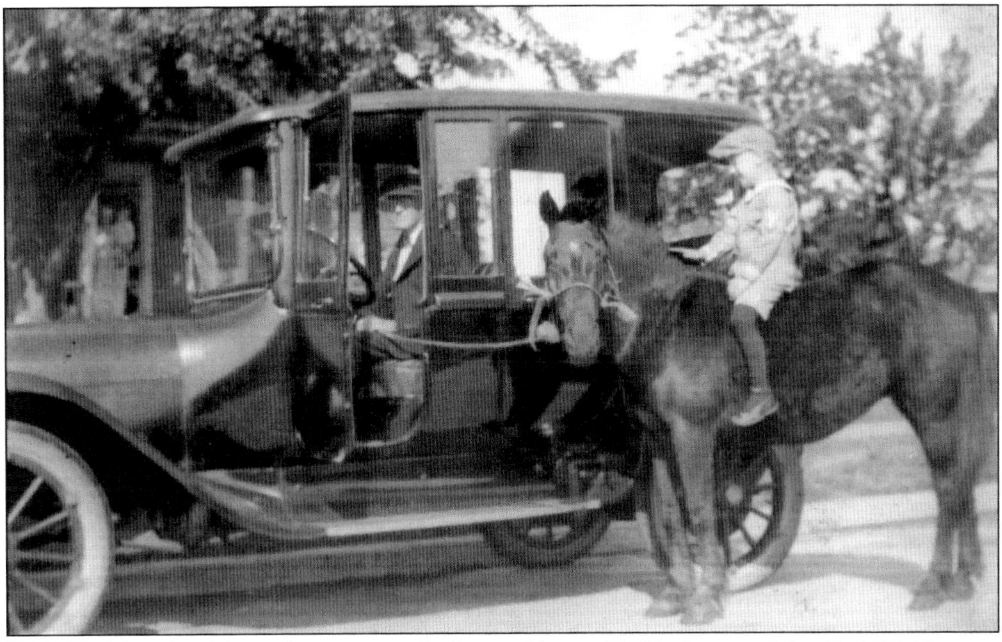

In the first decade of the 20th century, only the wealthy could afford automobiles. By 1910, Norman boasted a total of 15 cars. By 1923, when Henry Ford dropped the price of his Model T, one out of nine Cleveland County residents owned an automobile. That year, the state of Oklahoma issued 319,000 driver's licenses. (CCHS.)

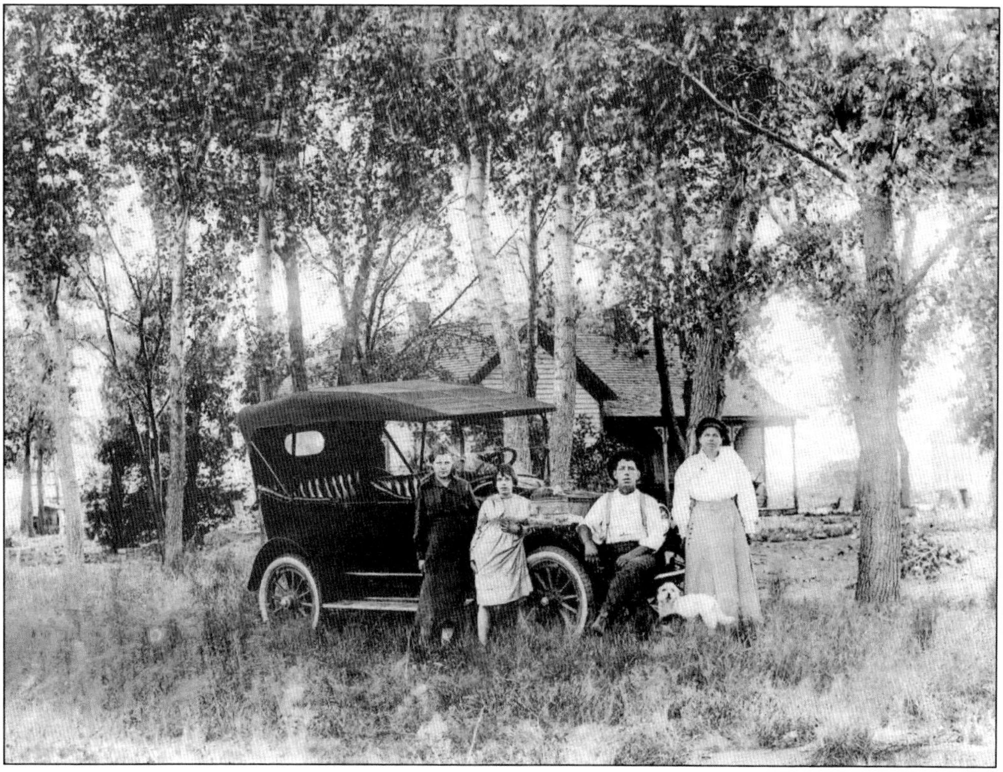

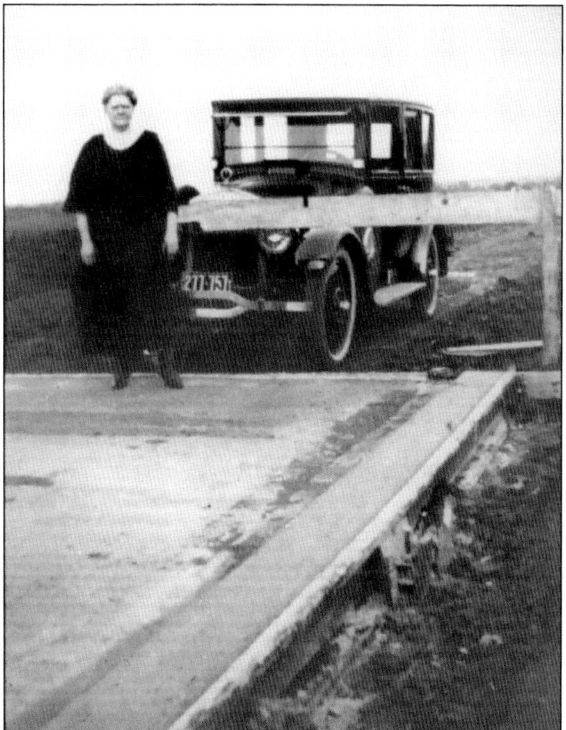

As automobiles became affordable for the average family, more people traveled throughout Oklahoma. Public parks were popular camping places, and towns accommodated visitors by developing overnight camps. By 1925, Norman allocated space in Andrews Park, in the center of town, for overnight camping. The park had bathroom and shower facilities, and each camp had a fire oven and a water hydrant. (CCHS.)

Until the late 1920s, most Oklahoma roads consisted of dirt or mud. To keep dust down in Norman, a city employee sprinkled and graded Main Street each day, until it was paved in 1913. The Federal Road Act of 1916 appropriated money to grade and gravel Oklahoma roads. In some towns, brick was used to provide an all-weather surface. By 1929, the state began paving the roadways. (CCHS.)

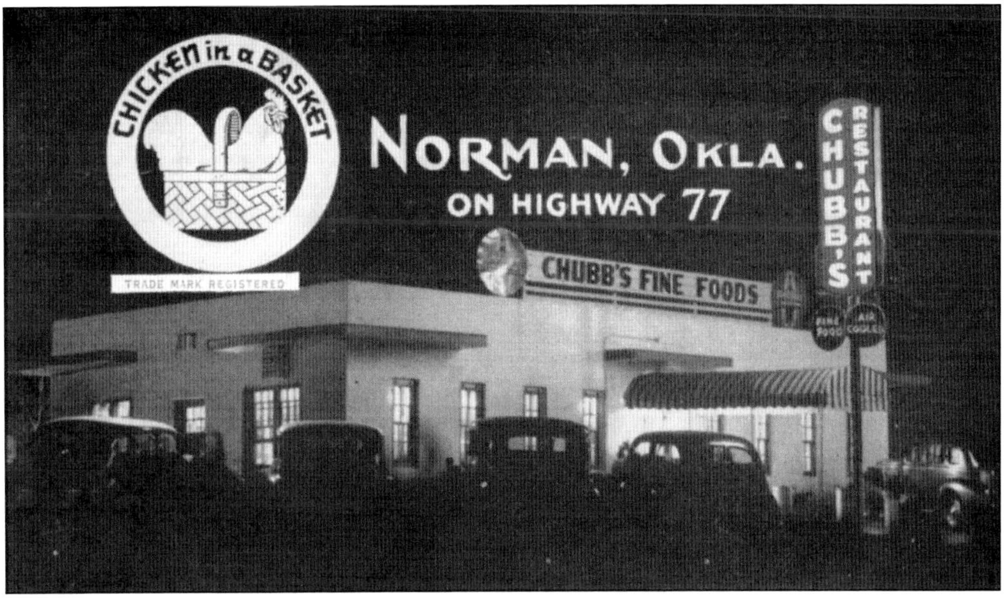


The Federal Interstate Highway Commission initially designated nine US highways for paving. US Highway 77, the north/south route from Iowa to Brownsville, Texas, came through Norman. It was known locally as the "football road," being the most heavily traveled route to University of Oklahoma football games. Highway 77 was the first highway in Oklahoma to be paved. Paving was completed in 1930. (CCHS.)

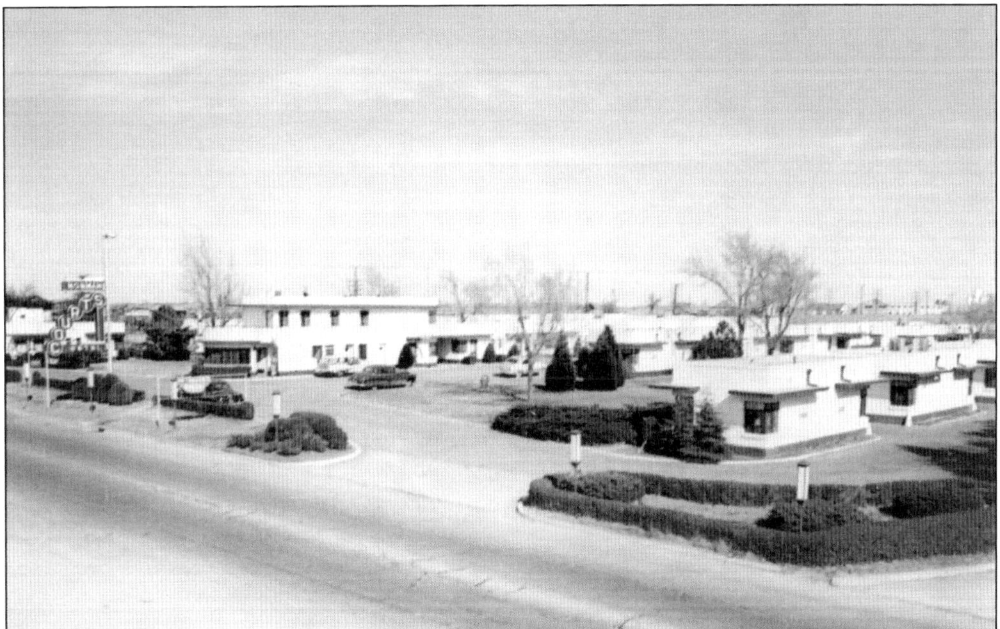

Along Route 77 in Norman were eating establishments, drive-in movie theaters, and motor courts. Norman Courts, which opened in 1939, was described as the "Nation's Outstanding Tourist Court." The air-conditioned motel had 85 rooms in 23 separate buildings. The key investor was Jack Foster, the youngest person to serve as mayor of Norman in 1929. Norman Courts was at the corner of US 77 (Porter Avenue) and Robinson Street. (CCHS.)

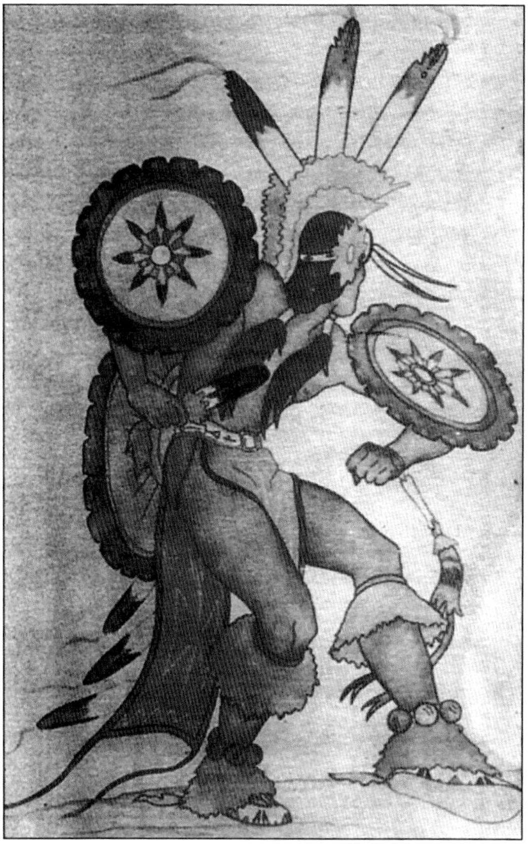

Inside the Norman Courts lounge were several murals by J. Craig Sheppard, an art student and instructor at the University of Oklahoma when he finished the murals in 1939. Sheppard became a distinguished Oklahoma artist and was known nationally for his depiction of Native Americans. He had been a student of Oscar Jacobson, dean of the School of Art at the university, and, later, Jacobson's son-in-law. (OHS.)

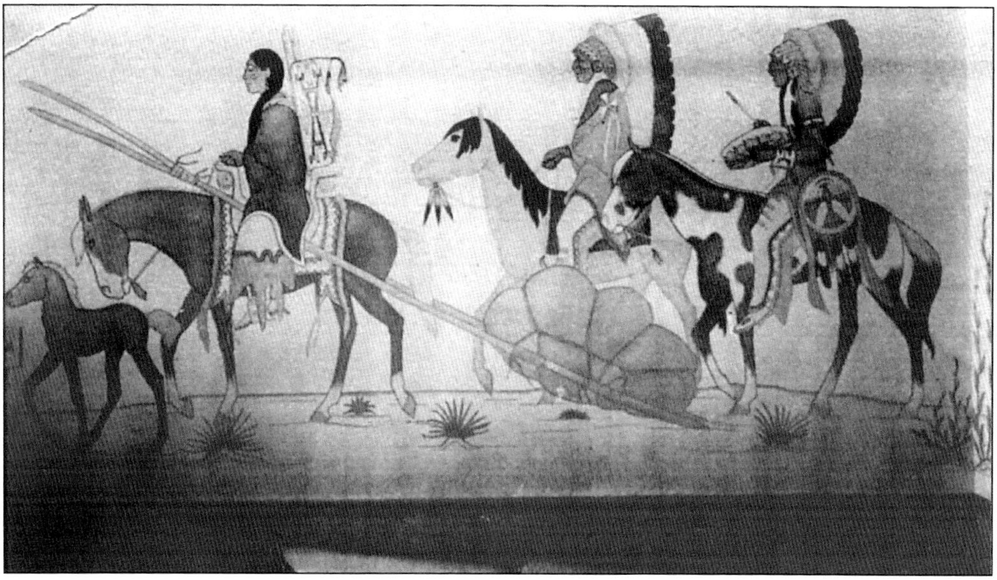

Sheppard used a new technique in his murals. He nailed white linoleum on the walls, then knife-sketched the outline of his picture. He then filled in the grooved outline with oil paint. Sheppard depicted Native American life and culture with figures that were more true to life than those of other artists, who depicted Native Americans as stick figures. (OHS.)

The Coterie Club (right) and Basketry Club (below) were two of Norman's first women's organizations. Women came together to establish the Coterie Club in the home of Carrie Holbrook in 1894. The first meeting was in the parlor of the Victoria Hotel. At first, Coterie was both literary and civic minded, the goal being to improve women's minds and to make improvements to the new prairie town. Coterie is the oldest club in Norman. Today, the women's main focus is literary. Women's clubs were successful in establishing the first library and raising funds each year to add books to the collection. The women also raised money to buy flags, pictures, and a new clock for Washington School. When the American Legion Hospital opened in 1925, the women raised money to furnish one room and bought the facility its first electric fan. (CCHS.)

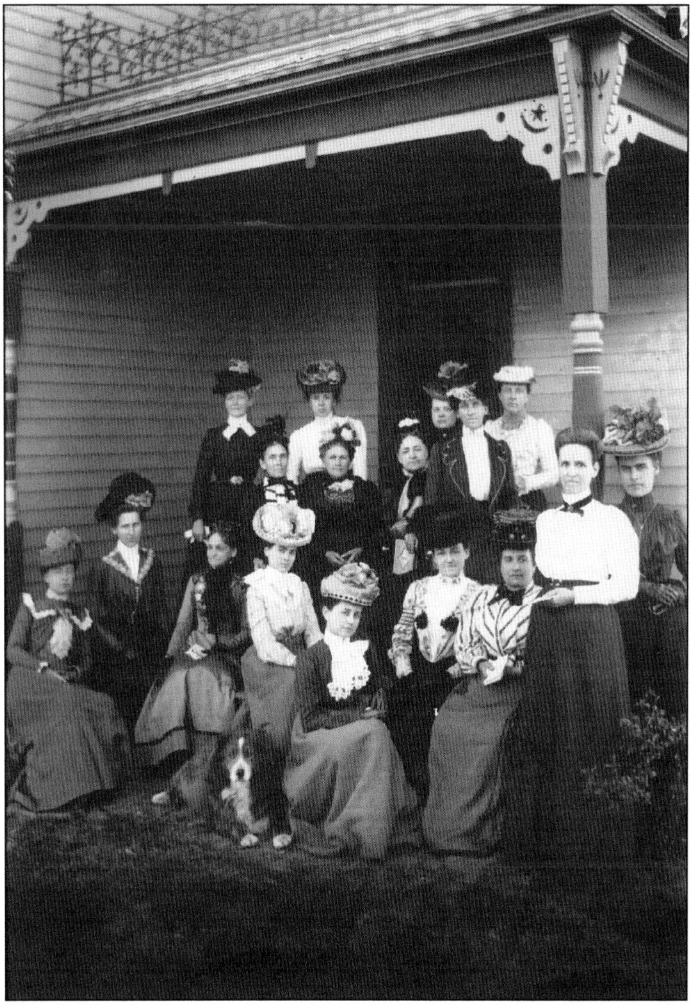

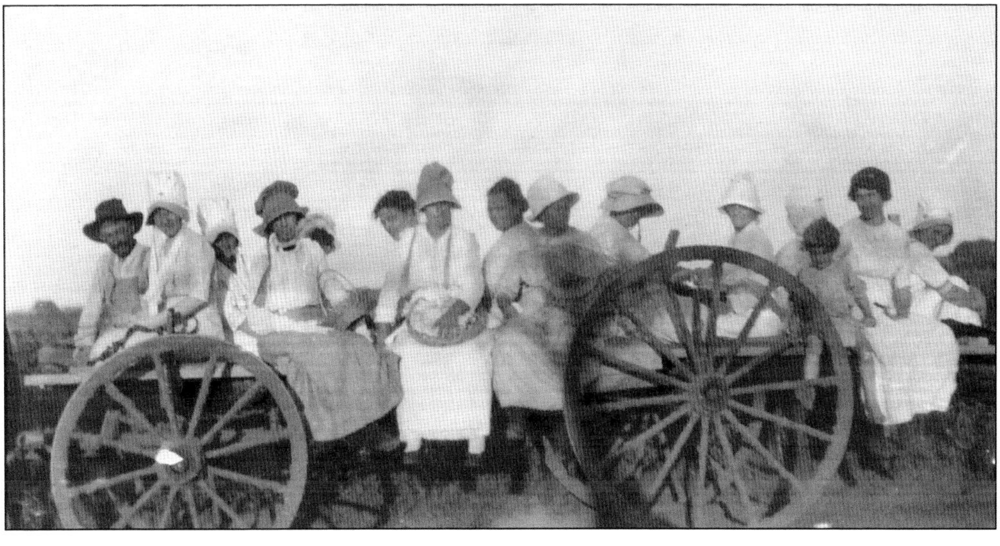

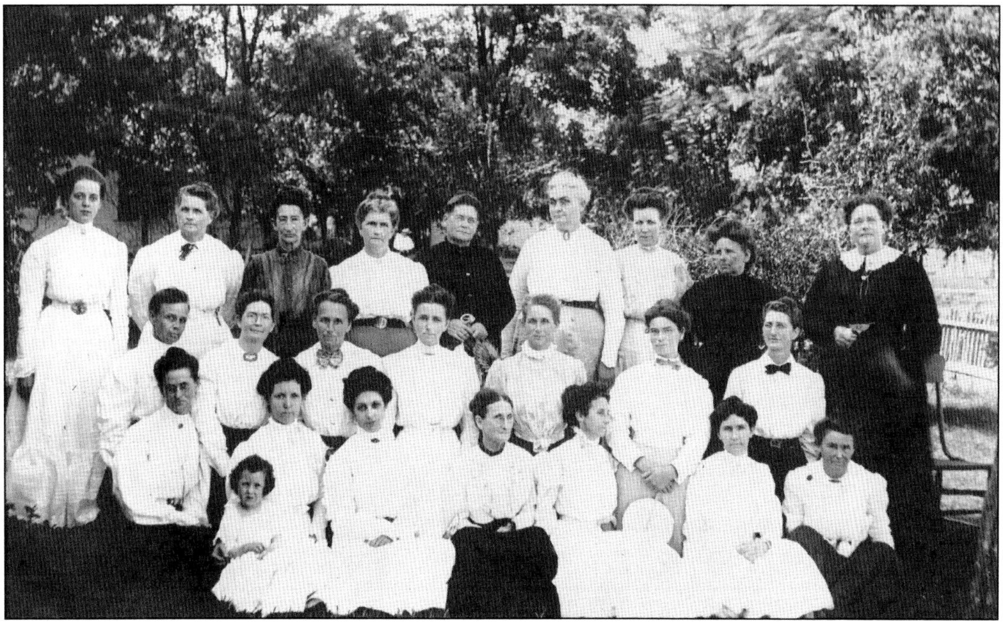

The New Idea Club was organized in Norman in 1909. This photograph of the cultural club was taken at the home of Mrs. J.J. Riley (top row, second from left). Among the prominent women seen here are Mrs. Briggs (top row, fourth from left), wife of Levi Briggs, town builder and merchant; Mrs. Capshaw (second row, second from left), whose husband was the town doctor; and Mrs. Bumgarner (second row, far right), daughter of Mrs. Briggs and grandmother of James Garner. (CCHS.)

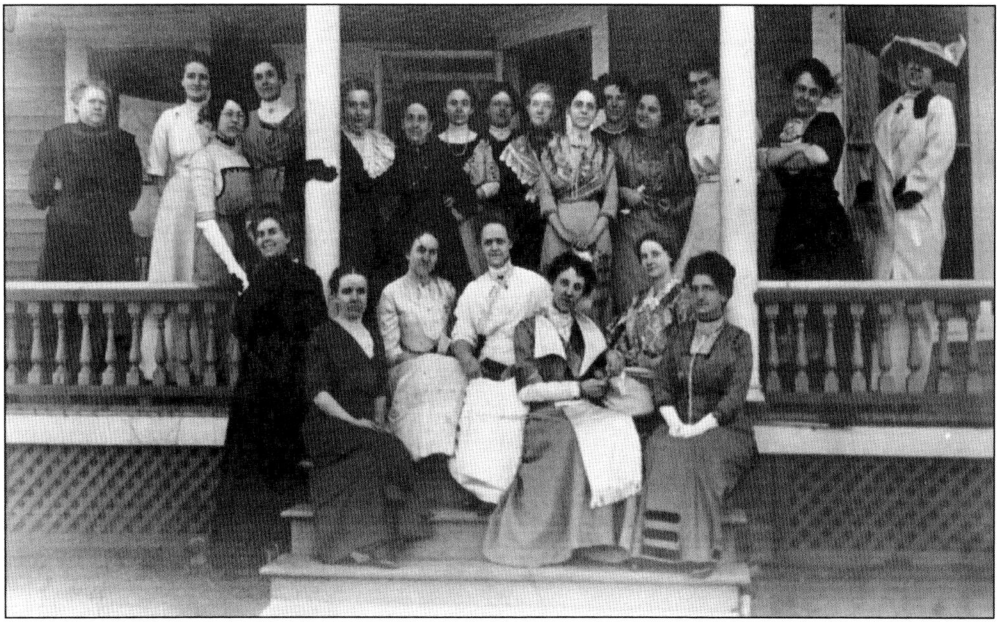

The Old Regime Study Club, seen here on the porch of Daisy Lindsay's home, was organized at her house in 1908. Lindsay was active in Norman's women's club movement. Along with her husband, Harry, they owned Barker Lumber Company. Daisy was known for her rose gardens and marketed her roses in town. The Lindsay house, at 508 North Peters Avenue, is now the Moore-Lindsay Historical House. (CCHS.)

The Norman Brass Band, which included the town's leading businessmen, made its debut in January 1890. Fred Reed and Tony Nolan were charter members. The band played at social activities in the new community and raised funds for various civic causes. They played at ice-cream socials for school supplies and at church socials to raise money for the needy. (CCHS.)

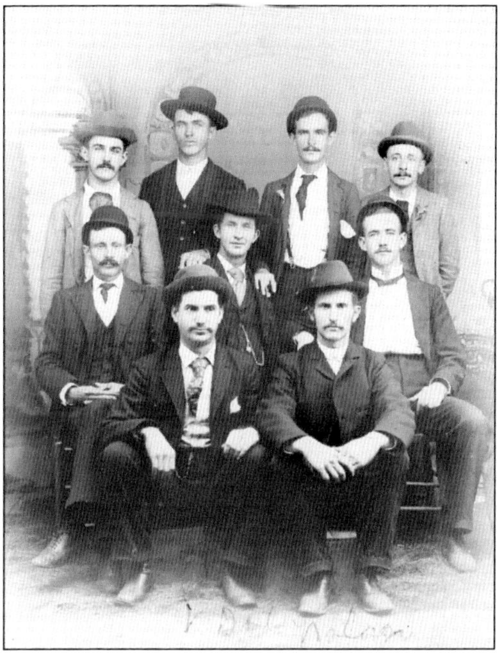

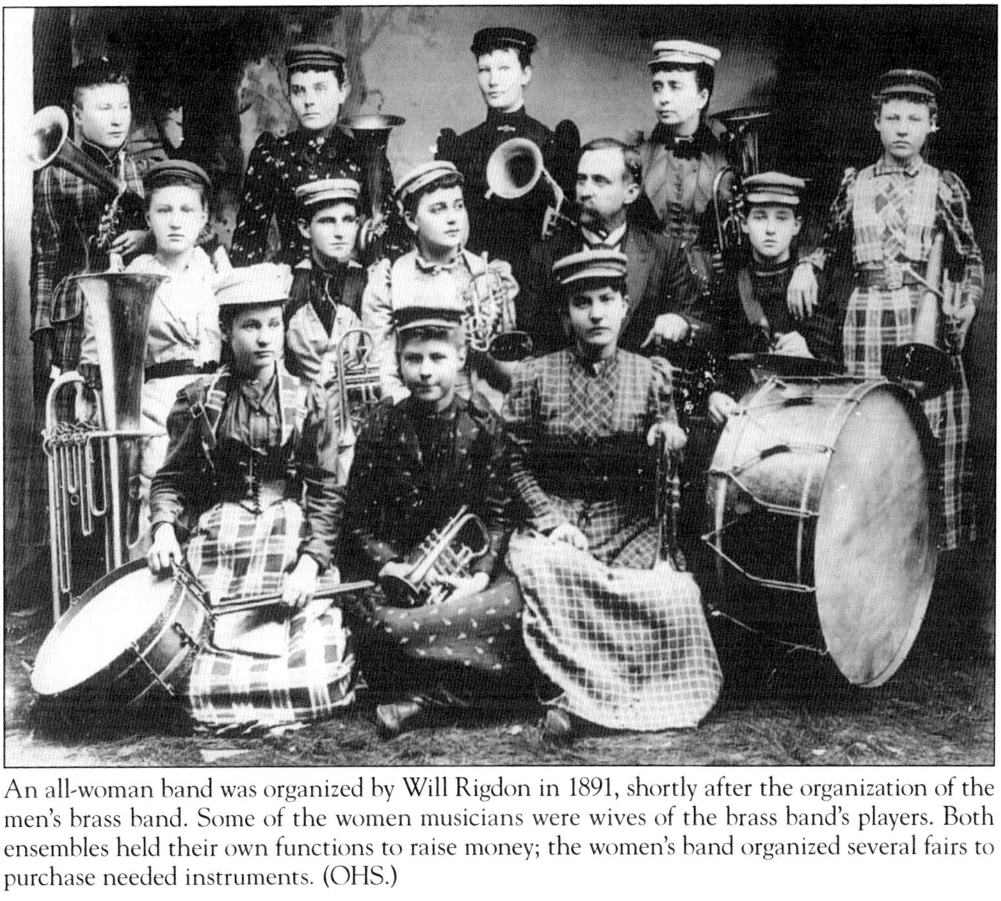

An all-woman band was organized by Will Rigdon in 1891, shortly after the organization of the men's brass band. Some of the women musicians were wives of the brass band's players. Both ensembles held their own functions to raise money; the women's band organized several fairs to purchase needed instruments. (OHS.)

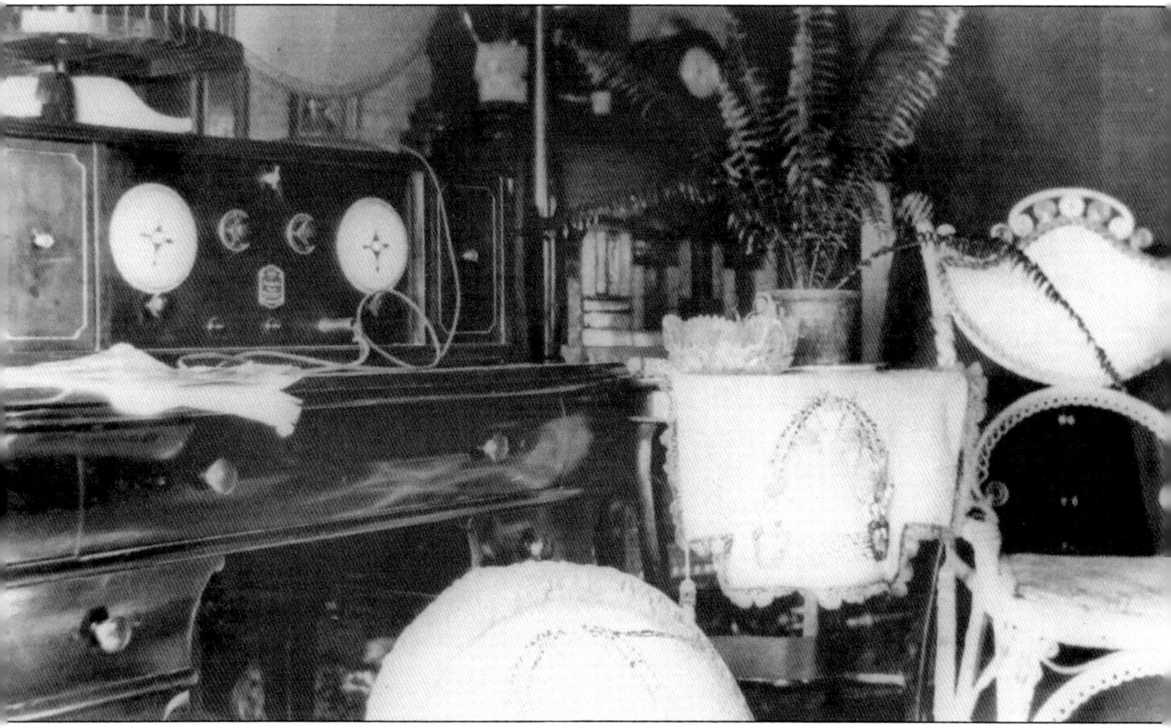

Norman residents adapted quickly to technological changes in the early 20th century. Shown here is Harry and Daisy Lindsay's wireless radio, which was proudly displayed in the entranceway to their home at 508 North Peters Avenue. Norman also had several phone companies connecting residents to one another in town and in the surrounding countryside. Purcell was the first town to offer phone service; in 1893, the first phone line connected Abernathy's drugstore in Lexington to the Purcell Santa Fe depot. The following year, 10 telephones were installed in Norman, and by 1895, the city of Norman had installed its own system. The switchboard was in the firehouse. In 1898, the city council granted a franchise to J.D. Phillips, who immediately connected 60 homes in town. By 1902, telephone lines extended into the countryside, connecting homes in rural Norman and Cleveland County. (CCHS.)

By the early 1900s, most small towns had opera houses. The Franing and Seawell opera houses were established in Norman in the 1890s. Seawell's Opera, at 111–113 East Main Street, was the first three-story building in downtown Norman. The building currently houses Mr. Roberts Furniture Store. Seawell's opening play was *Esmeralda*; its cast was made up of local citizens. From 1890 to 1929, most theaters in downtown Norman showed silent movies; "talkies" became the norm by 1930. The Varsity Theatre (right), at 108 East Main Street, started in 1910 as an "electric theater." The evolution from silent films to talkies kept the Varsity open until 1954. The University Theatre (below), an Art Deco structure at 225–227 East Main, showed films from 1925 to 1959. The most elegant theater in Norman was the Sooner Theatre, at 101 East Main Street. (OHS.)

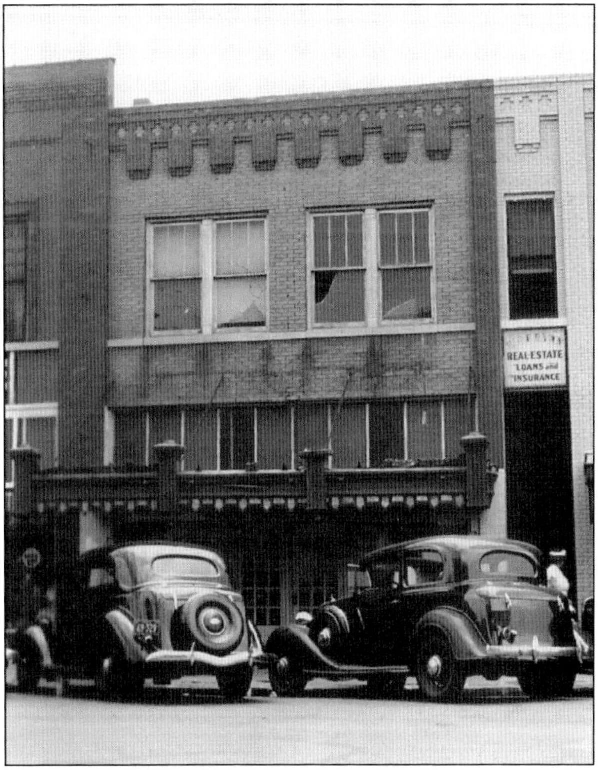


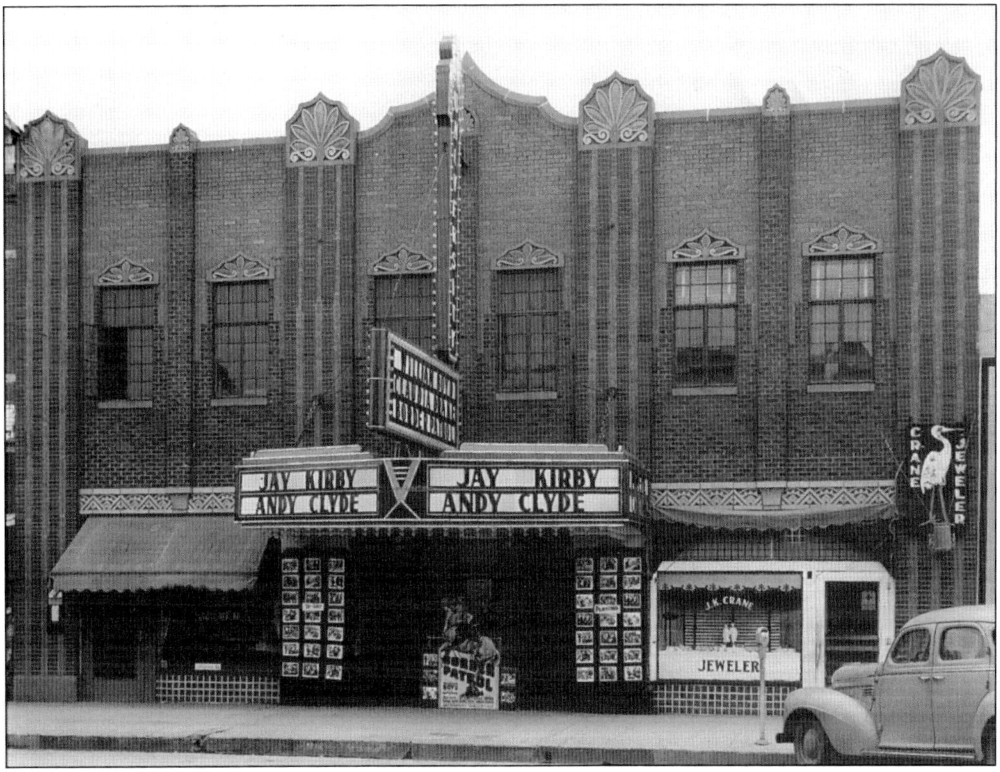

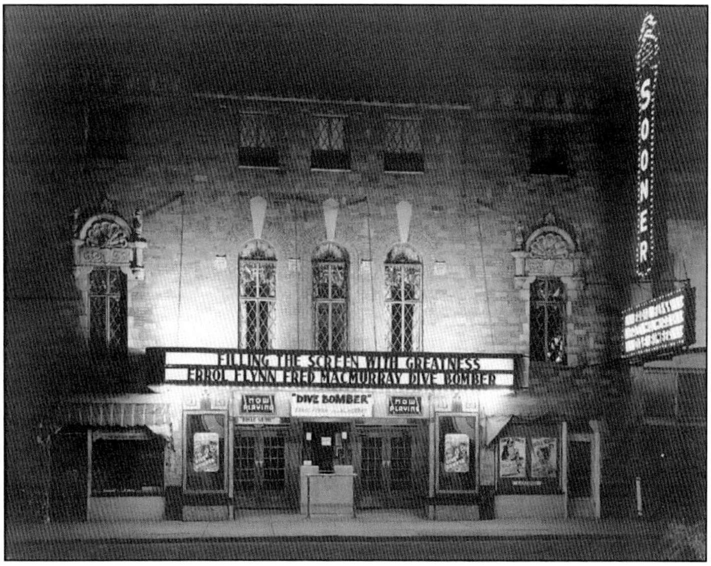


The Sooner Theatre was built in 1929 at 101 East Main Street. The theater occupies the town lot where Pryor Adkins erected the Planter's Hotel, the first brick building in Norman. Adkins's building was used as a gathering place for Christmas and New Year's dances and as the location of the first play in Norman, *Among the Breakers*. The Adkins building was razed in 1928 to make room for the Sooner. (OHS.)

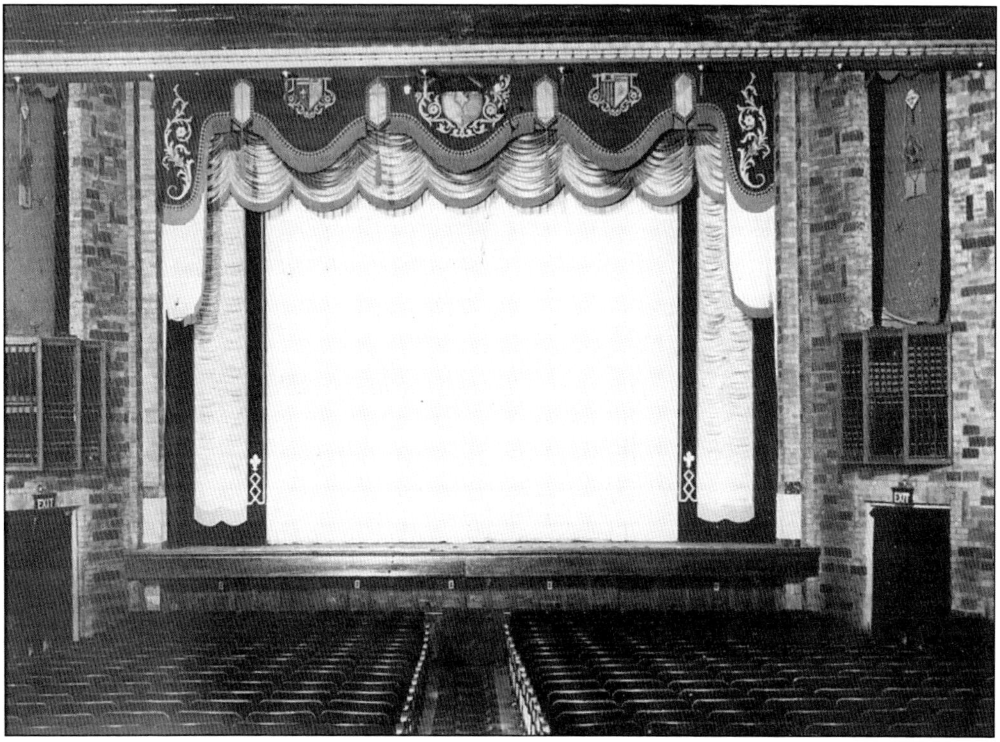

The Sooner Theatre's architect, Harold Gimeno, designed a Spanish Colonial interior emphasizing imported mosaic tile and Italian marble. The ceiling has 252 hand-painted Spanish coats-of-arms. Amenities included "refrigerated air" and cooled water fountains. Gimeno and his father, Patricio, hand painted the high beams and wall decorations. The theater, which also boasted specially designed lights and stained-glass windows, cost more than $200,000 to build. (OHS.)

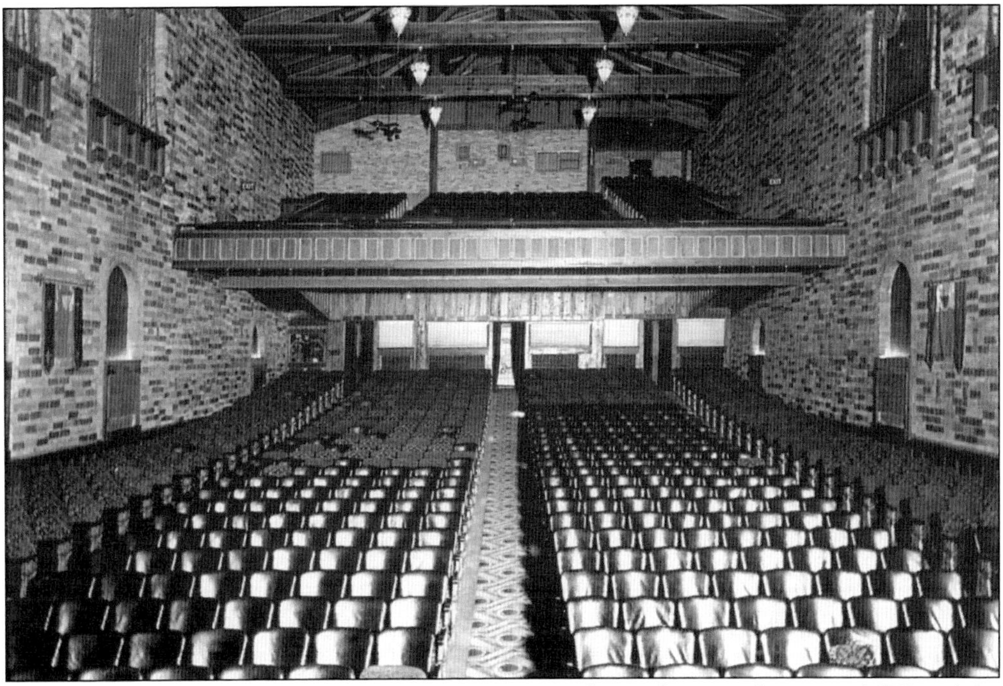

The three-story Sooner Theatre had a seating capacity of 819. The main floor seated 585, and the balcony had 234 seats. There was a special ladies lounge on the mezzanine and a cry room for families with babies at the orchestra level. When the theater opened in February 1929, the management boasted that the facility was one of the first "talkie" motion picture theaters in the country. (OHS.)

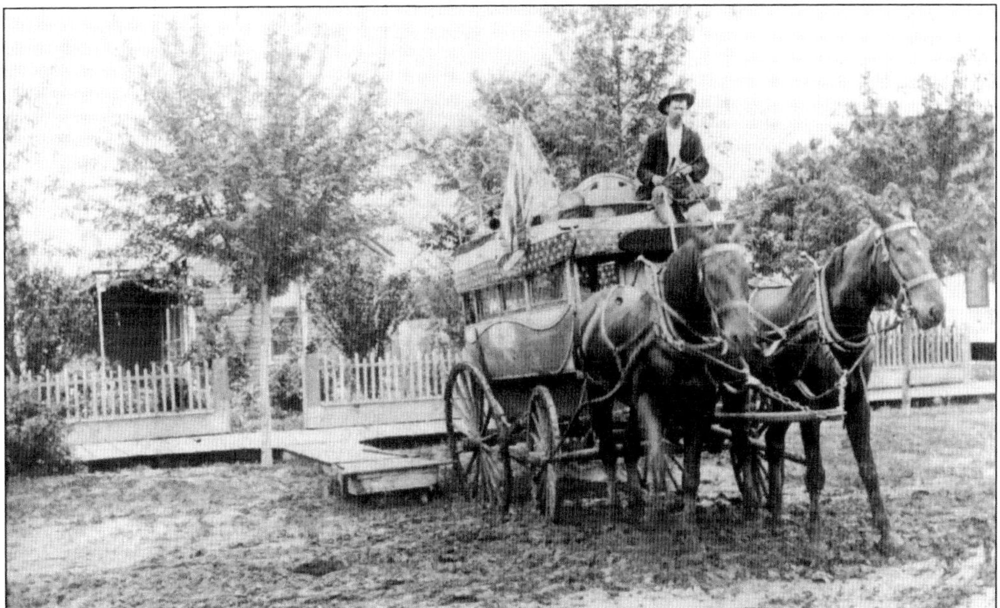

Norman residents celebrated the Fourth of July and 89er Day with parades and picnics. The parade started on East Main Street and headed west to Andrews Park. The town fire engine led the parade, and the band played from the park grandstand. Activities in the park included sock races, climbing the greased rope, bronco riding, Native American dances, and, at night, fireworks. (CCHS.)

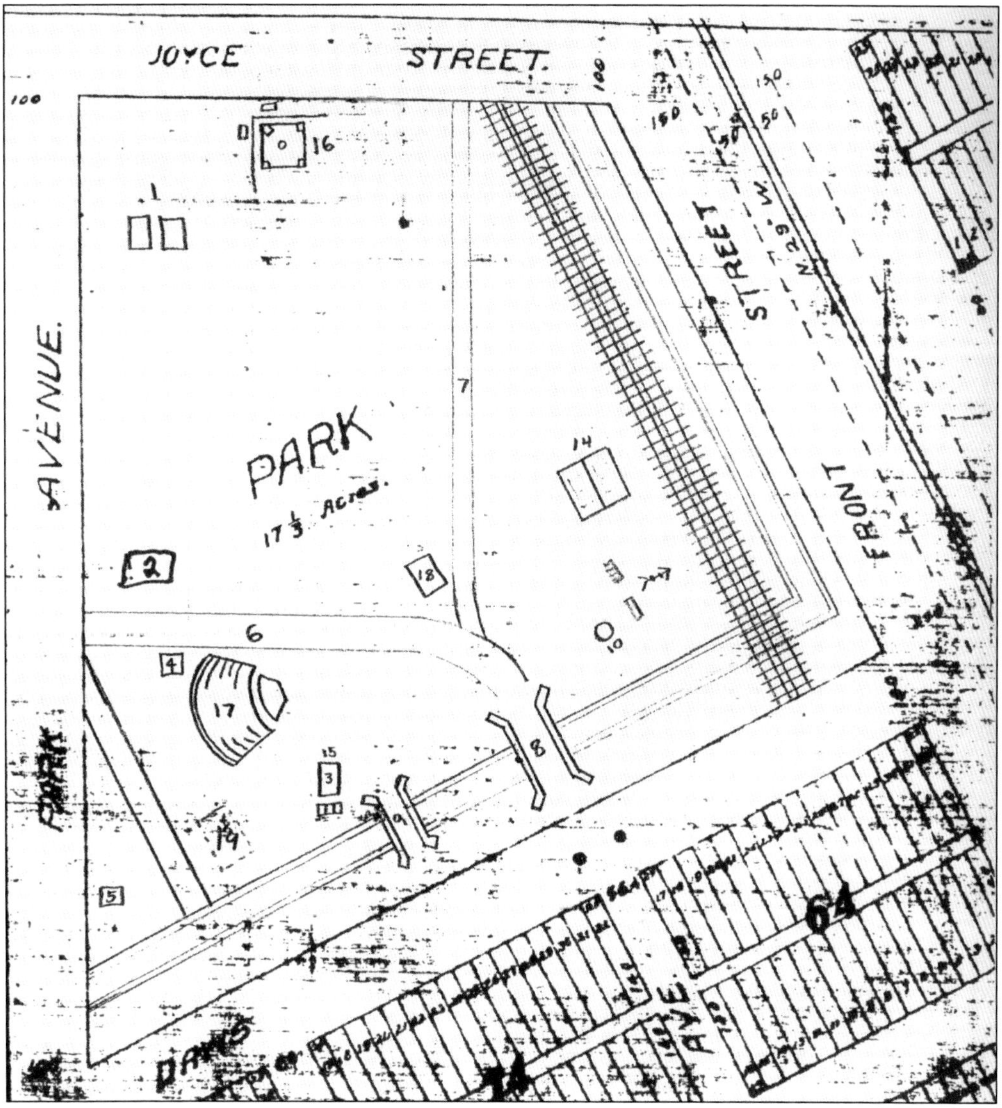


A park was included in the original 1889 town plat. Until 1925, the park was used for holiday celebrations and the Cleveland County fair. The only structures in the park were stock barns. In June 1926, James Adson "Abe" Andrews became superintendent of Norman Parks. Beginning in 1926 and throughout the Great Depression, the park provided free recreation and a cool respite from economic difficulties. Free movies were shown for children, and food was handed out to the needy. In 1926, Andrews started a zoo, which housed deer, bobcats, pheasants, and an ocelot. The park was bordered on the south by Daws Street, on the east by Front Street, on the west by Park Avenue, and on the north by Acres Street. Two gravel streets bisected the park. In 1927, Andrews added a merry-go-round, a slide, swings, trapeze bars, and a wading pool. This sketch notes the interurban's path along the railroad tracks. In 1937, Works Projects Administration laborers built an amphitheater, park pavilion, and stone ditches that are still in place today. (CCHS.)

# *Five*

# UNIVERSITY TOWN

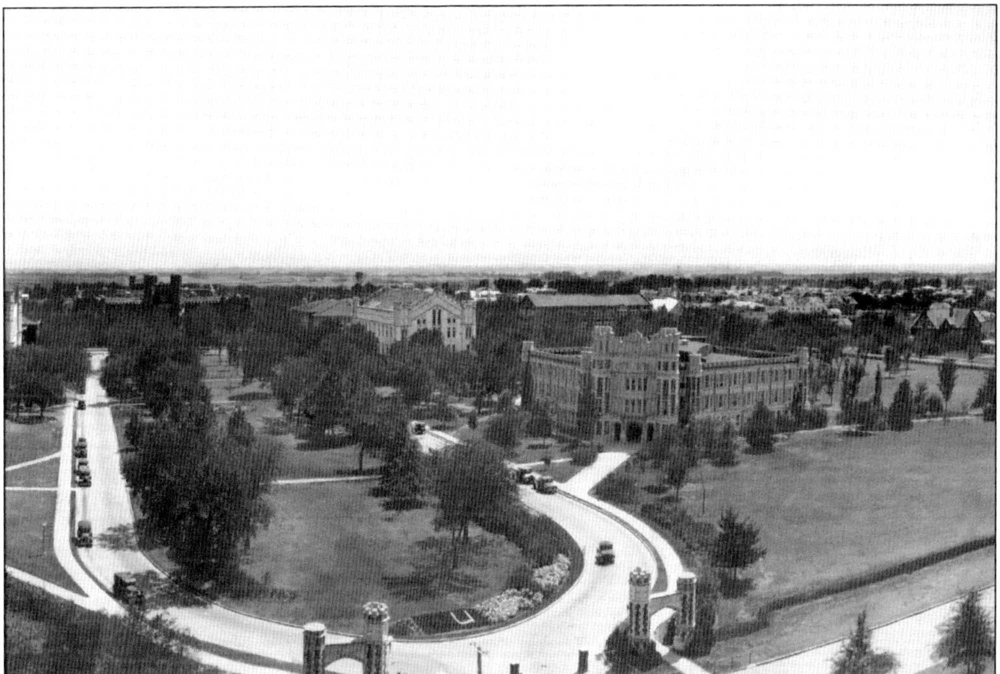

The Territorial Legislative Act of 1890 provided for the establishment of a state university in Norman. The university improved the struggling town economy and helped to define its culture. Once again, the eastside and westside political factions strongly debated an institution's location. The predominately Republican west side won. In July 1891, Seth M. Moore donated 40 acres southwest of town, land originally owned by his father-in-law, Charles Gorton. (CCHS.)

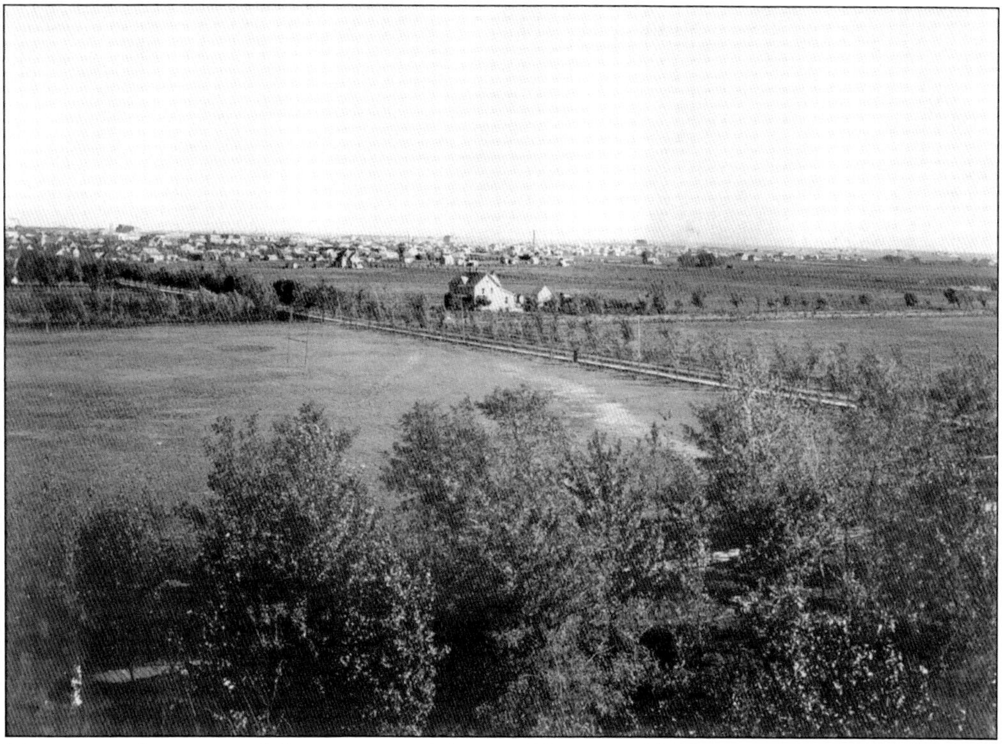

To connect the town and the university, Thomas Waggoner, Norman's first mayor, and Dilbert Larsh, a Norman founding father and initial organizer of the Norman Townsite Company, donated a strip of land 100 feet wide and a quarter of a mile long, from West Main Street to the university; the connecting corridor became University Avenue. (CCHS.)

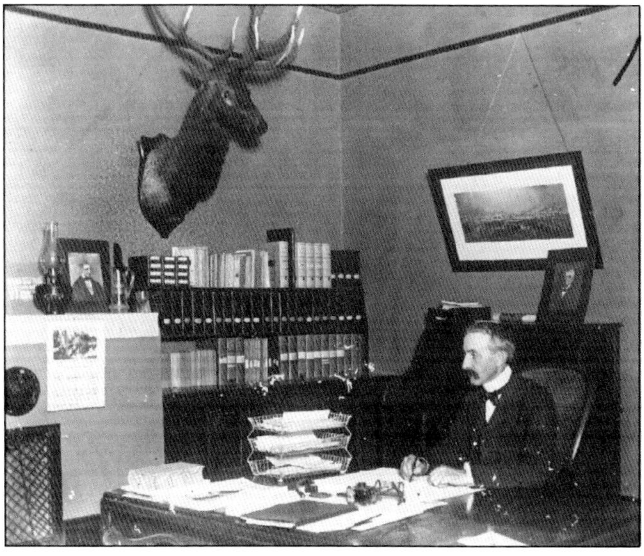

The first president of the University of Oklahoma was David Ross Boyd. Before his appointment, Boyd was superintendent of schools in Arkansas City, Kansas. University regents offered Boyd the position of president in 1891 after two regents traveled to Kansas to inquire about a heating system recently installed in the town's school system. After meeting Boyd and hearing his presentation in Oklahoma City on heating systems, the regents offered him the job. (CCHS.)

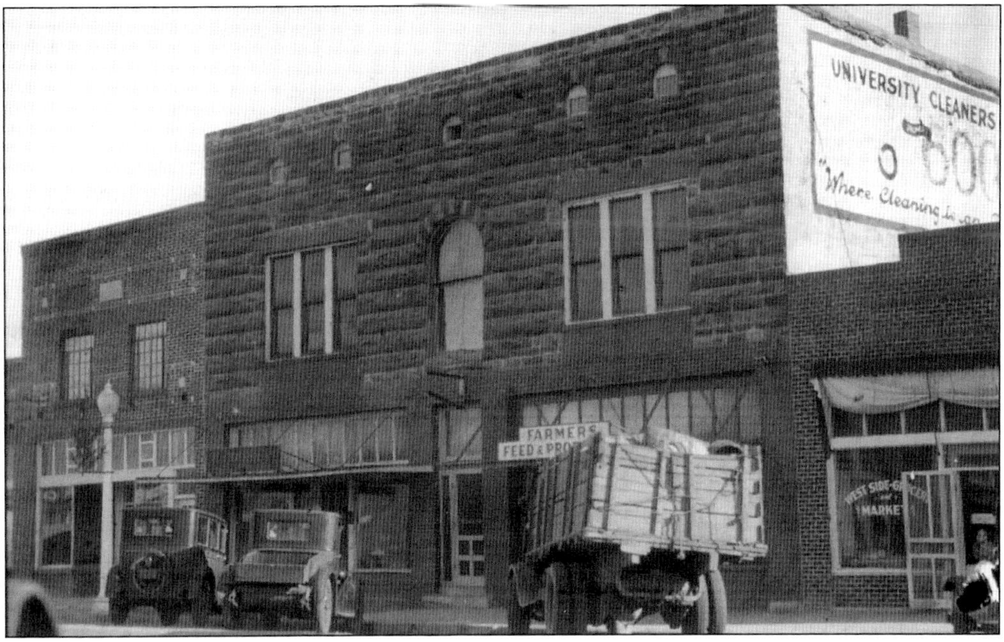

The territorial legislature allocated $10,000 to erect the first campus building, and work on it began on March 29, 1892. While construction was under way, classes began on September 15 in the Adkins-Welch building, 202 West Main Street. Boyd rented the second floor for $20 a month for four classes. The last occupant of the Adkins building was Landsaw's Furniture. Today, First Baptist Church owns what is now an empty lot. (OHS.)

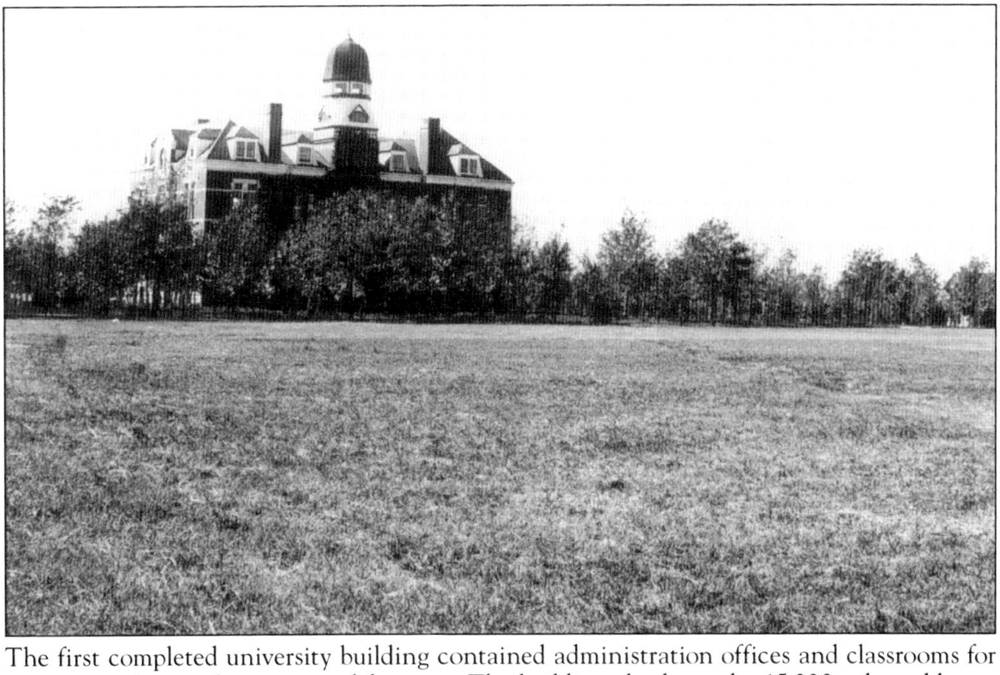
The first completed university building contained administration offices and classrooms for science, math, social science, and fine arts. The building also housed a 15,000-volume library. On the first day of class, there were 57 students. By December, 83 students attended, and in the spring of 1893, the enrollment was 119. (CCHS.)

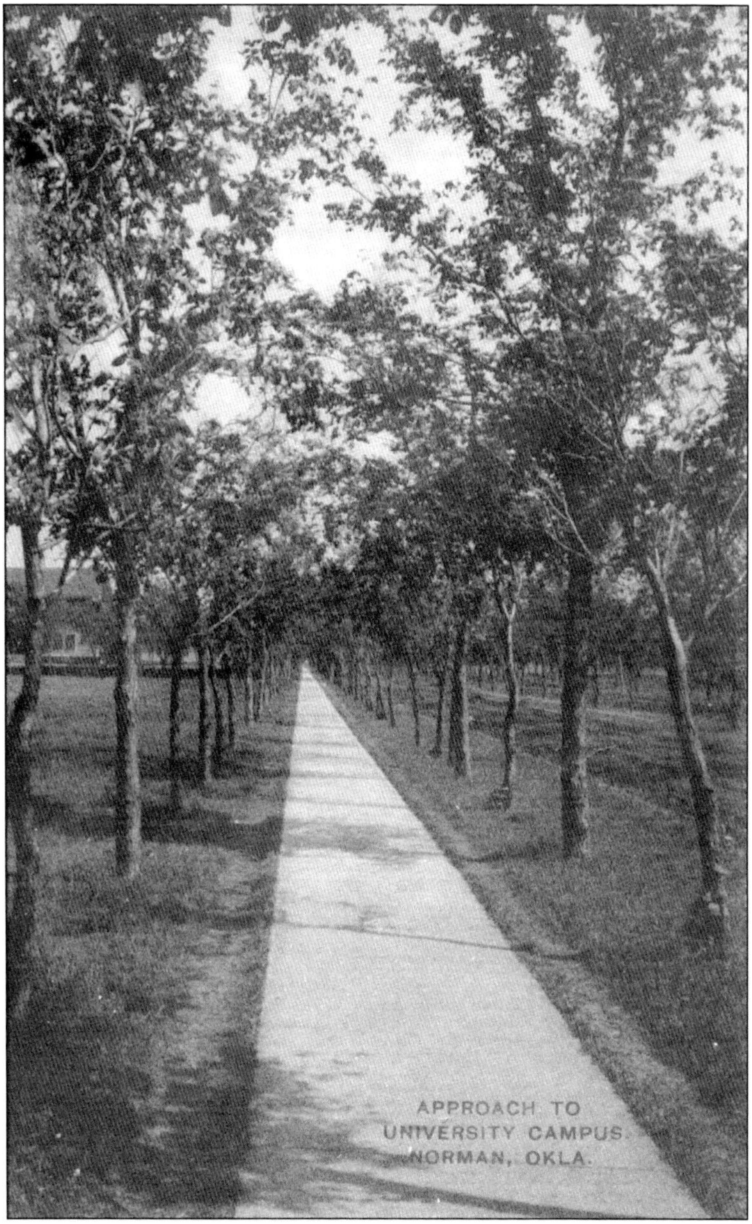


President Boyd worked hard to transform the prairie countryside, initiating a tree-planting campaign. In 1893, he ordered young saplings dug from creek beds to be planted on campus. None of the saplings survived the dry season. Next, Boyd bought trees from a nursery in Kansas. He planted five acres in rows behind the campus building. He watered the trees himself with water he purchased for 15¢ a barrel. He offered trees to citizens; if the trees lived, they were free, but if the trees died, the citizen owed Boyd for the loss. For a while, Boyd's tree nursery augmented university revenue. Trees were planted in double rows on each side of University Boulevard, and a bicycle path extended down the middle of the row of trees on the west side. Eventually, a boardwalk was built from Main Street to the university. In 1903, the boardwalk was replaced with a cement walkway. Bicycles became so popular a mode of transportation for students that walking to campus along University Boulevard was a perilous proposition. (CCHS.)

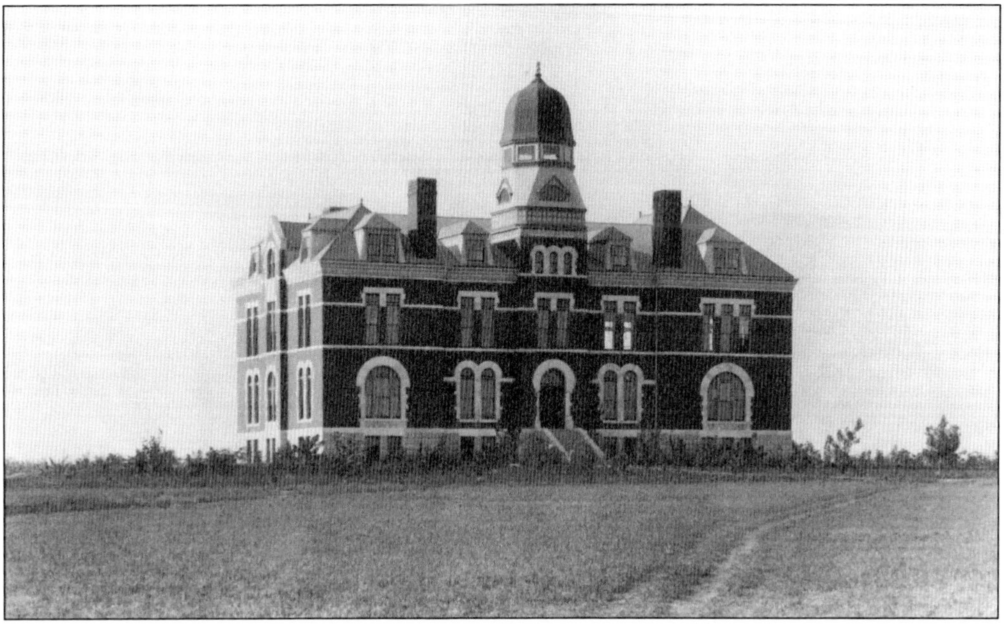

In 1903, a fire broke out in the southeast corner of University Hall's basement. There were few resources to fight the fire. Those who witnessed it tried to save what they could of the furniture and papers, including students' grades in the president's office. The 15,000-volume library, however, was destroyed. A new building campaign started while classes were resumed in the Adkins-Welch Rock building on East Main Street. (CCHS/WHC.)

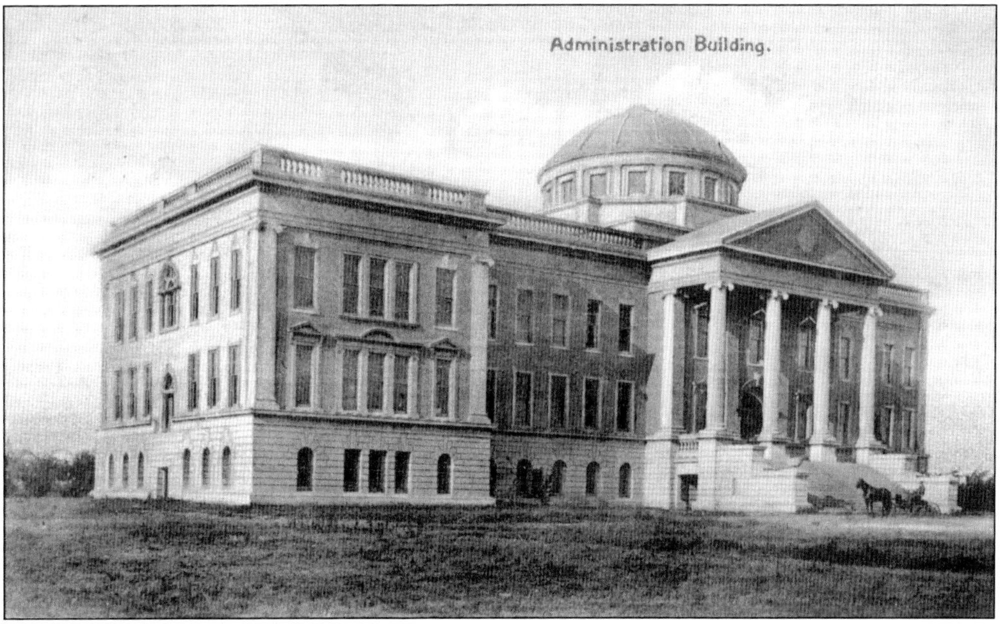


Expanding the new campus was a slow process, due to monetary constraints. However, before the fire destroyed the university building, the territorial legislature had appropriated $90,000 for a new classroom building and administrative offices. The appropriation and insurance money made it possible to renovate the fire-stricken building, which became the science hall, and at the same time build the new University Hall. (CCHS.)

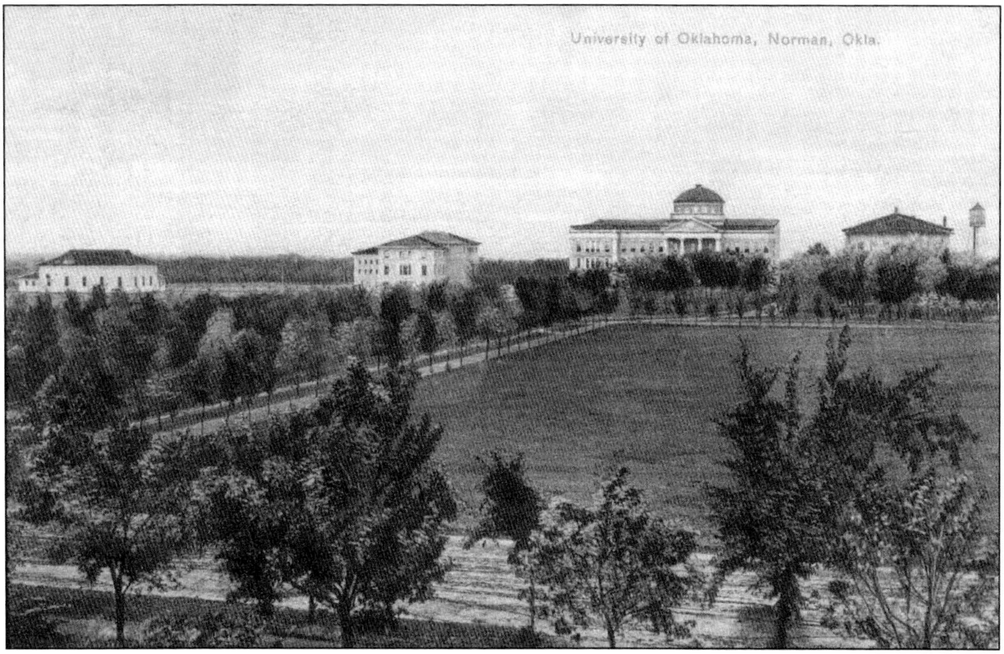


In spring of 1904, the new University Hall opened. The building was east of the original building and faced north. The $68,040 structure, of Renaissance design, had tall white pillars in front, which supported a gable with the new university seal. A pinewood dome covered with tin topped the three-story structure. The new building opened with an enrollment of 400 students. (CCHS.)

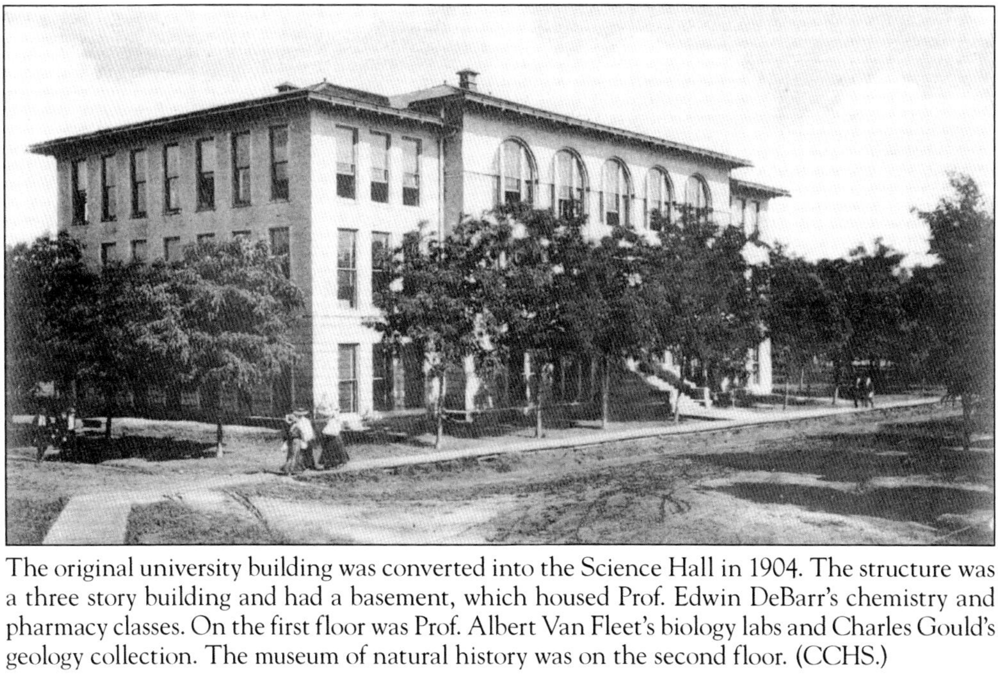

The original university building was converted into the Science Hall in 1904. The structure was a three story building and had a basement, which housed Prof. Edwin DeBarr's chemistry and pharmacy classes. On the first floor was Prof. Albert Van Fleet's biology labs and Charles Gould's geology collection. The museum of natural history was on the second floor. (CCHS.)

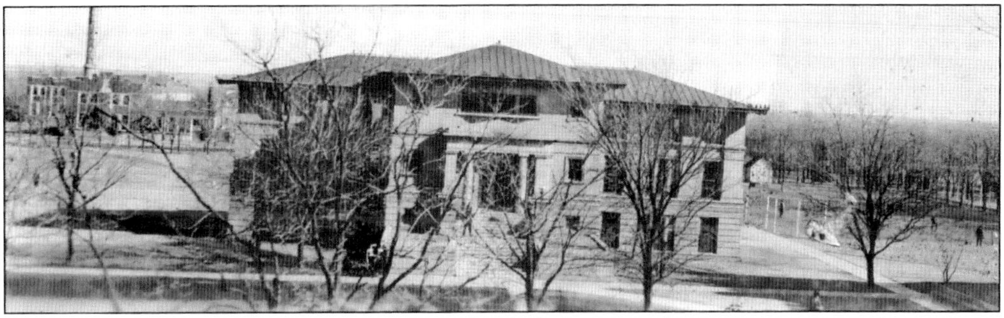

The Carnegie library was constructed with funds from an Andrew Carnegie Foundation grant in 1904. Between 1883 and 1929, Andrew Carnegie, businessman and philanthropist, donated funds for the construction of public and university libraries throughout the United States and Europe. The University of Oklahoma was the first university to receive a Carnegie library grant. (CCHS.)

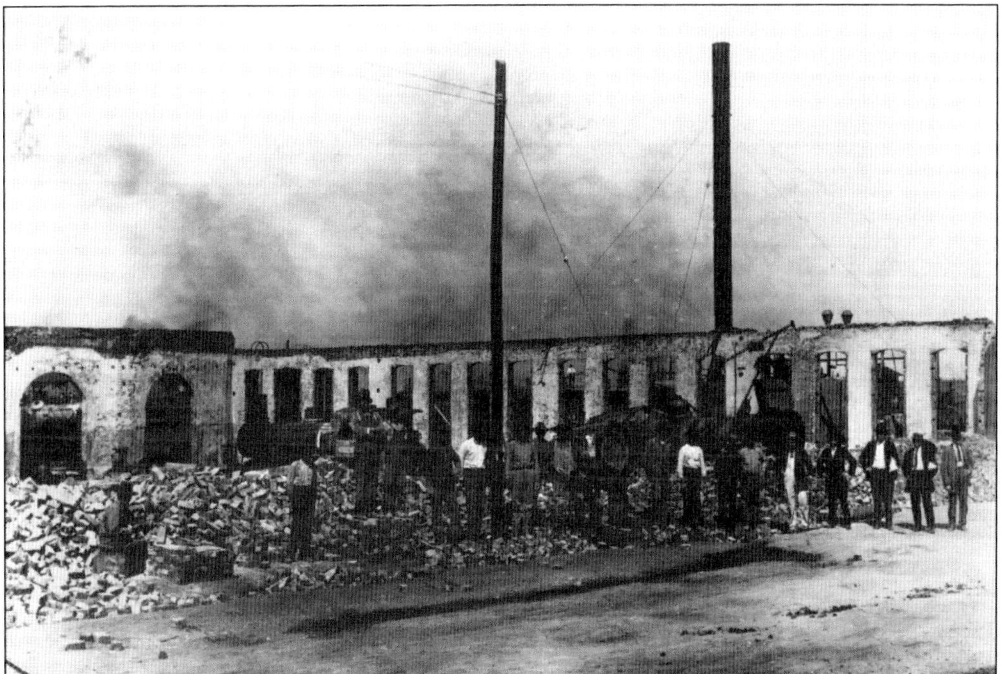

In December 1907, a fire destroyed the new University Hall. This blaze, however, did not destroy valuable records housed in administrative offices. Learning from the 1903 fire, all records were kept in a vault. The fire started on the roof, where workmen were heating paint on a gasoline stove to refinish the dome. The stove exploded, sending burning paint over the dome; the fire quickly spread to the interior of the building. (CCHS.)

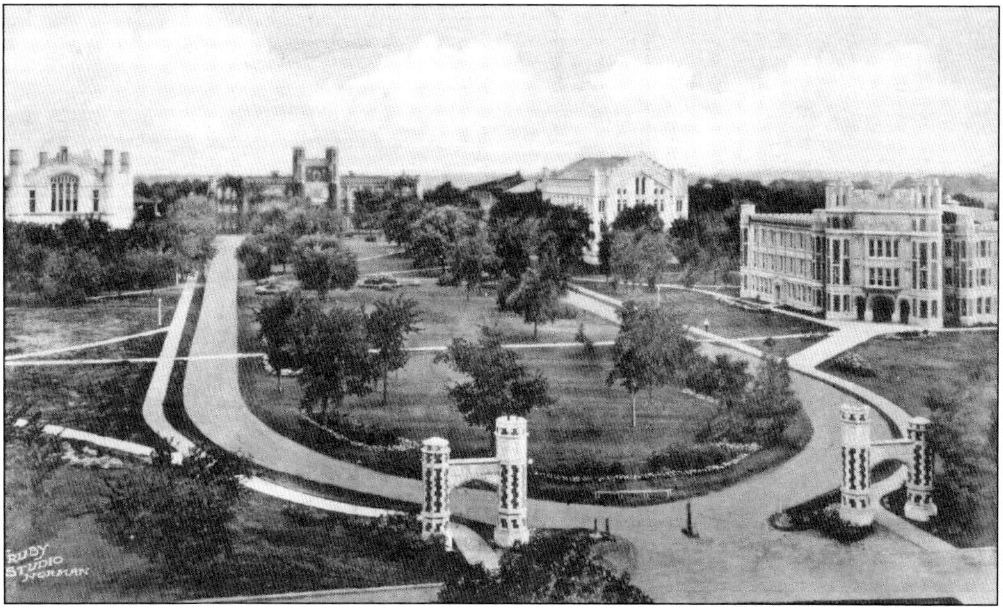

After the 1907 fire, Vernon Louis Parrington, who joined the faculty as an English instructor in 1897, devised a plan to organize core university buildings along an oval. This north oval became the Parrington Oval. Parrington coached football from 1897 to 1891. In 1908, after democrat Charles N. Haskell became Oklahoma's first governor, he fired Parrington and six other faculty members, including President Boyd, all of whom were Republicans. (CCHS.)

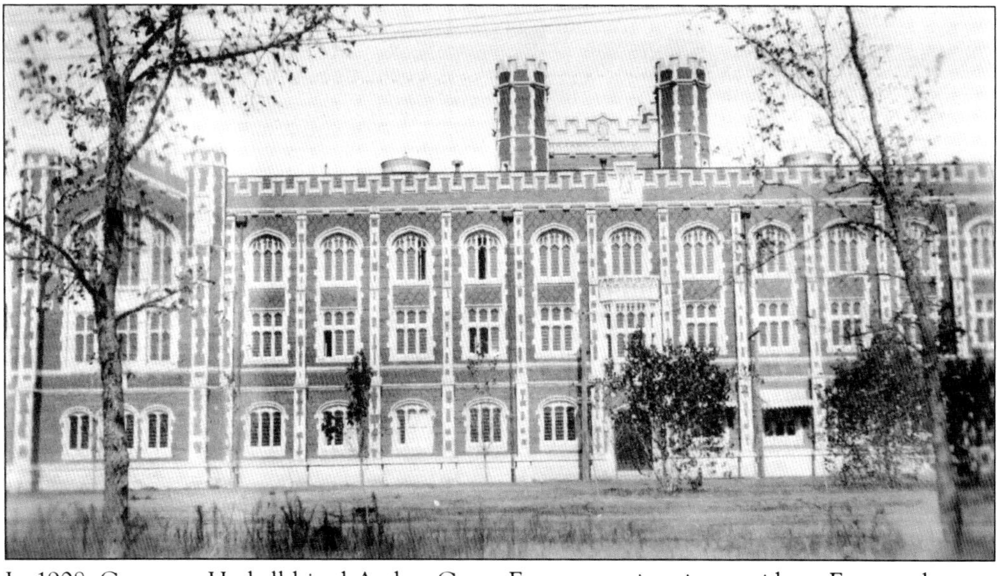

In 1908, Governor Haskell hired Arthur Grant Evans as university president. Evans, who was born in India of British parents, was a Democrat and a prohibitionist. He had immigrated to the United States as a missionary to the Cherokees. The regents hired 28 new faculty members that year to teach in new and reorganized programs. Shown here in 1911 is the third University Hall, which served as the administration building. (CCHS.)

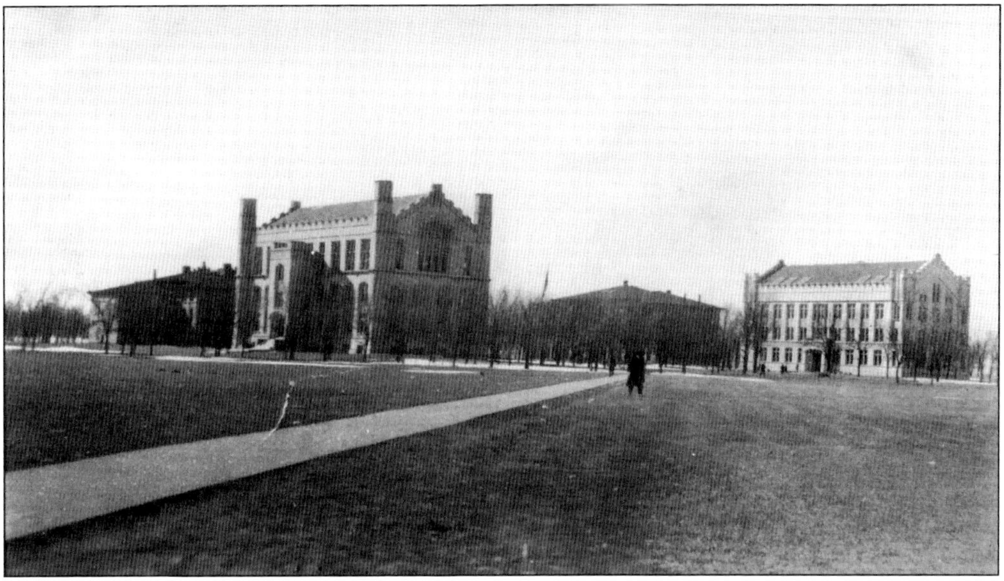

One of the new buildings along the Parrington Oval was the School of Law. The building stood on the east side of the oval, north of the Carnegie library (seen in the foreground). It was finished in 1914 and honored Julian Charles Monnet, a Harvard Law School graduate and the first dean of the university's law school. Today, Monnet Hall houses the University of Oklahoma's Western History Collection. (CCHS.)

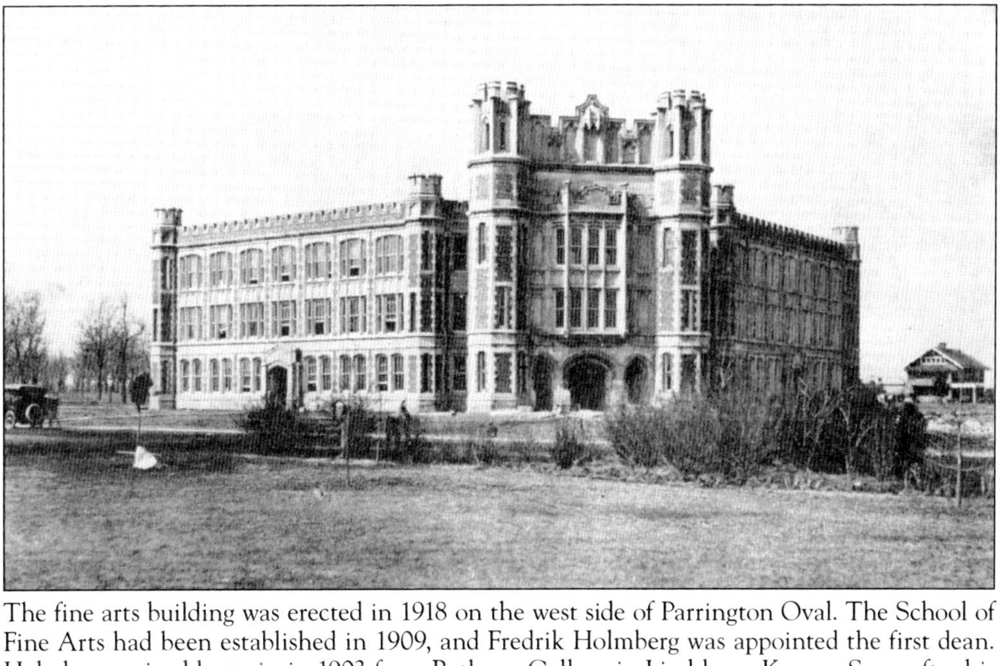

The fine arts building was erected in 1918 on the west side of Parrington Oval. The School of Fine Arts had been established in 1909, and Fredrik Holmberg was appointed the first dean. Holmberg arrived by train in 1903 from Bethany College in Lindsborg, Kansas. Soon after his arrival, he organized the glee club, band, and orchestra. Holmberg conducted student concerts throughout the state. (CCHS.)

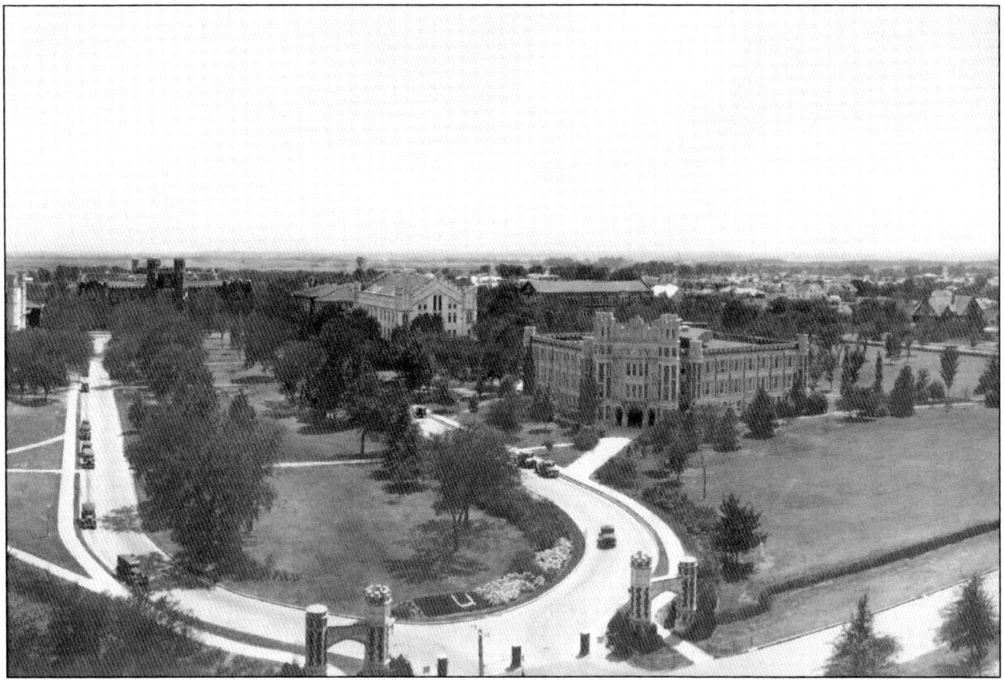

The fine arts building (on the near right) was named Holmberg Hall in 1938. At the time it was built, the structure was considered a fine specimen of European-style opera house. Its style exemplifies what architect Frank Lloyd Wright termed "Cherokee Gothic," a combination of European Gothic and Native American cultural motifs. In 2005, after extensive renovations, the hall became the Donald W. Reynolds Performing Arts Center. (CCHS.)

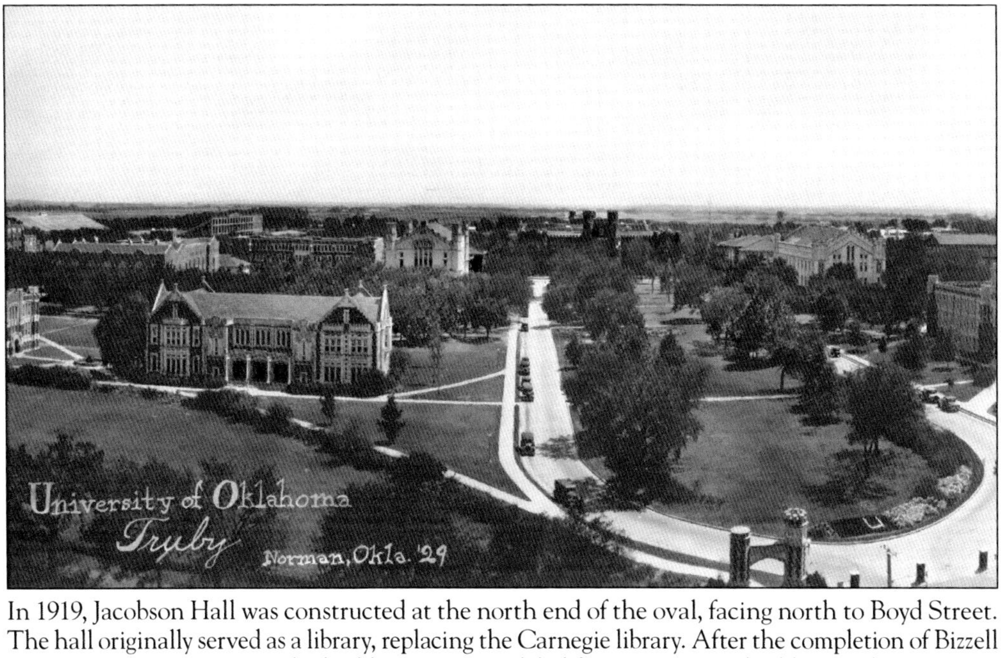


In 1919, Jacobson Hall was constructed at the north end of the oval, facing north to Boyd Street. The hall originally served as a library, replacing the Carnegie library. After the completion of Bizzell Memorial Library in 1930, the building was remodeled for use as an art building and museum. It was named after Oscar B. Jacobson, first dean of the School of Fine Art. (CCHS.)

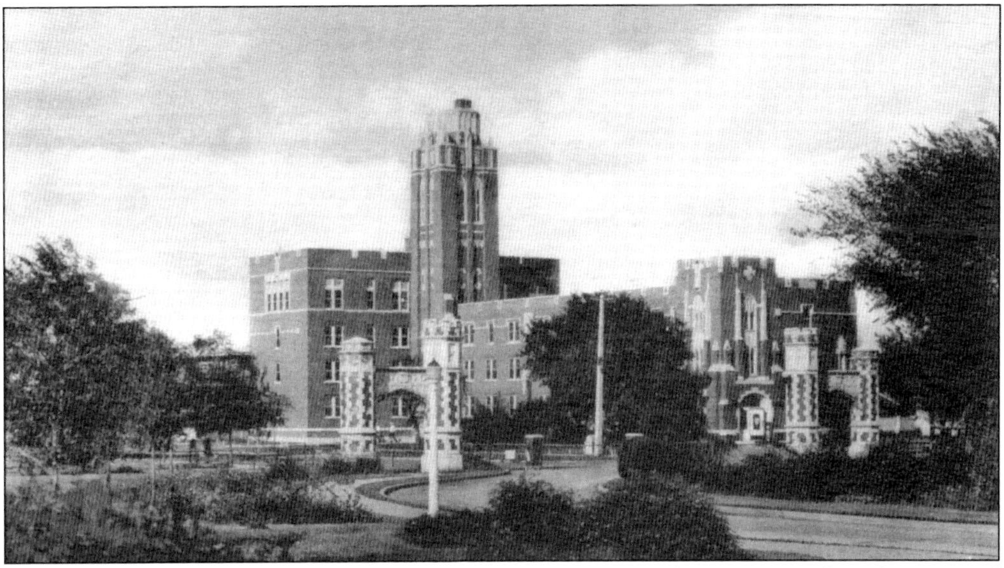

The Masonic Lodge of McAlester built Albert Hall, on the northeast corner of Boyd Street and University Boulevard, in 1921 as a men's dormitory. The Masons had a strong presence on OU's campus since its founding; President Boyd and the first three faculty members were Masons. The university bought Albert Hall in 1946 and renamed it for OU drama professor Robert Whitehand, who was killed in World War II. (CCHS.)

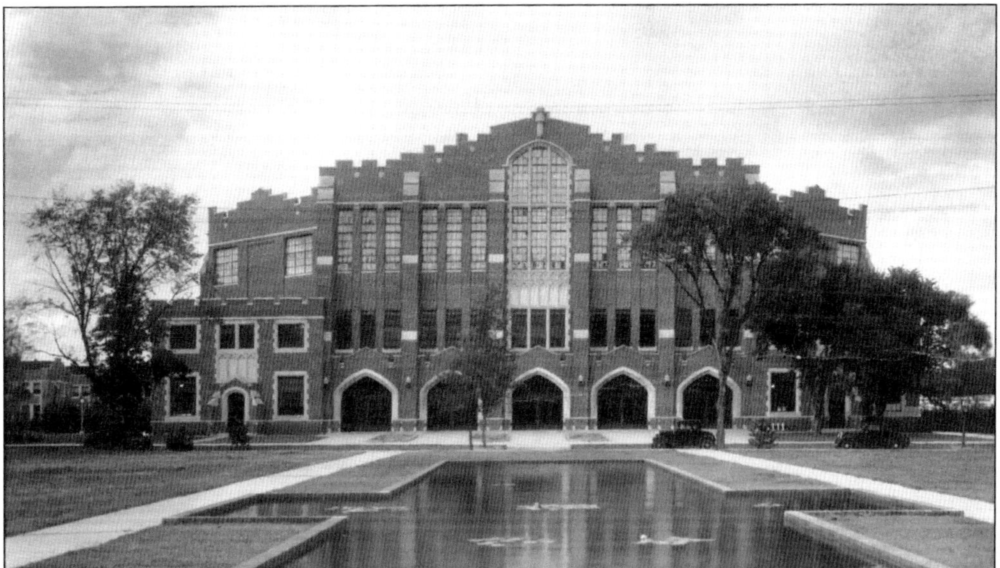

McCasland Field House, finished in 1928, served as the physical education building. It was home to the varsity basketball team. The reflecting pool in front faced south to the university's football field. In 1895, Jack Hart coached the university's first football team, whose initial game was against Methodist College in Oklahoma City. OU lost 30-0. (CCHS.)

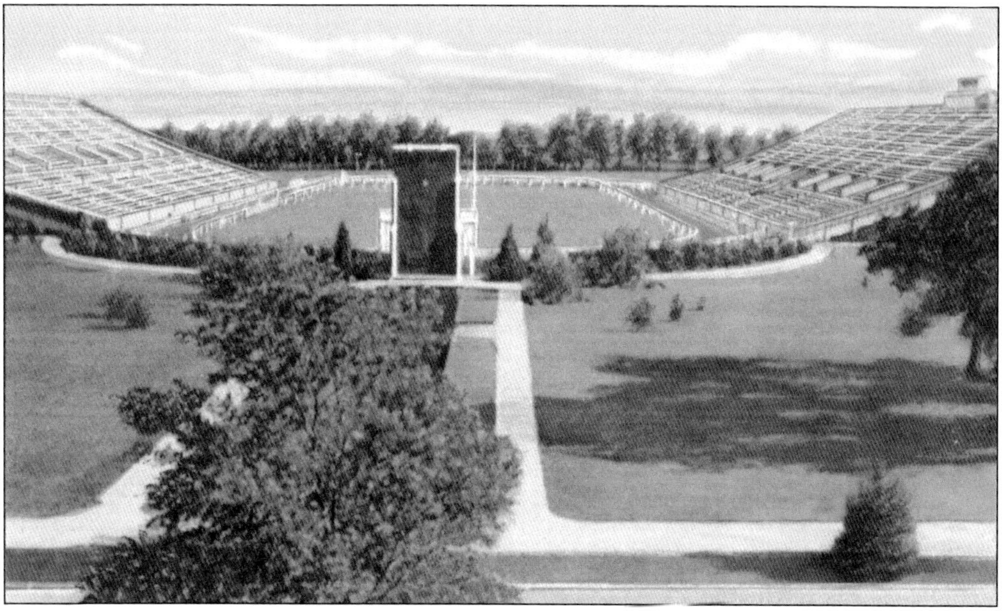

Jack Hart lasted one game as OU's football coach. As the story goes, Hart, 20, had the idea of organizing a team while getting a haircut at Bud Resinger's Barber Shop on Main Street. While there, he discussed strategy and recruited a few players. After the defeat, Hart gave up and headed North to prospect for gold. Pictured here is Memorial Stadium, finished in the late 1920s. (CCHS.)

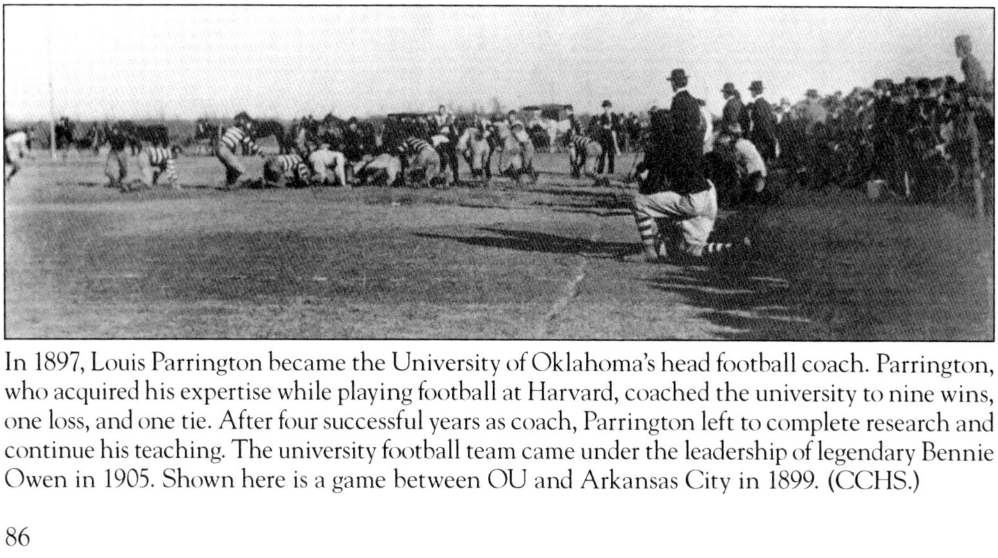

In 1897, Louis Parrington became the University of Oklahoma's head football coach. Parrington, who acquired his expertise while playing football at Harvard, coached the university to nine wins, one loss, and one tie. After four successful years as coach, Parrington left to complete research and continue his teaching. The university football team came under the leadership of legendary Bennie Owen in 1905. Shown here is a game between OU and Arkansas City in 1899. (CCHS.)

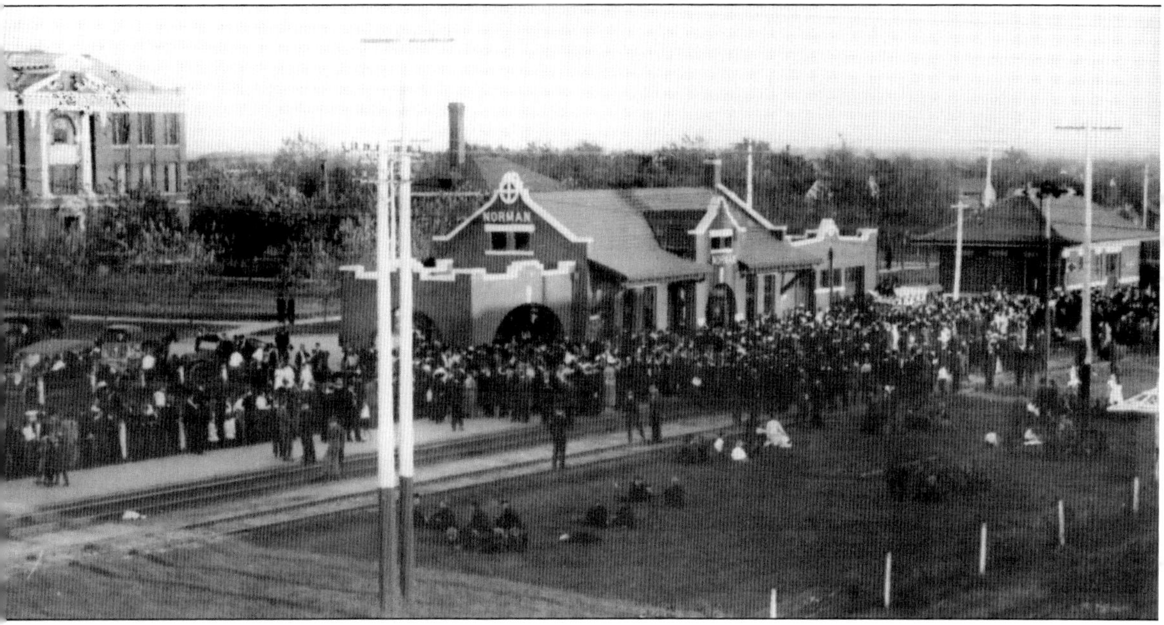


Fans gathered at the Santa Fe depot in 1916 to welcome home the University of Oklahoma football team after they defeated Texas 14-13. The win capped two undefeated seasons for coach Bennie Owen. As a student at the University of Kansas in 1899, the 130-pound Benjamin G. Owen played quarterback for the undefeated team. Although his academic interest was medicine, his success on the football field changed his career direction. Owen left his academic goals behind when he was offered the coaching job at the University of Oklahoma in 1906. The university did not have the budget to offer Owen a 12-month contract; he was offered, and he accepted, a three-month position. In his first year as coach, OU beat Texas 2-0. By the end of his 22-year tenure, Owen had a 67.7 winning percentage over 122 games. He was the first Oklahoma player inducted into the College Football Hall of Fame. (CCHS.)

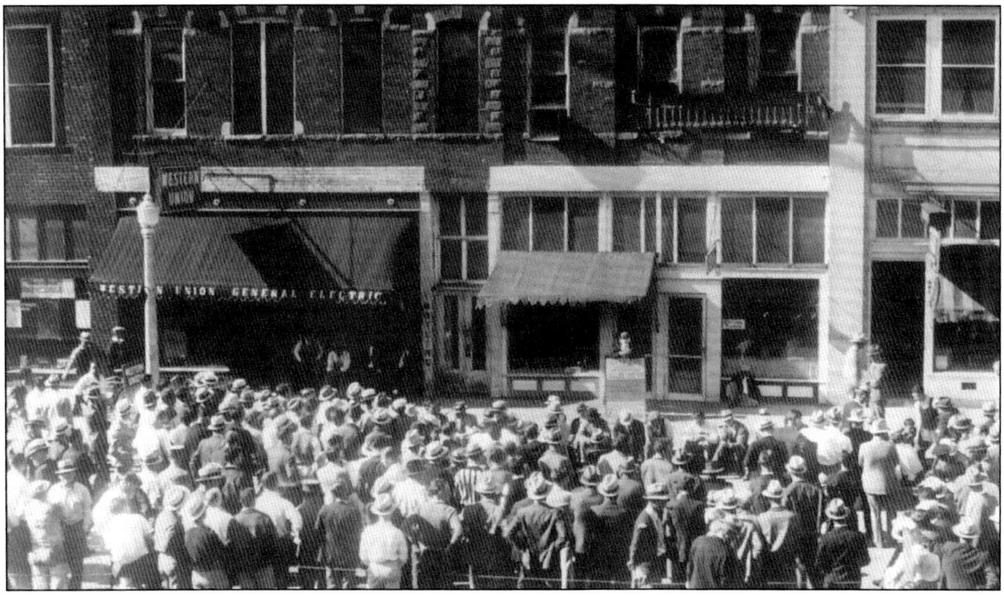


Football fans gathered in downtown Norman during away games to hear the latest score, which was available at the Western Union telegraph office and Barbour Drugs. On the drugstore building at 104 East Main Street, a wooden football on a football-field-shaped scoreboard helped fans visualize the action. When the telegraph came in at Western Union, the football would be placed at the corresponding point on the field. (CCHS.)

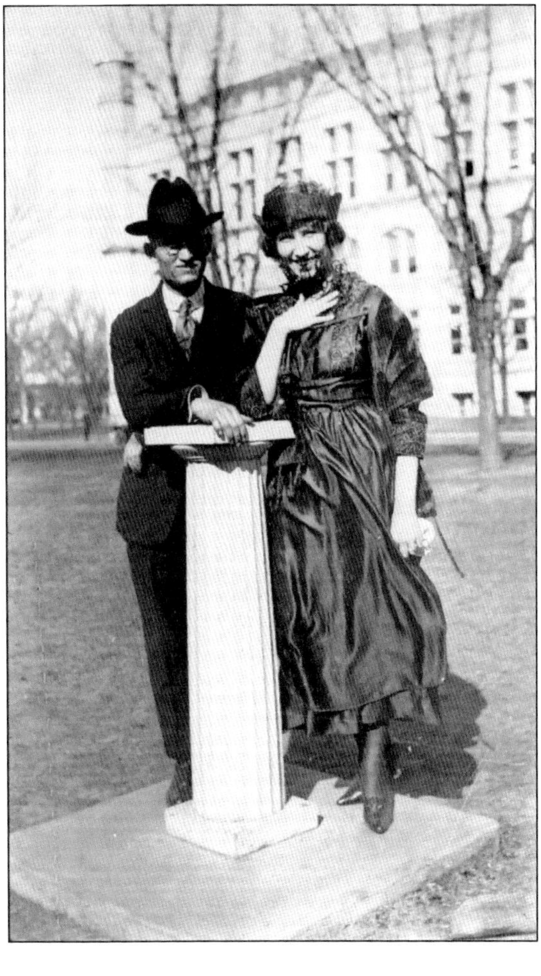

By the second decade of the 20th century, student life and activities at the University of Oklahoma mirrored those of Eastern universities. The first fraternity at OU was begun on November 17, 1905, when Kappa Alpha established the Beta-Eta chapter. Sororities began at the university in 1915 with the establishment of Kappa Kappa Gamma and Alpha Chi Omega. (CCHS.)

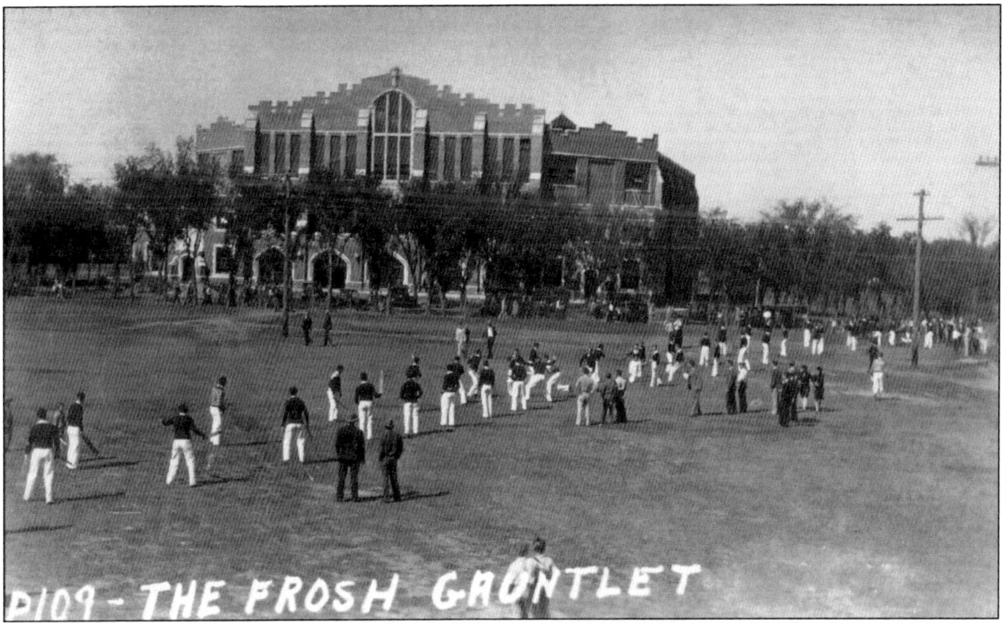


Initiation into a fraternity was part of the freshman experience. One rite of passage was running the gauntlet of senior members swinging paddles. In 1929, the board of regents ruled to eliminate the custom of using paddles in such ceremonies. Students challenged this ruling by continuing initiations without paddles. (CCHS.)

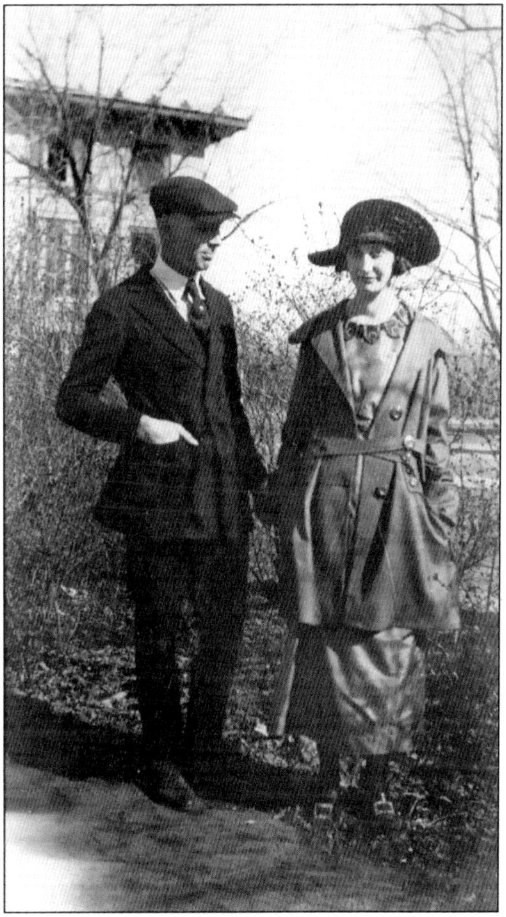

Fraternities and sororities frequented the Davis Dance Hall in downtown Norman. To make a competitive evening, the men and women formed dance clubs. The fraternities sent six members to form their group, Tabasco, and the sororities sent six women to form their group, Enchiladas. Each group vowed to win the night's competition. The students often rode to town in a small Ford used as a jitney service. (CCHS.)

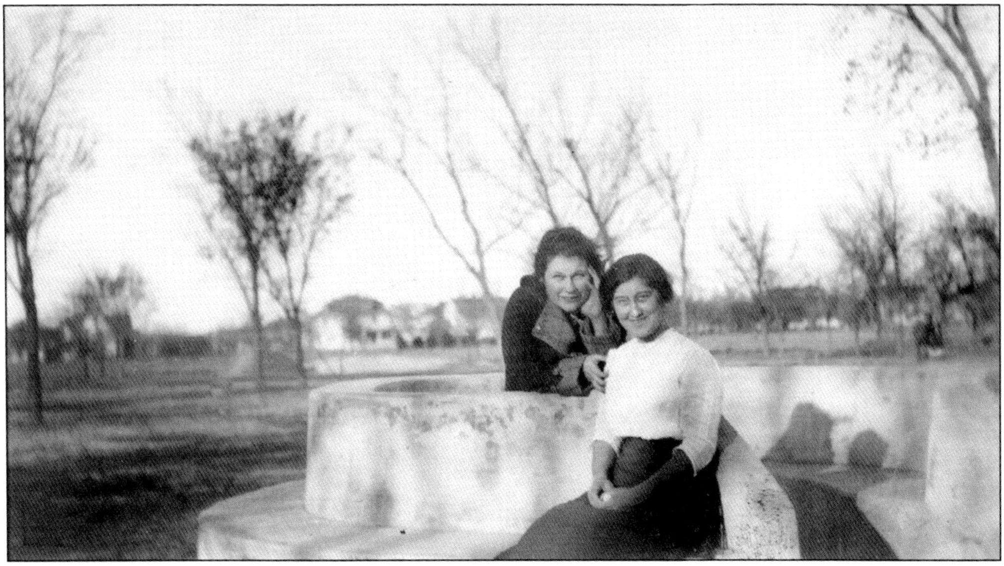

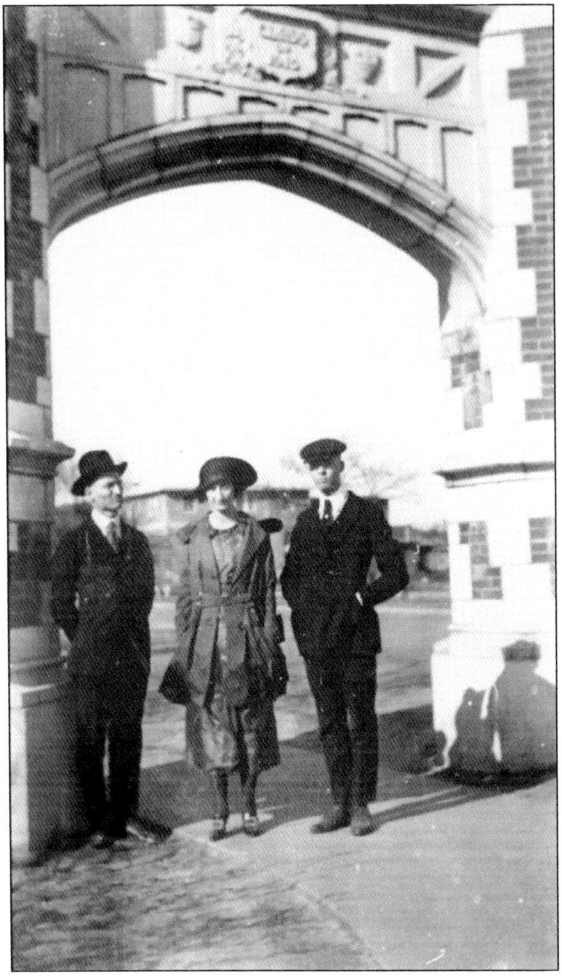

The class of 1910 presented the university with a cement circular bench called the "spoon holder," which was located north of the administration building. The legend was that if a couple kissed sitting inside the spoon holder, they were destined to marry. In 1999, the bench was removed for repair and reinstated on the north oval. In this 1914 photograph, Helen Biggers (right) sits with an unidentified friend. (CCHS.)

The class of 1919 gave as a departing gift to the university a stone arch at the entrance to the north oval. Altogether, Harold Gimeno designed four oval arches for the university. He was the son of Patricio Gimeno, a professor of architecture at OU. Father and son designed over eight houses and buildings in Norman, including the Sooner Theatre. (CCHS.)

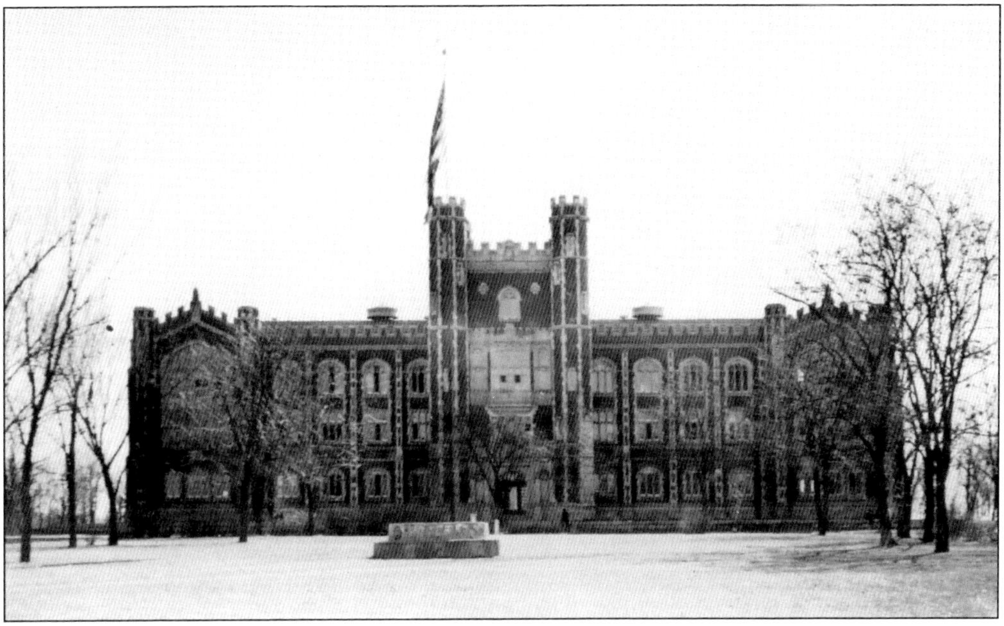

Another custom unique to the University of Oklahoma started in the 1920s, when engineering students celebrated St. Patrick's Day with the firing of a cannon. When officials tried to stop this custom, students formed a secret society, Loyal Knights of Old Trusty (LKOT). To avoid being detected while firing the cannon, the students wore black sheets and hoods. Today, LKOT is still a secret society within the School of Engineering. (CCHS.)

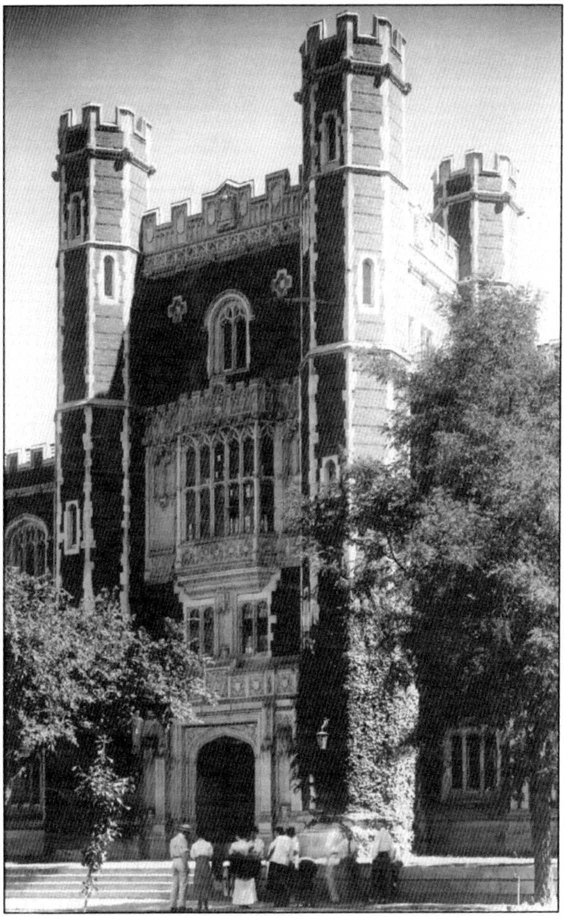

Territorial residents paid no tuition or enrollment fees, but each student had to take an entrance exam for placement. Of the 57 students in the first class in 1892, none qualified as freshmen. Therefore, the university started as a preparatory school and held that status until 1907, when college students outnumbered those at the high-school level. A majority of the students were from Norman families. (CCHS.)

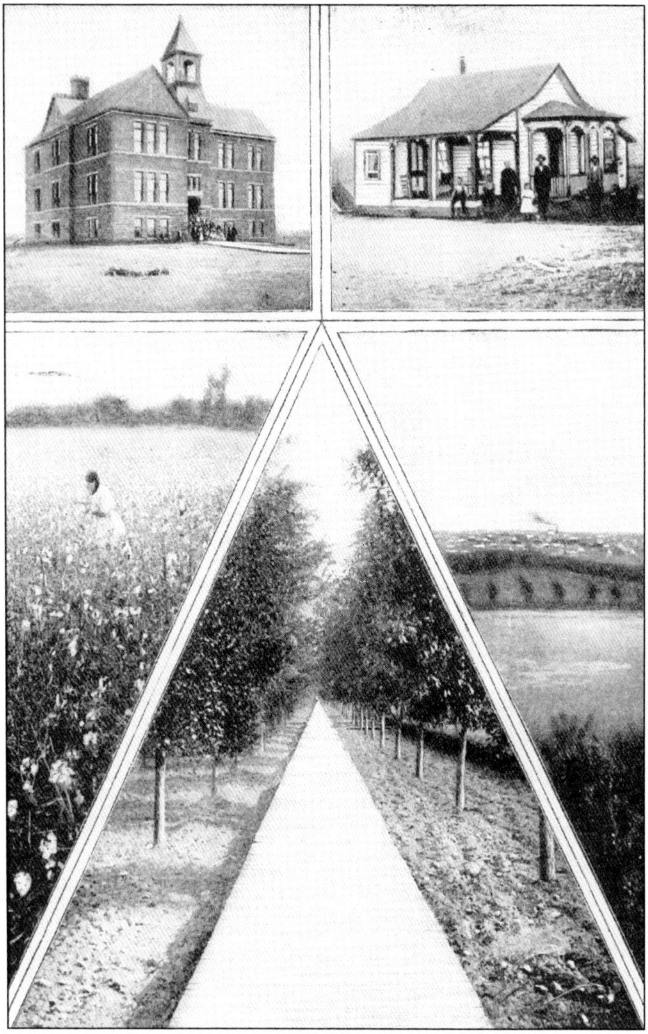

In a 1901 article in *The Outlook* entitled "The Next Commonwealth: Oklahoma," the author summed up the experience of pioneers in the initial settlement and development of a town and a new society. This composite photograph from *The Outlook* sums up Norman at the turn of the 20th century. The images depict, clockwise from lower left, a field of cotton, the Eastside School, a prairie home, agricultural fields, and President Boyd's trees lining University Avenue. (CCHS.)

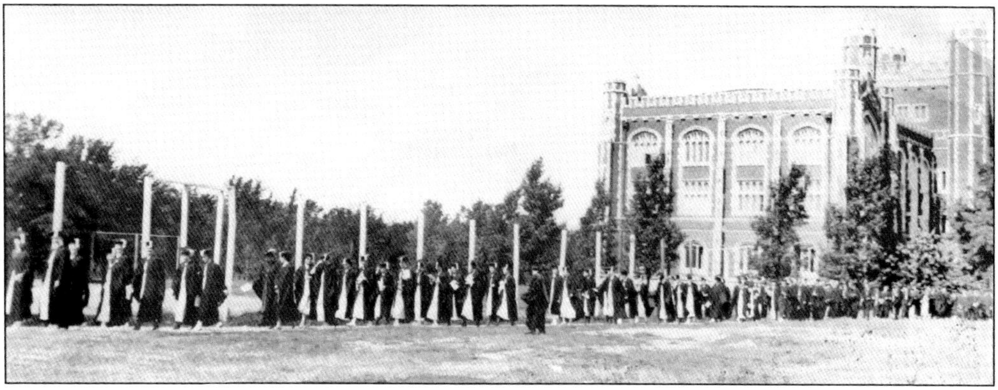

Students who graduated from the University of Oklahoma in the early part of the 20th century had expectations of starting their careers and establishing families. By the late 1920s, however, the Great Depression affected the lives of young graduates and the economic well-being of the university and Norman. (CCHS.)

# *Six*

# Depression Years

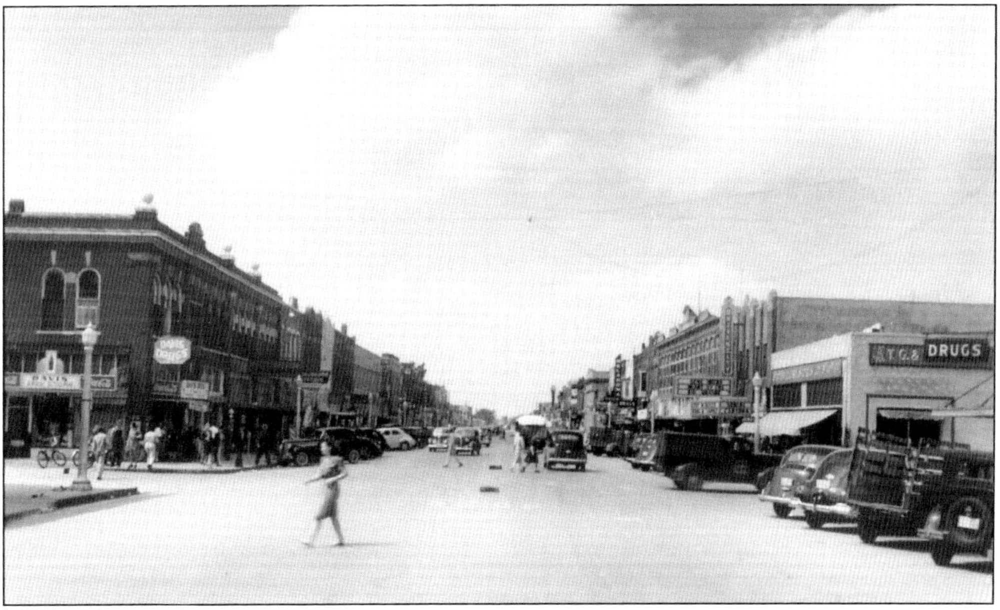


Norman's population in 1930 was 9,603. The main source of income for citizens was employment in small businesses and at two major institutions, the University of Oklahoma and Central State Hospital. But by 1933, Oklahomans struggled to overcome the hardships brought on by the Great Depression. For those unemployed, Pres. Franklin D. Roosevelt's New Deal brought economic relief via employment on federally funded construction projects and cultural programs. (CCHS.)

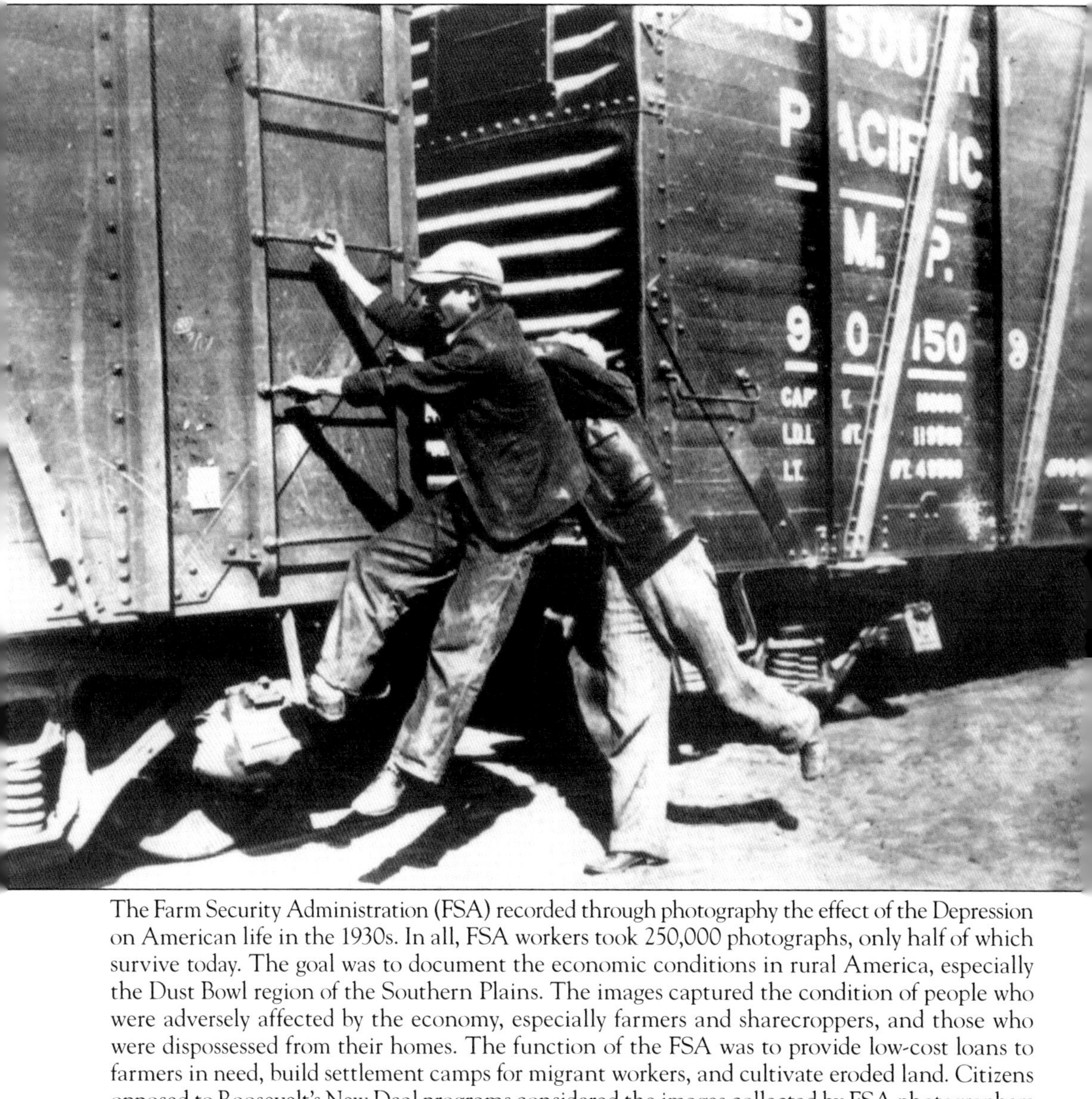


The Farm Security Administration (FSA) recorded through photography the effect of the Depression on American life in the 1930s. In all, FSA workers took 250,000 photographs, only half of which survive today. The goal was to document the economic conditions in rural America, especially the Dust Bowl region of the Southern Plains. The images captured the condition of people who were adversely affected by the economy, especially farmers and sharecroppers, and those who were dispossessed from their homes. The function of the FSA was to provide low-cost loans to farmers in need, build settlement camps for migrant workers, and cultivate eroded land. Citizens opposed to Roosevelt's New Deal programs considered the images collected by FSA photographers as government propaganda, selected for their tragic content of the human condition. Regardless, photographs of Oklahoma do tell part of the story of the 1930s. Men "rode the rails" in search of work, as seen in this photograph taken in central Oklahoma. (WHC.)

Dorothea Lange was a well-known documentary photographer from Berkeley, California. Her photographs were famous worldwide for depicting rural poverty and the condition of sharecroppers. Hired by the FSA in the 1930s, Lange is most famous for her photograph "Migrant Mother." While in Oklahoma in search of rural victims of a depressed farming economy, she took this photograph of a secondhand store in downtown Norman. (WHC.)

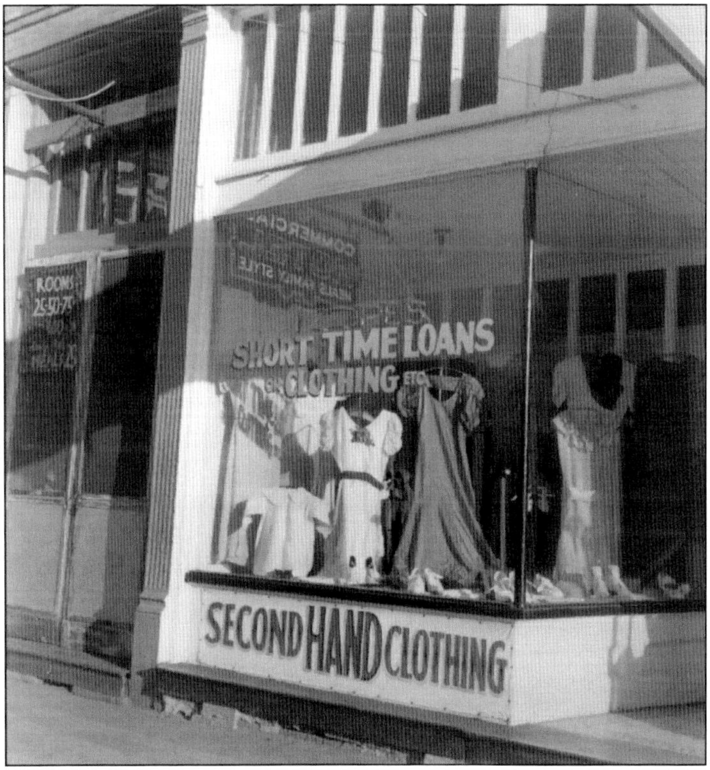


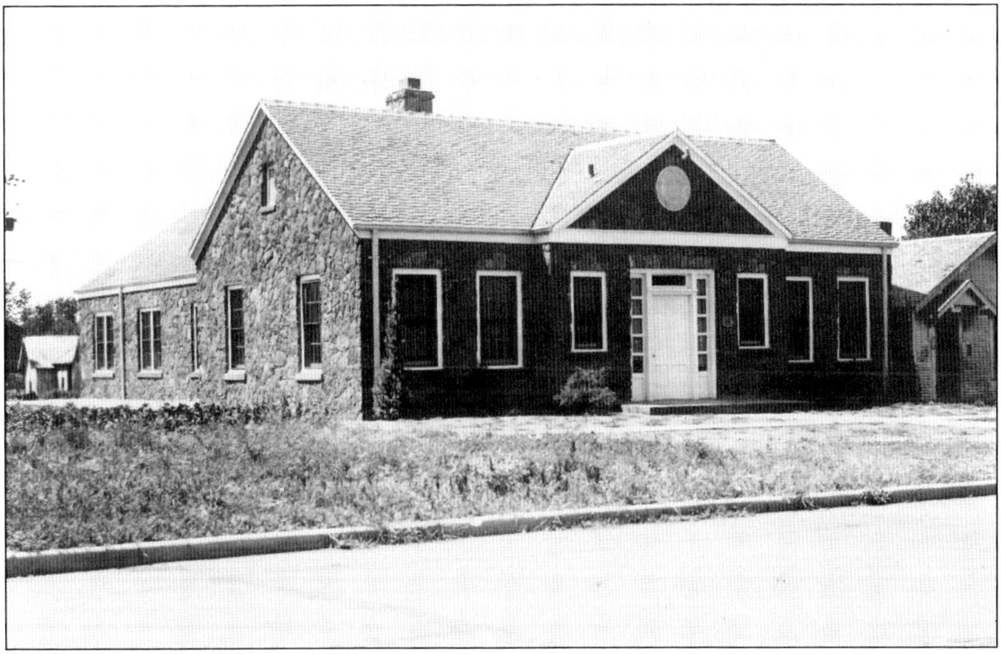

Federal New Deal programs were designed to offer training and ultimately employment for those in need. In Oklahoma, 166,000 people qualified for WPA jobs. Several projects in Norman and at the University of Oklahoma were supported by New Deal financing. Most construction projects added to the town's infrastructure, such as the community building shown here. (CACA.)

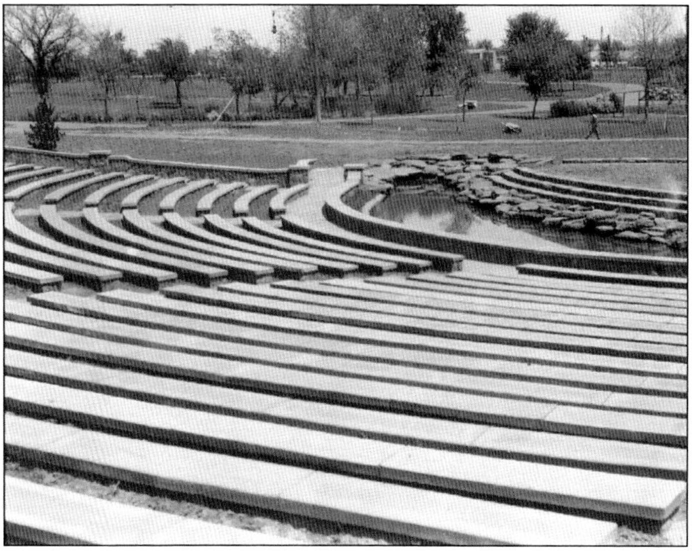

The WPA made improvements to Abe Andrews Park by building an amphitheater and adjacent community building. Park enhancements also included native stone drainage ditches. Whenever possible, materials used in government projects were of native sources. Another WPA project was stone fences, which can be seen today at Andrews Park and at the University of Oklahoma duck pond. (CCHS.)

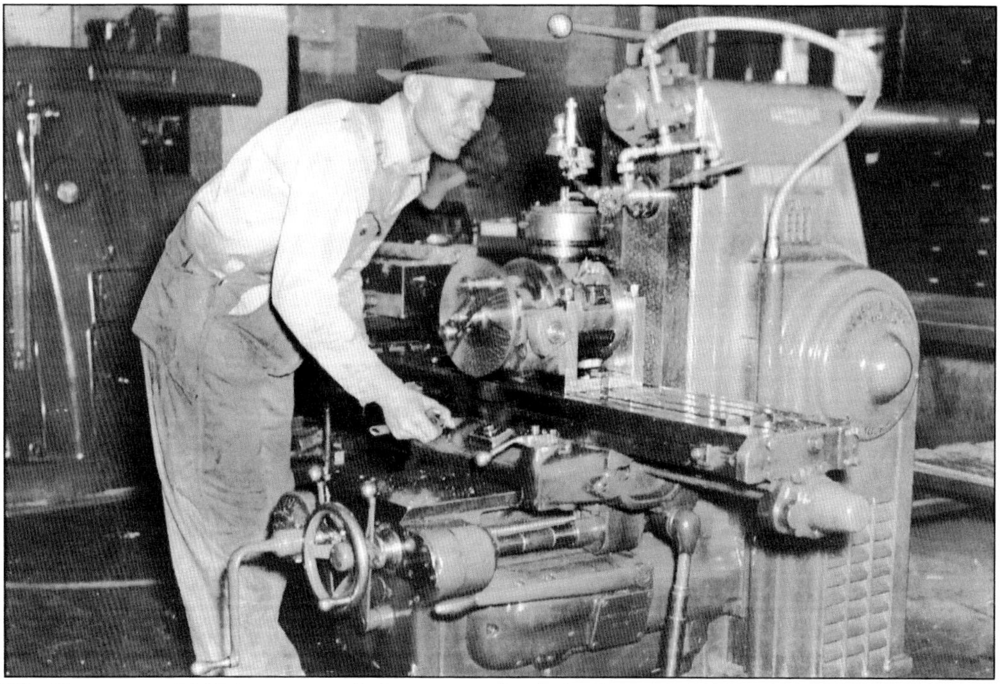

The University of Oklahoma provided programs that helped out-of-work men maintain or augment their skills. In OU's College of Engineering, under the Federal Vocational Defense Training Program, 12 men from the WPA rolls received an eight-week machinist course, which included instruction on grinders, milling shapers, planers, and turning lathes. (CACA)

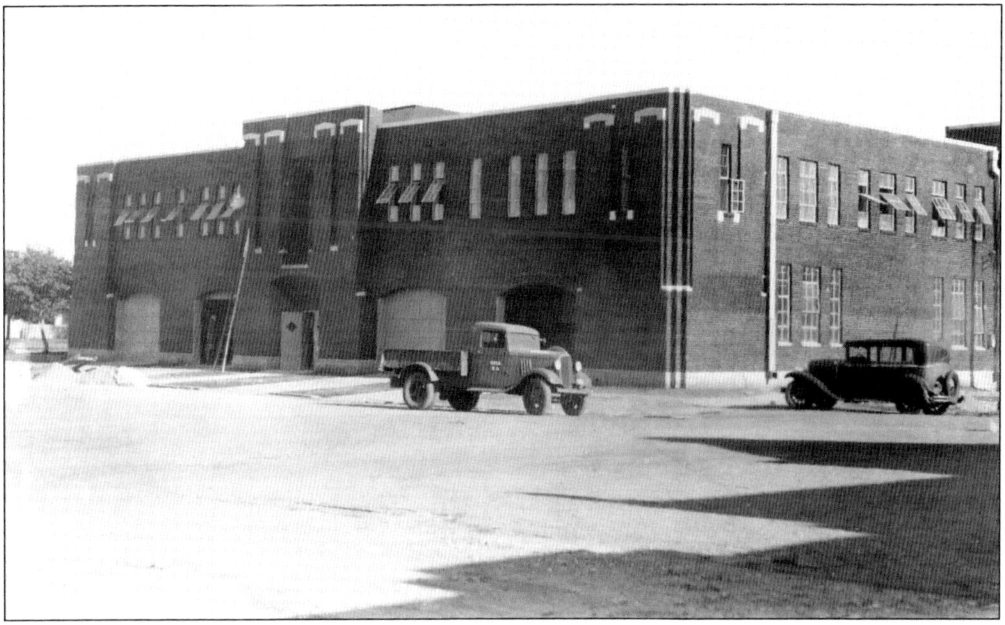

The Norman National Guard Armory, completed in 1936, employed 85 WPA workers in its construction. The building, 125 feet by 150 feet, served as headquarters for two National Guard units, Company C of the 120th Engineers and Company D, 179th Infantry. The two-story structure, which also served as a community building, contained a garage, drill room, recreation room, and offices. (CACA.)

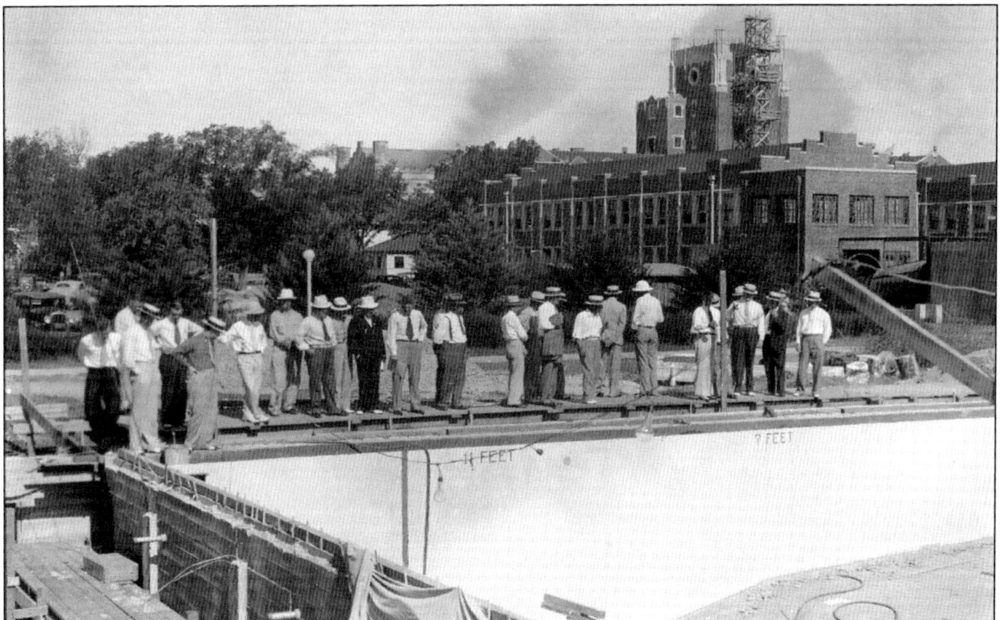

The University of Oklahoma requested WPA funds for several projects. Among the projects was a proposed men's swimming pool. In 1935, Bennie Owen, former football coach and intramural athletic director, landed federal aid for a nine-hole golf course and an Olympic-sized swimming pool. The pool facility was built to provide showers, dressing rooms, and seating for 1,000. (CACA.)

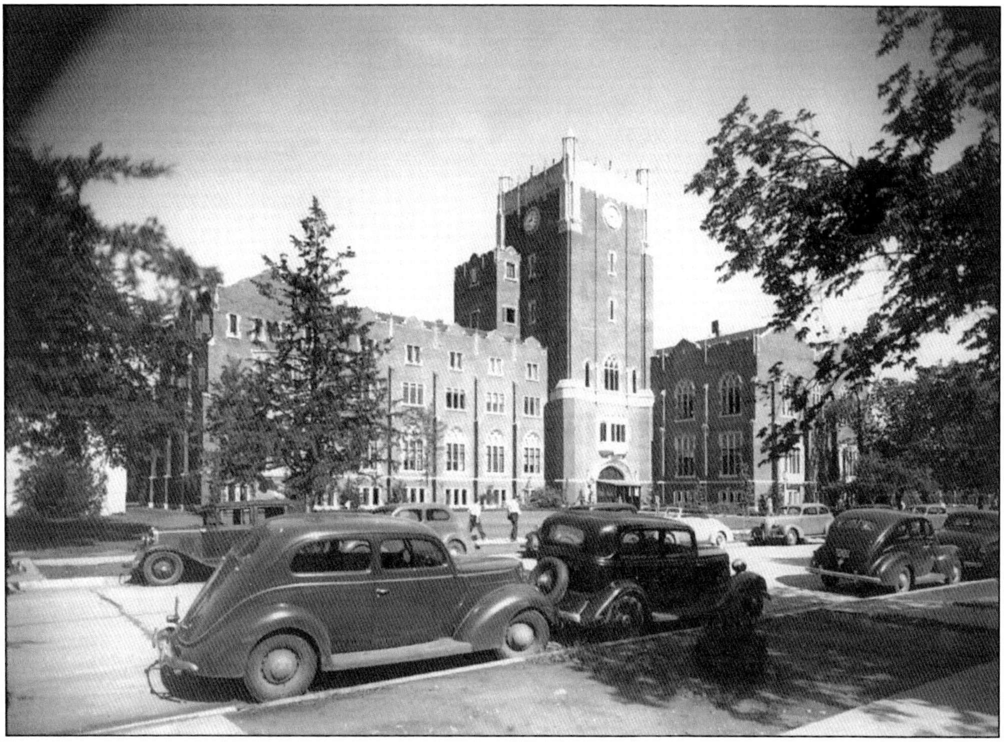

The University of Oklahoma Student Union was built in 1928. Funding for the building came from student fees and donations from alumni, faculty, and friends of the university. The union housed a variety of organizations, including the University of Oklahoma Association, the Men's Council, the University Christian Association, and various student religious groups. (CCHS.)

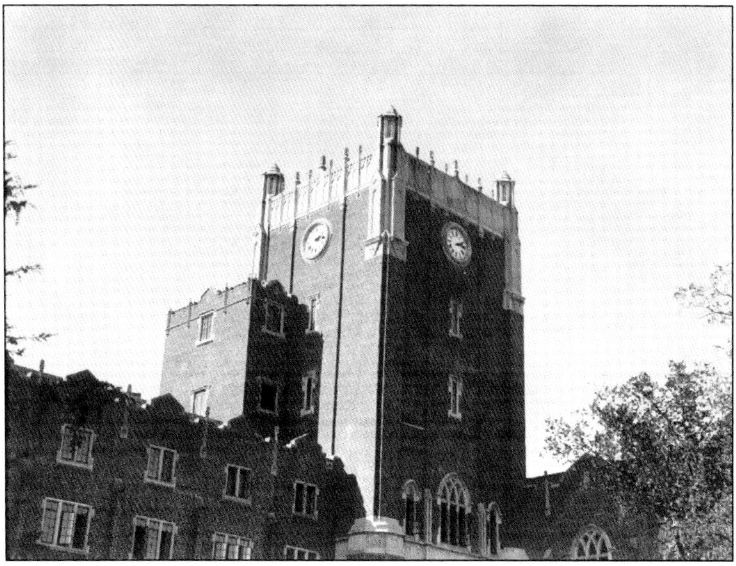

In 1936, federal money paid for the tower at the University of Oklahoma Student Union building. WPA work crews constructed the tower and installed the first passenger elevator in Norman, which rose to the fifth floor. The tower housed offices and studio rehearsal rooms for radio station WNAD, the radio voice of "Soonerland." (OHS.)

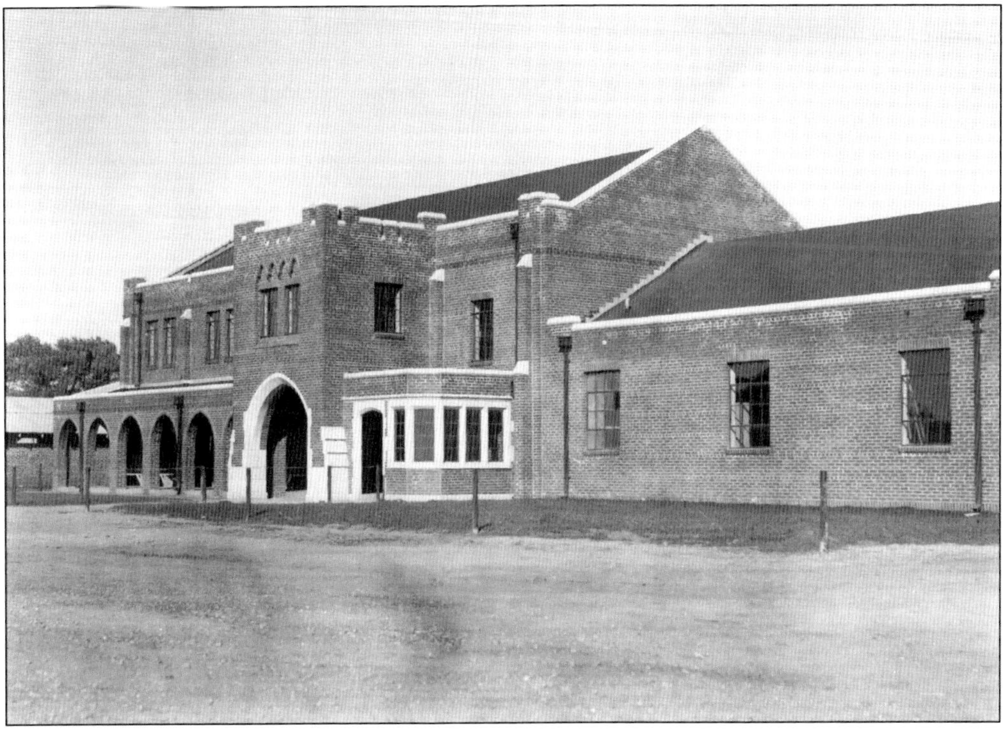

The WPA funded the ROTC Armory building on campus, erected in 1936. In 1948, the building became the J. Willis Stovall Museum of Science and History. The museum housed a vast vertebrate paleontology collection, much of it collected by Dr. Stovall and WPA workers in the field. In 1935, Stovall received a WPA grant to research, collect, and prepare the fossil vertebrate collection. The result was 60,000 to 80,000 man-hours devoted to collecting and preparing the specimens. This was the beginning of the world-renowned Sam Noble Museum of Natural History. (CACA)

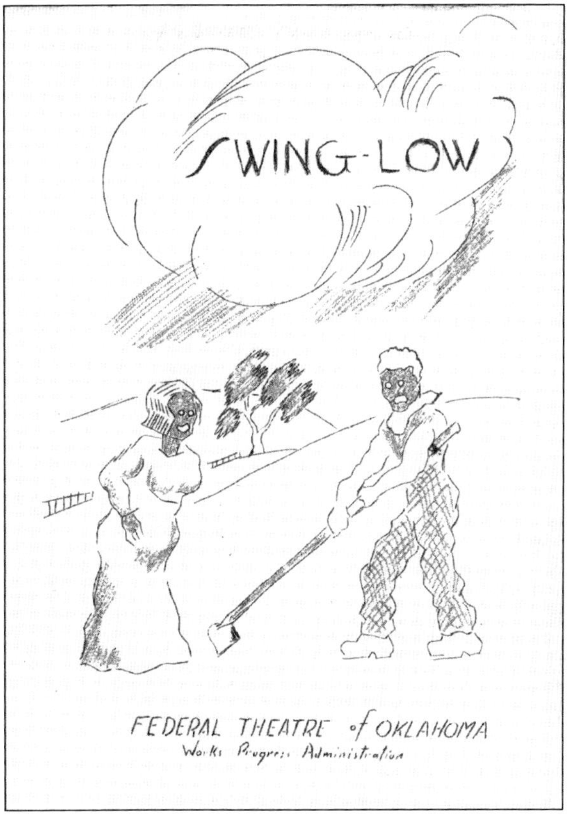


The Roosevelt administration believed that artists, musicians, actors, and writers needed work relief to maintain their talent and skills and to preserve American culture. Federal One was an important cultural program within the WPA. Two projects, Federal Theatre and Federal Art, flourished under the instructors at the University of Oklahoma. (CCHS.)

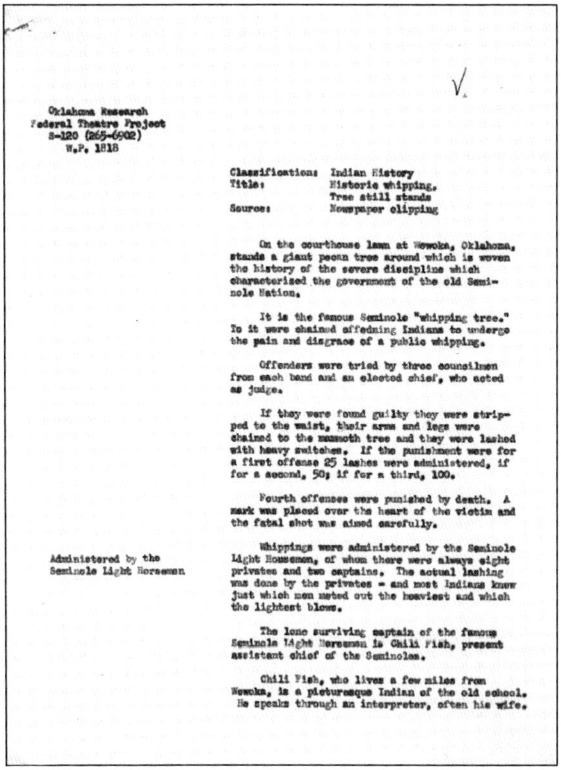

Oklahoma Research
Federal Theatre Project
S-120 (265-6902)
W.P. 1818

Classification: Indian History
Title: Historic whipping. Tree still stands
Source: Newspaper clipping

On the courthouse lawn at Wewoka, Oklahoma, stands a giant pecan tree around which is woven the history of the severe discipline which characterized the government of the old Seminole Nation.

It is the famous Seminole "whipping tree." To it were chained offedning Indians to undergo the pain and disgrace of a public whipping.

Offenders were tried by three councilmen from each band and an elected chief, who acted as judge.

If they were found guilty they were stripped to the waist, their arms and legs were chained to the mammoth tree and they were lashed with heavy switches. If the punishment were for a first offense 25 lashes were administered, if for a second, 50; if for a third, 100.

Fourth offenses were punished by death. A mark was placed over the heart of the victim and the fatal shot was aimed carefully.

Administered by the Seminole Light Horsemen

Whippings were administered by the Seminole Light Housemen, of whom there were always eight privates and two captains. The actual lashing was done by the privates - and most Indians knew just which men meted out the heaviest and which the lightest blows.

The lone surviving captain of the famous Seminole Light Horsemen is Chili Fish, present assistant chief of the Seminoles.

Chili Fish, who lives a few miles from Wewoka, is a picturesque Indian of the old school. He speaks through an interpreter, often his wife.

The Federal Theatre Project in Oklahoma, under the leadership of School of Drama professor John Dunn, developed a research bureau to employ drama teachers to canvas the state, interviewing people and collecting their stories about early Oklahoma. The researchers then categorized the stories within the following subject fields: Pioneer, Cowboy, Indian, and Outlaw. In all, Federal Theatre Project workers collected 450 stories. (CCHS.)

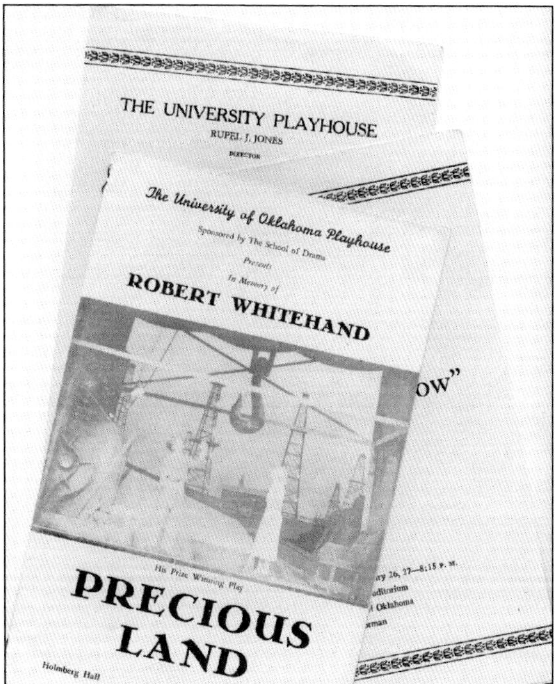


The University Playhouse was used for the staging of Federal Theatre Project plays written by drama students. John Whitehand was perhaps the most promising student in 1935. His play, *Precious Land,* won the School of Drama's Oklahoma Playwright Prize. In 1936, the play was added to the Federal Theatre playlist and produced throughout the country. Whitehand's promising career was cut short when he died fighting in France during World War II. (CCHS.)

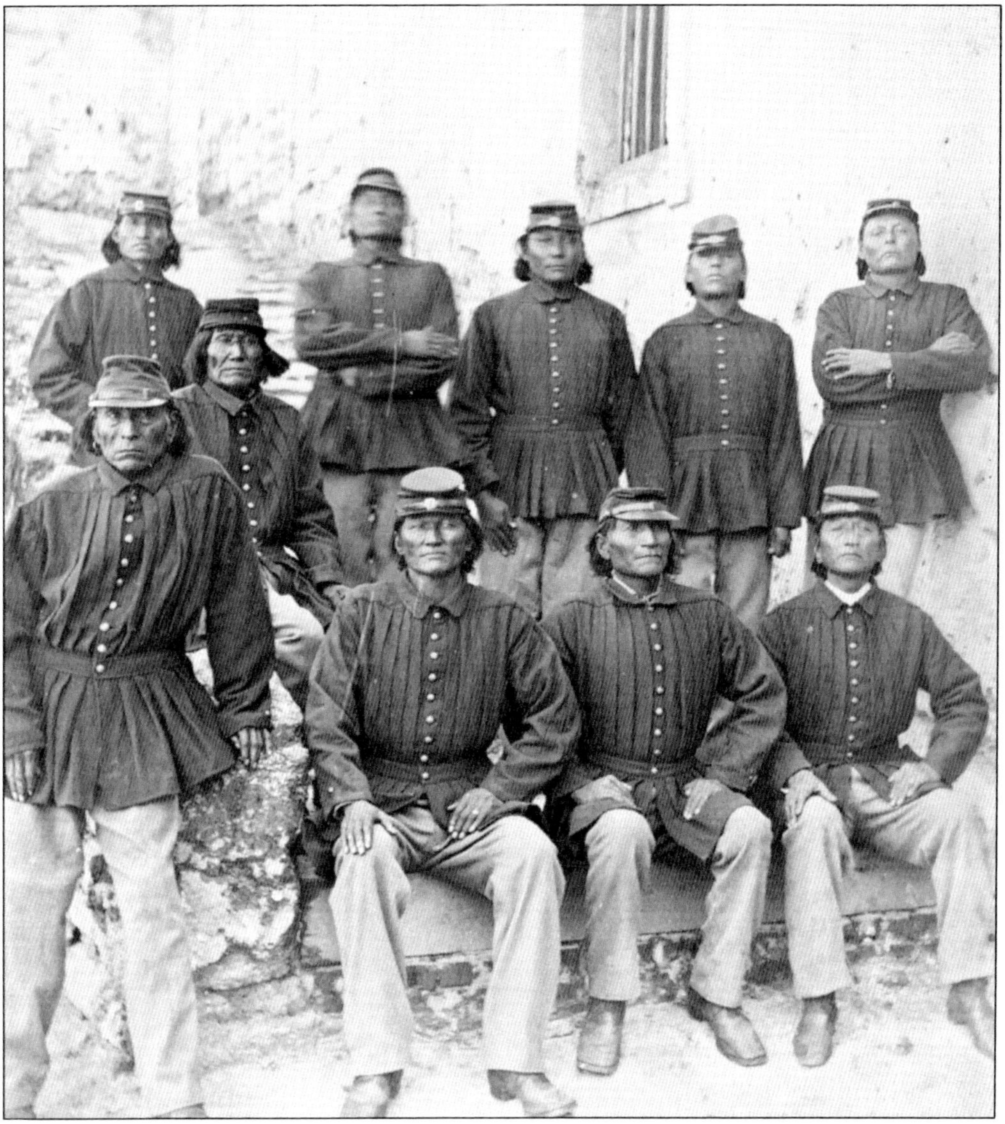

The Federal Art Project also utilized the talent of students at the University of Oklahoma, especially five Kiowa artists, who learned their distinctive artistic style from their ancestors, once imprisoned in Florida. In the late 19th century, members of Native American tribes on the Plains told the history of their people through their drawings of stick figures and one-dimensional animals. The native people narrated their story on paper, hide, or cloth, and in ledgers or account books that were available to them from traders, missionaries, government agents, and military officers. Ledger art also became a form of expression for Native American prisoners sent to Fort Marion in St. Augustine, Florida, after the end of the Red River War in 1874. The prisoners were encouraged to continue their art and to sell it to those who had an interest in Western Native American culture. The Kiowa, in particular, continued to express their culture through art, passing this artistic tradition to their sons and daughters on the Kiowa Reservation in Oklahoma. (NCM.)

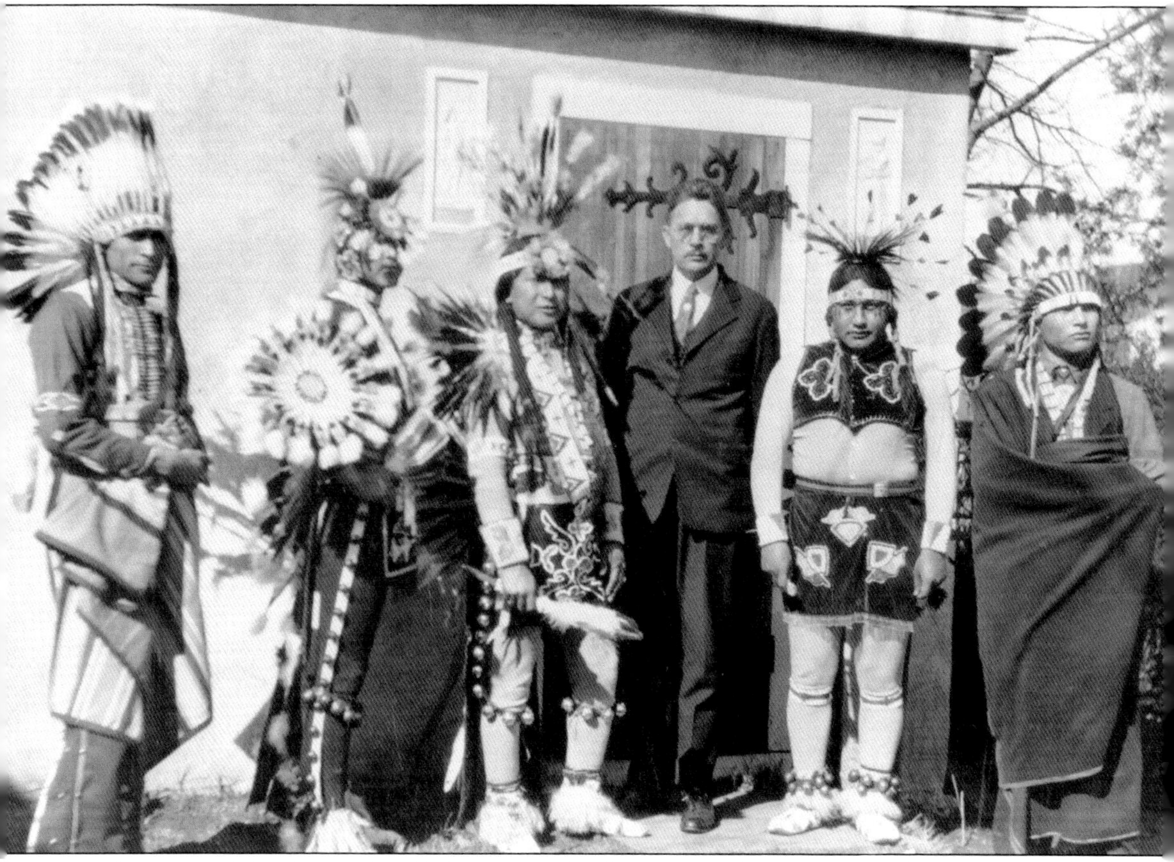

The Federal Art Project in Oklahoma brought Kiowa art to the attention of American as well as international art critics. The state Federal Art Project was under the leadership of Nan Sheets of Oklahoma City; Oscar Jacobson, director of the School of Art at the university, was technical advisor for President Roosevelt's Public Works of Art in Oklahoma. In 1926, Susan Peters at the Kiowa Agency in Anadarko wrote Jacobson about the artistic quality of the work of five of her students. Impressed with their work, Jacobson brought the five Kiowa from the reservation to work at the university under Jacobson's tutelage. Shown here are, from left to right, Monroe Tsatoke, Jack Hokeah, Stephen Mopope, Jacobson, Spencer Asah, and James Auchiah. During the 1930s, the five Kiowa painted murals in post offices, museums, schools, and public buildings in Oklahoma, New Mexico, Louisiana, and Washington, DC. (NCM.)

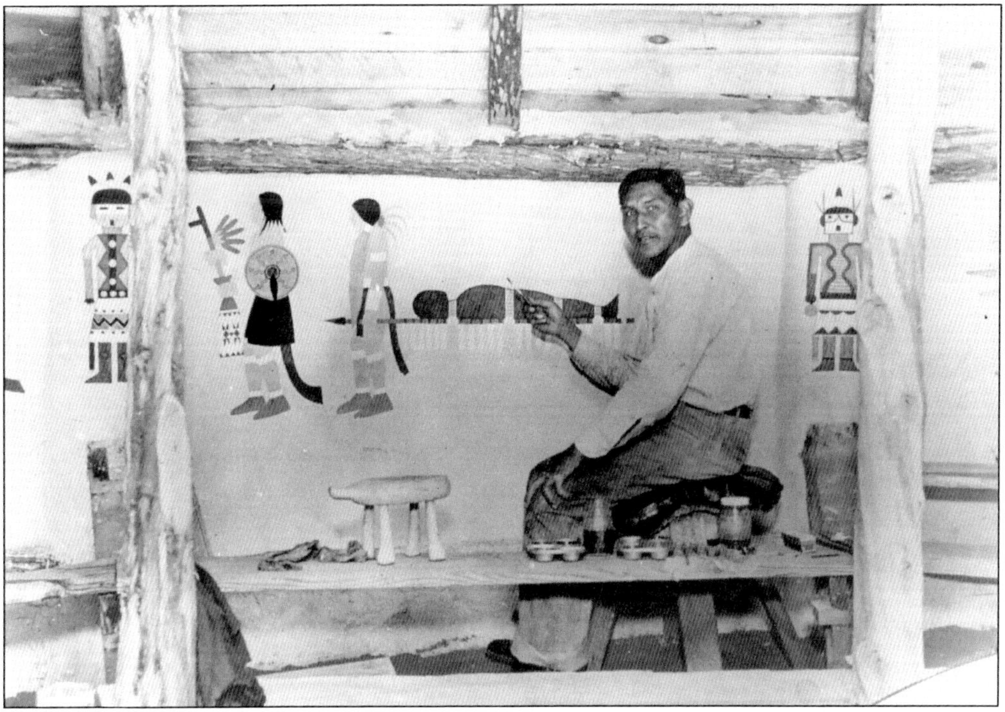

Interior post office walls were ideal canvases on which to paint murals of Native American culture. The Kiowa style was both representational and narrative, rooted in their native culture. Jack Hokeah (shown here), along with Spencer Asah, James Auchiah, and Stephen Mopope, painted 16 murals on the upper walls of the Anadarko, Oklahoma, post office in 1936 and 1937. (NCM.)

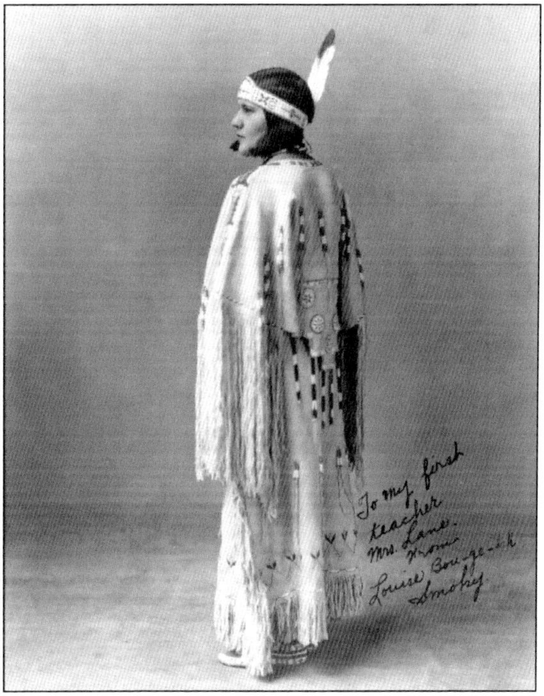


Lois Bougetah Smoky was one of the original Kiowa Five who studied art at the University of Oklahoma under Oscar Jacobson. She was at a disadvantage in expressing her artistic talent, as Kiowa custom did not allow women to draw in a representational style. She left the Kiowa Five after a few years, and James Auchiah took her place. (NCM.)

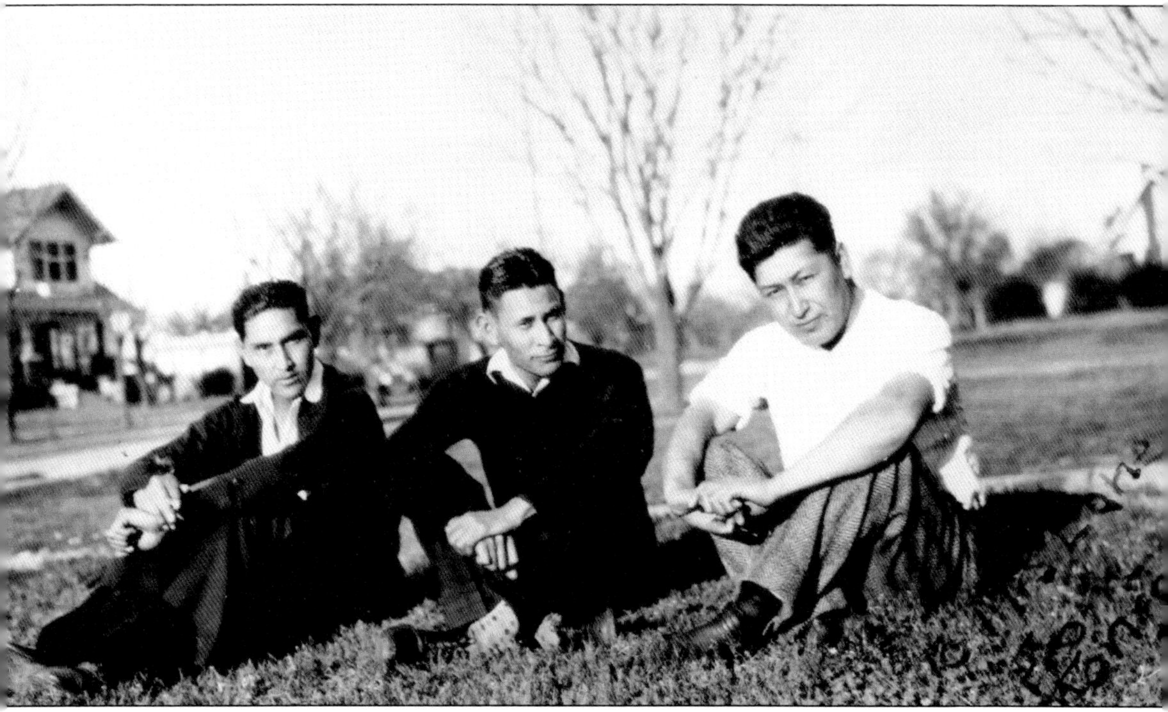

Shown here are three of the Kiowa Five, from left to right: Jack Hokeah, Monroe Tsatoke, and Stephan Mopope. Hokeah, born in 1902, was orphaned at a young age and brought up by his grandmother. He was an artist and a talented dancer. Tastoke was born in 1904 and excelled in singing and beadwork, as well as painting. A member of the Peyote religion, his paintings reflected his religious experiences. He died in 1937 of tuberculosis while completing WPA murals for the Oklahoma Historical Society. Stephen Mopope was born in 1898 and grew up on the Kiowa Reservation. Tribal elders recognized his artistic talent and taught him the traditional art of painting on tanned skins. He was also a tribal dancer. Mopope was the most prolific artist of the Kiowa Five. (NCM.)

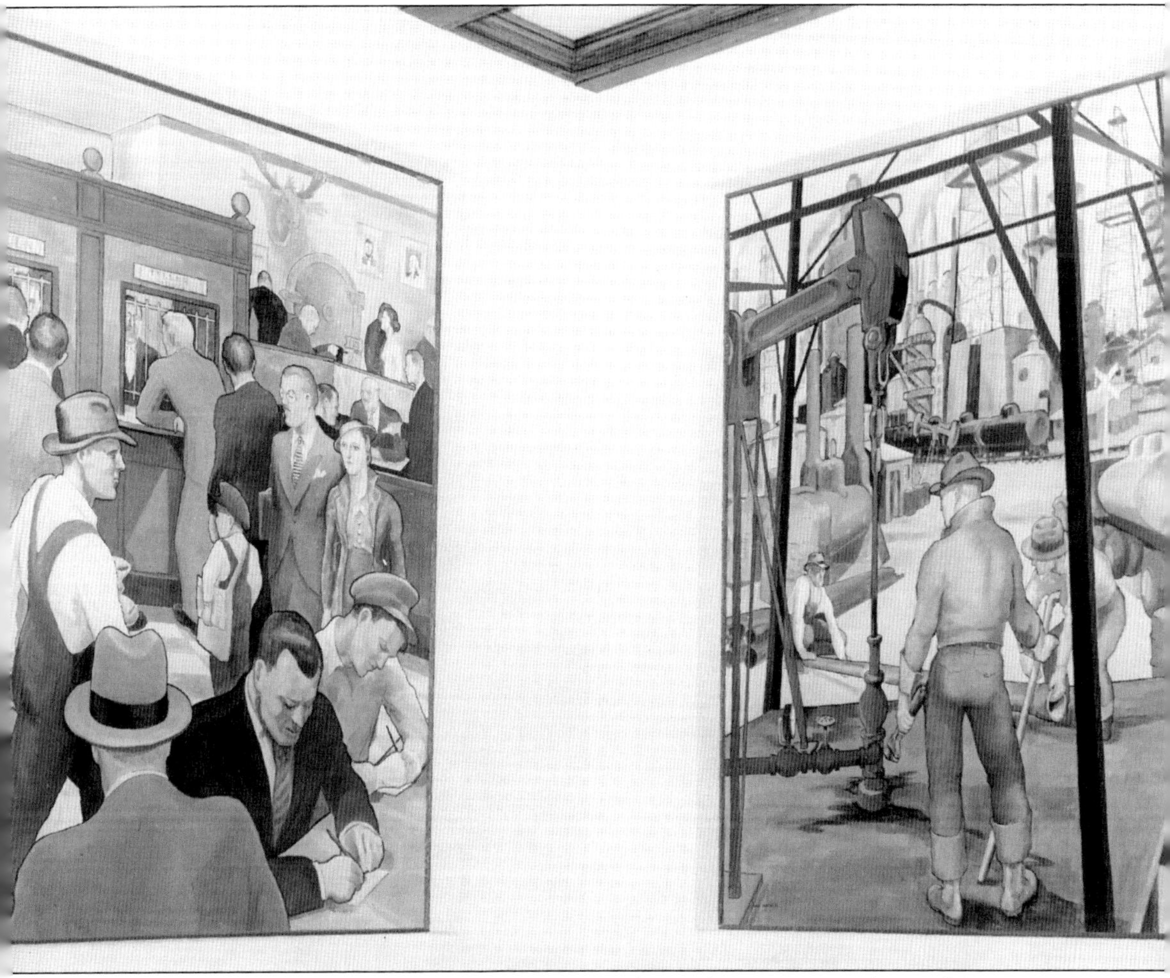

An underlying goal of the Federal Arts Projects was to depict the positive attributes of America's historic and economic culture. The themes of WPA murals in the foyer of Adams Hall at the University of Oklahoma followed the federal art mandate by illustrating prominent Oklahoma industries. The mural on the left depicts the banking industry, and the theme of the opposing mural is the oil and extractive industries. The murals were planned and executed by University of Oklahoma art student Craig Sheppard. Adams Hall was also a product of New Deal funding. In 1935, the Oklahoma legislature appropriated $250,000 for the construction of a business administration building. New Deal funding matched that amount. With labor from men working with the WPA, the building was completed in 1936 and named after the dean of the College of Administration, Arthur Barlo Adams. In 1997, the college was renamed the Michael F. Price College of Business. (UNR.)

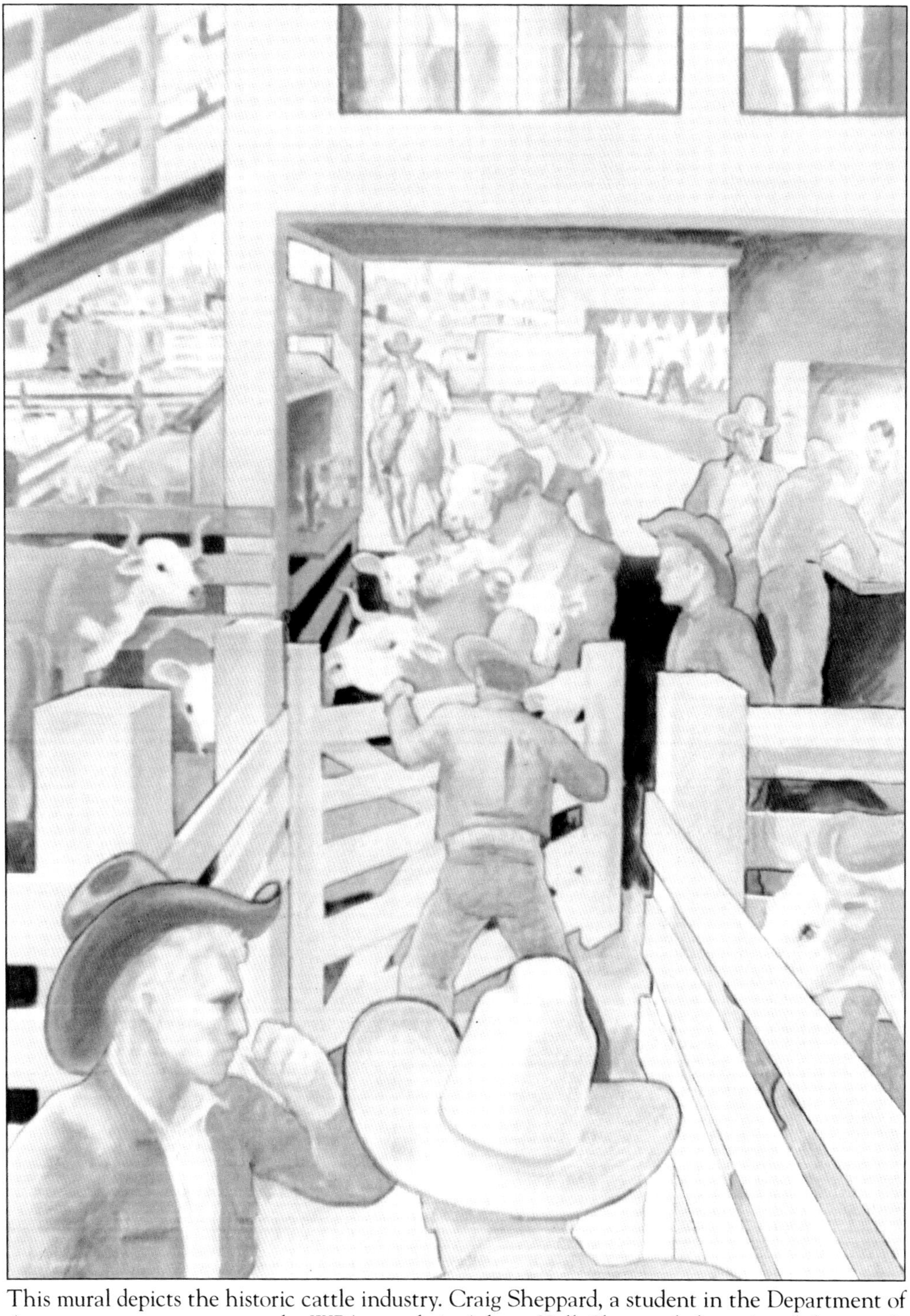

This mural depicts the historic cattle industry. Craig Sheppard, a student in the Department of Art, won a contest to create the WPA murals in Adams Hall. Sheppard also painted the murals in the Courts Motel. He painted his self-portrait into the mural; he is just inside the opening gate looking directly at the cattle pen. (UNR.)

# *Seven*

# War Years

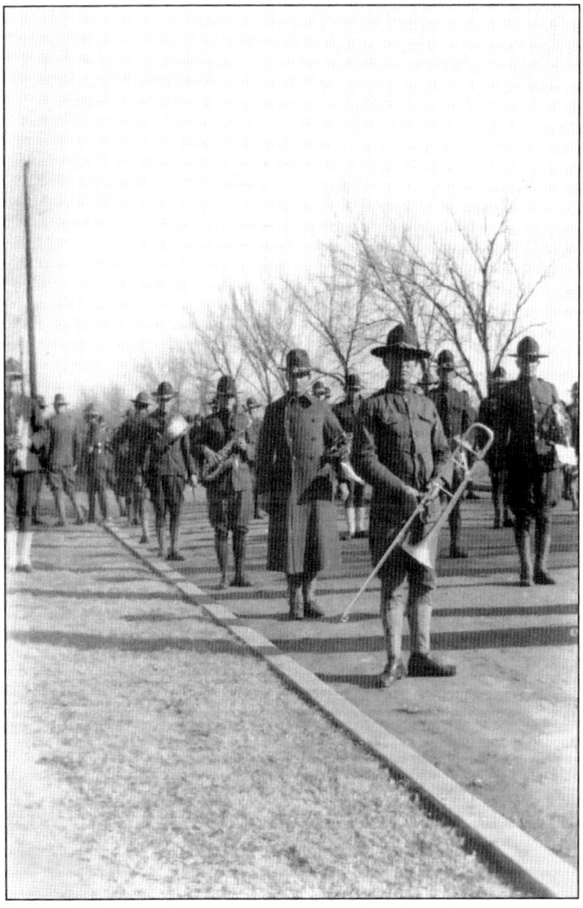

In April 1917, the US Congress declared war on Germany and entered the war in Europe. Militarily and industrially, the nation was ill prepared. University of Oklahoma president Stratton D. Brooks attended a conference in Washington, DC, on war preparedness. Brooks brought home the message that Oklahoma farmers needed to increase food production and that the state needed to prepare young men for service in the armed forces. (CCHS.)

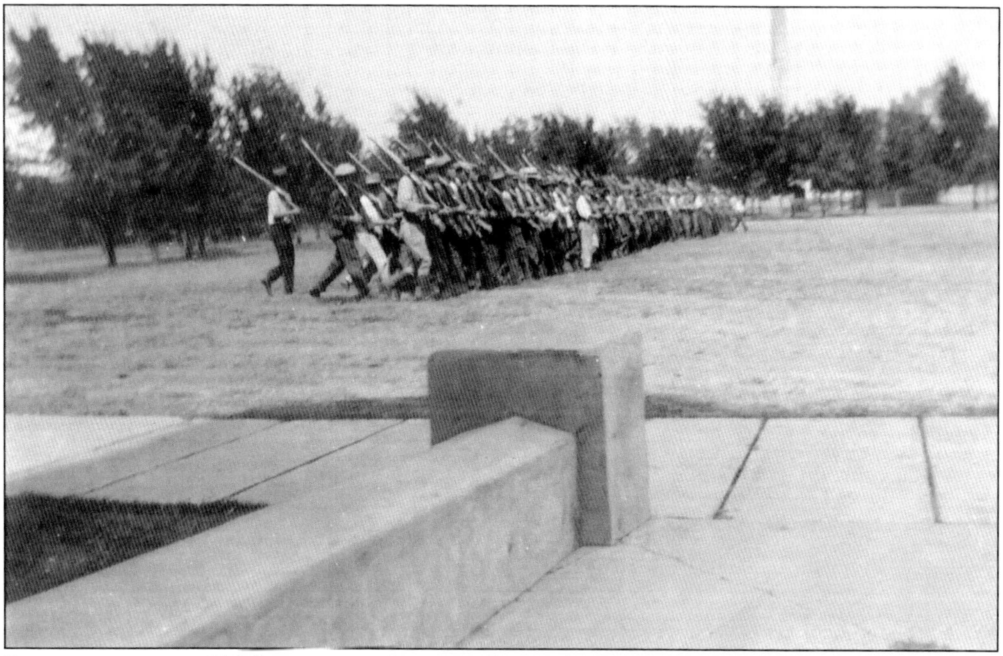

Five universities in Oklahoma trained men in the Student Army Training Corps (SATC). Every male student who was fit and enrolled at the university in 1918 was required to enroll in the SATC. The university had to follow Army regulations in providing barracks, mess halls, and infirmaries for the men. (CCHS.)

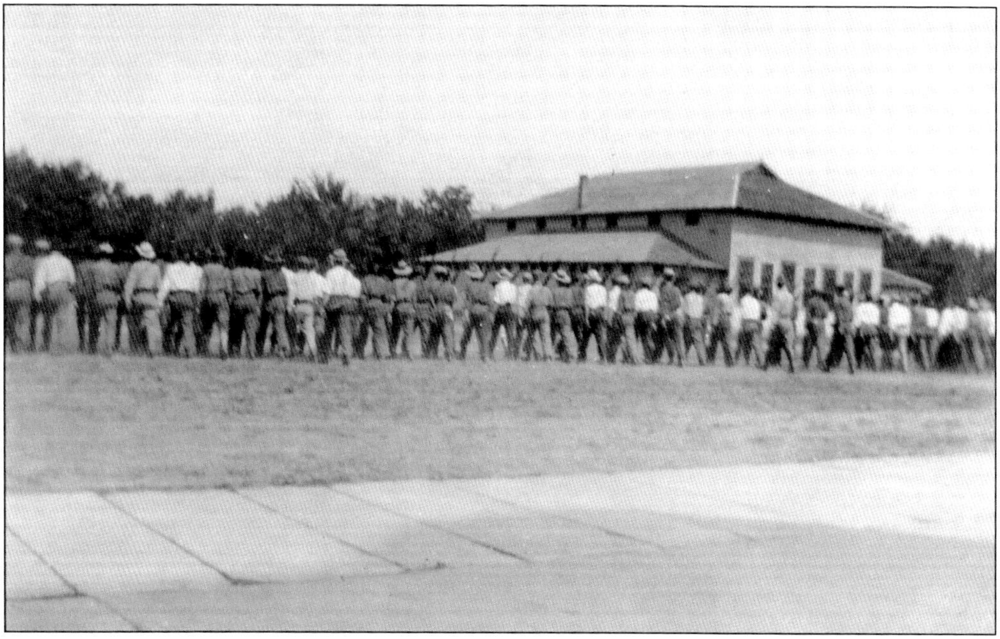

OU student Joseph Benton was assigned to Company C. He later wrote that he started training without a uniform and that he slept in the old gym "on bags of old straw." The gym is where the student union is today. As seen here, the men marched on the parade grounds in front of the gym. (CCHS.)

The University of Oklahoma also established a vocational training unit for young men not enrolled at the university. Instructors from OU's School of Engineering and the US Army taught general mechanics, auto mechanics, radio operation, and surveying. The trainees received room and board, uniforms, equipment, and $30 a month. The War Department paid the state $14,000 annually for the use of university buildings. (CCHS.)

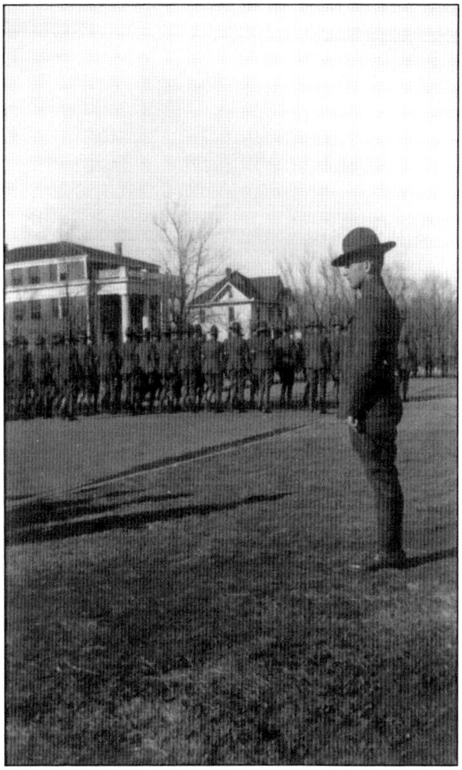

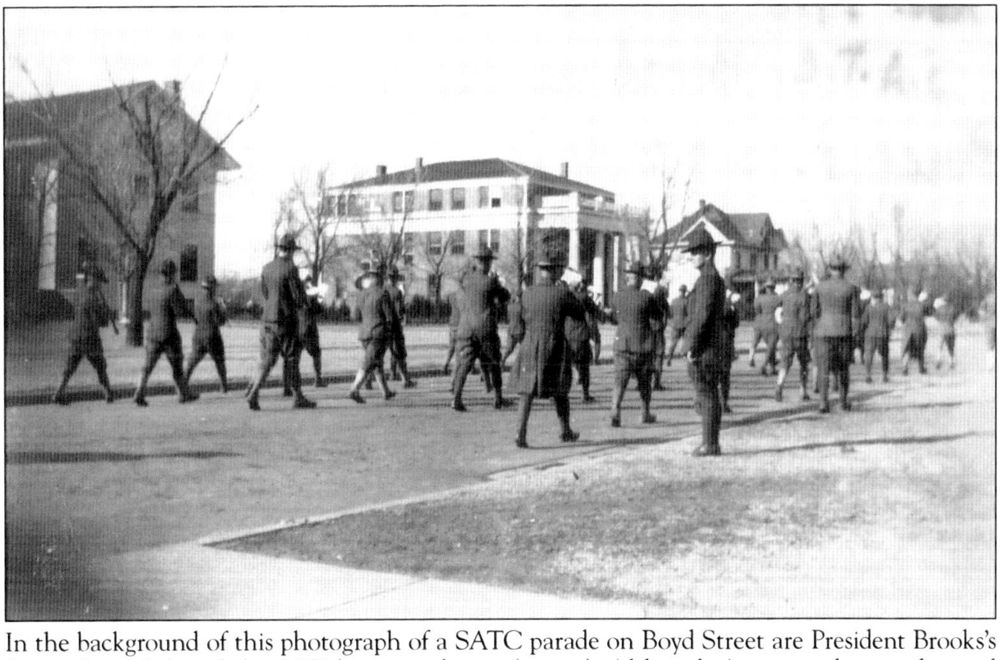

In the background of this photograph of a SATC parade on Boyd Street are President Brooks's home (far right) and the SAE fraternity house (center). Although Army regulations dictated the kind of facilities to be used by servicemen, other options were available. At the University of Oklahoma, several fraternity and sorority houses were taken over to provide barracks for the men in SATC. (CCHS.)

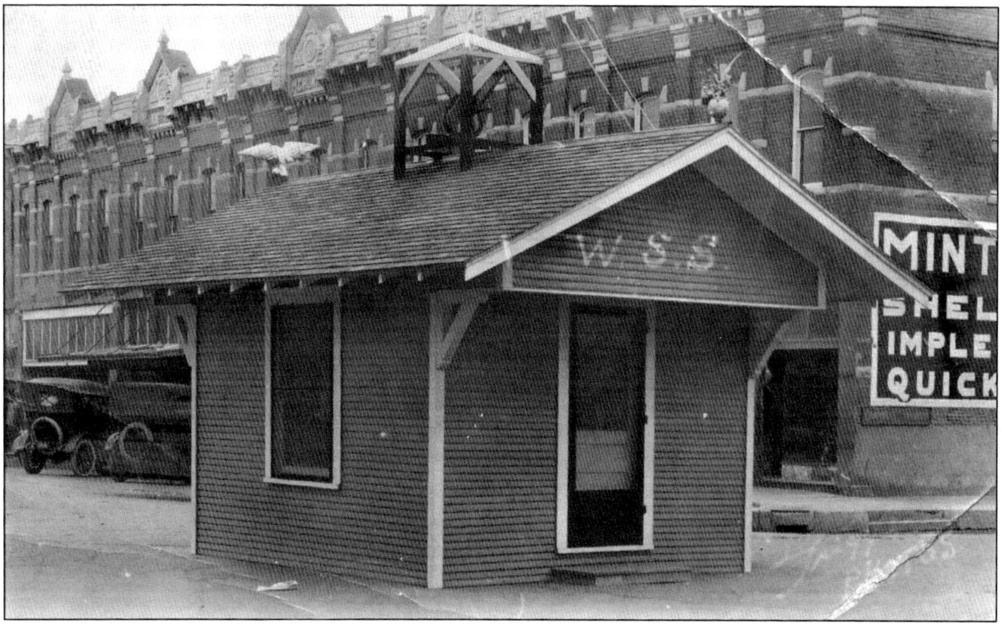

To fund the war, Americans were encouraged to buy US Treasury bonds. The federal government encouraged the American people to buy bonds as their patriotic duty to help defeat the enemy. Oklahoma was the first state in the nation to build war savings banks. Norman's war savings bank (shown here) was just east of Main Street and Peters Avenue. (CCHS.)

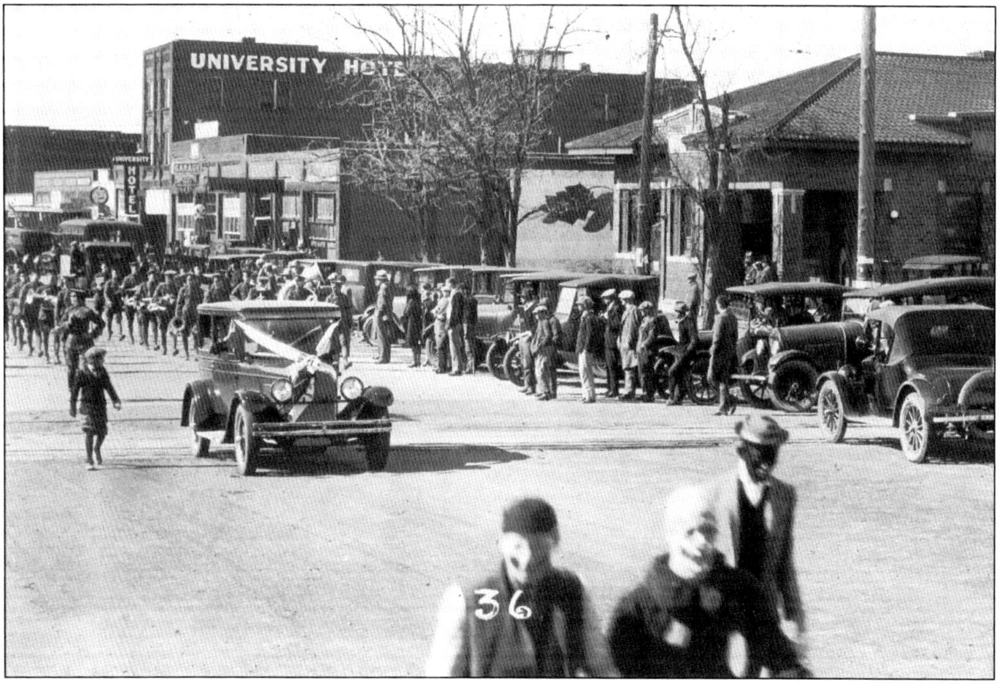

Parades were an effective tool in uniting citizens for the war effort. Often, the parade would terminate at a park, where a picnic made it a festive day. In March 1918, these patriotic individuals marched from the University of Oklahoma to Main Street, ending at the War Savings Bank, where many participants lined up to purchase war bonds. (CCHS.)

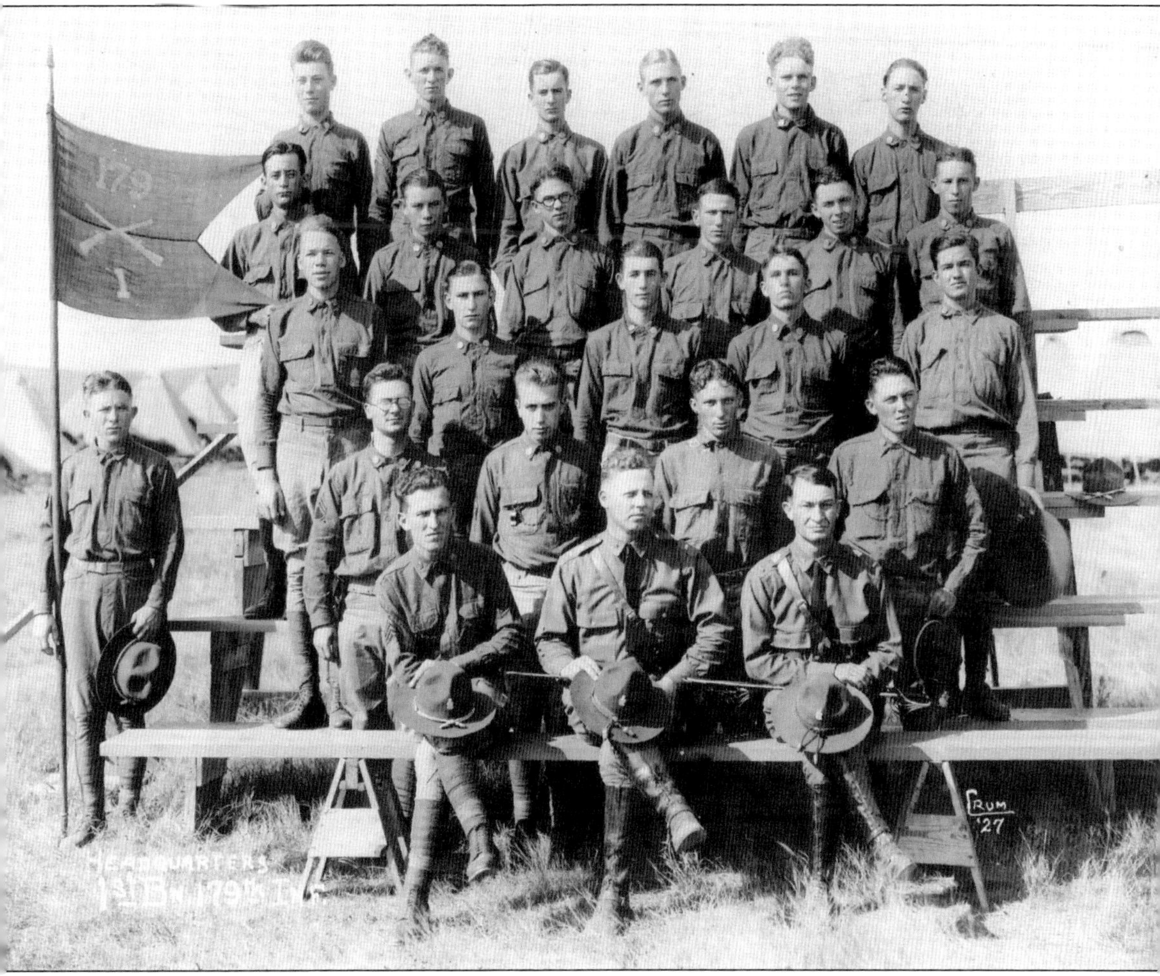


Oklahoma's National Guard 1st Infantry Division was mobilized to the Mexican border in 1916. In July 1918, the 1st Division arrived in France, where it fought at Blanc Mont Ridge in the Ferme Forest. Elmer Capshaw (first row, far right) was an officer in the 179th Regiment. The Norman native was an All-American football player at OU. The 1st Division troops returned and were discharged in 1919. By November 1918, there were over 1,000 OU students in SATC, including 80 in the naval reserve. By the end of the war, 700 OU students had served in the armed forces. Of these, 250 were commissioned officers, 100 in aviation, and 100 in coast and field artillery. An additional 250 OU students served as infantry in France with the American Expeditionary Force. (CCHS.)

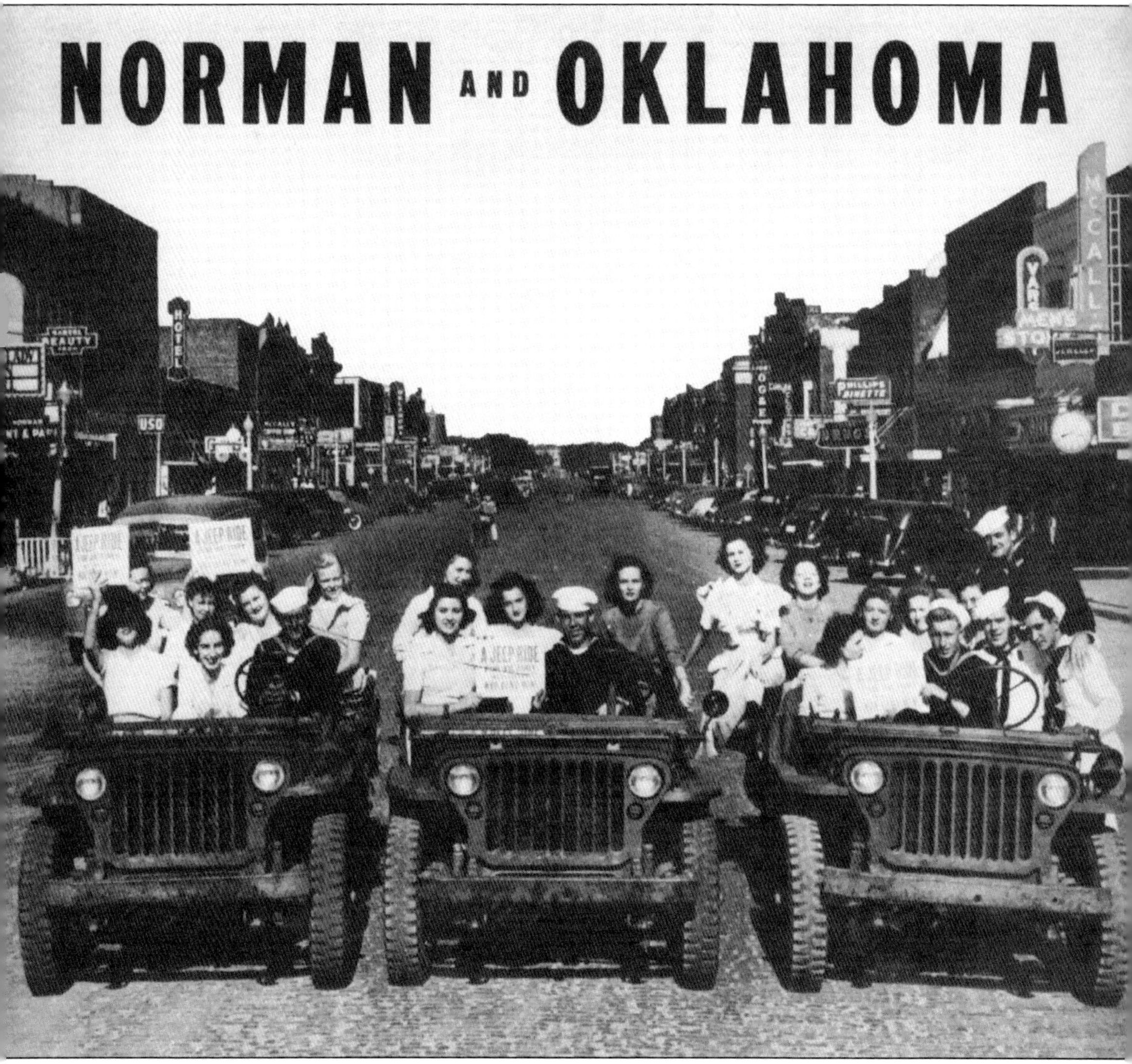


Beginning in 1942, Norman became part of the US Navy's effort to prepare the country for another war. In all, the Navy purchased 62,000 acres in the state. In March 1942, the Navy acquired 2,537 acres in Norman to build a naval air station, a naval air technical training station, and a naval hospital. The naval air station was located north of the university (north base) at Max Westheimer Airfield. The air technical training center, military barracks, and hospital were constructed southeast of the university (south base). The training facilities north and south of town educated young men and women in skills that helped maintain naval aircraft and ground equipment. The acquisition of properties, and the increased number of military personnel in Norman, was a well-needed economic boost that moved Central Oklahoma out of the Great Depression. (CCHS.)

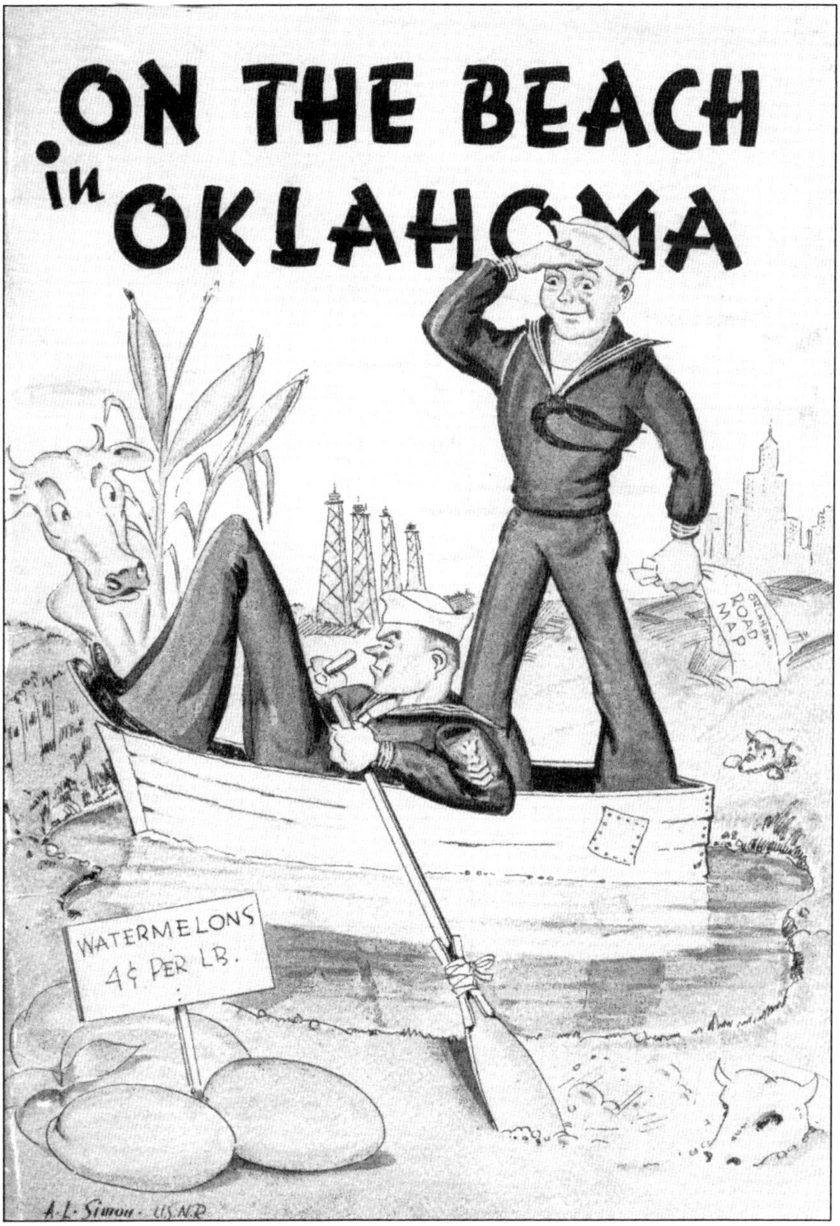


The establishment of a naval base in Norman, a city far from any ocean, resulted from a fortuitous encounter between Savoie Lottinville, director of the University of Oklahoma Press, and K.B. Salisbury, captain in the US Navy. In 1941, Lottinville, eastbound on the Santa Fe Railroad, met Salisbury, who was returning to the Bureau of Aeronautics at the Department of Navy in Washington, DC. As Lottinville and Salisbury were getting acquainted, the Navy captain asked Lottinville if there was an interest at the University of Oklahoma in flying. Lottinville proudly told the captain about the university's new airfield north of town, named after World War I pilot Max Westheimer. Salisbury then asked, "Would you be willing to lend it [the airfield] to the Navy for the duration of the war?" Lottinville discussed the possibilities with university president Joseph Brandt, who gave Lottinville the green light to pursue the matter. Brandt and university regents were excited about the prospects of a naval training station in Norman. (CCHS.)

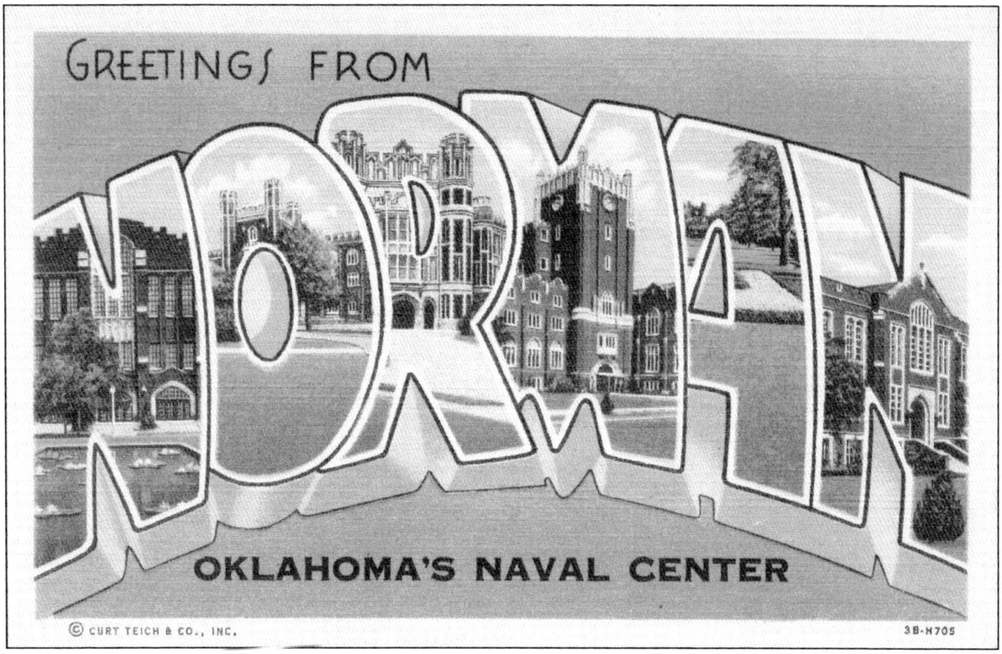


In 1939, OU had 6,935 students; by 1945, the enrollment declined to 3,769—the effect of young men and women joining the armed services during the war. By offering training classes to naval personnel, whose tuition was paid for by the federal government, the university made up for the loss of students and tuition. (CCHS.)

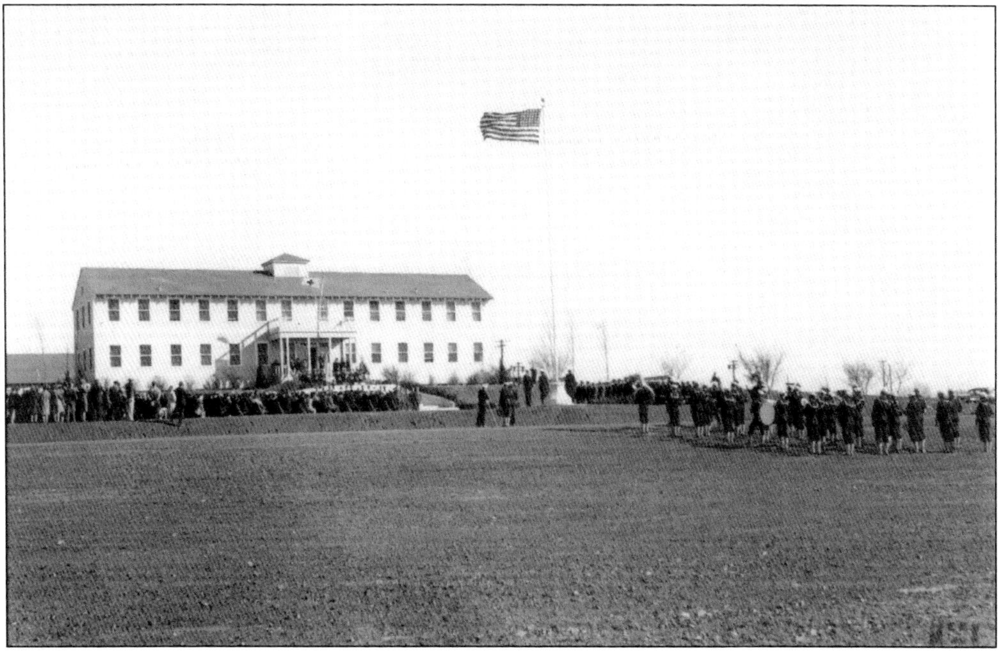

By April 1942, hundreds of workmen, carpenters, electricians, masons, and engineers crowded into Norman, ready to build the naval facilities. Santa Fe Railroad cars filled the Norman sidings with lumber, steel beams, and building materials awaiting the work crews. Construction began on April 28. The base was officially commissioned on May 20, 1942. (WHC.)

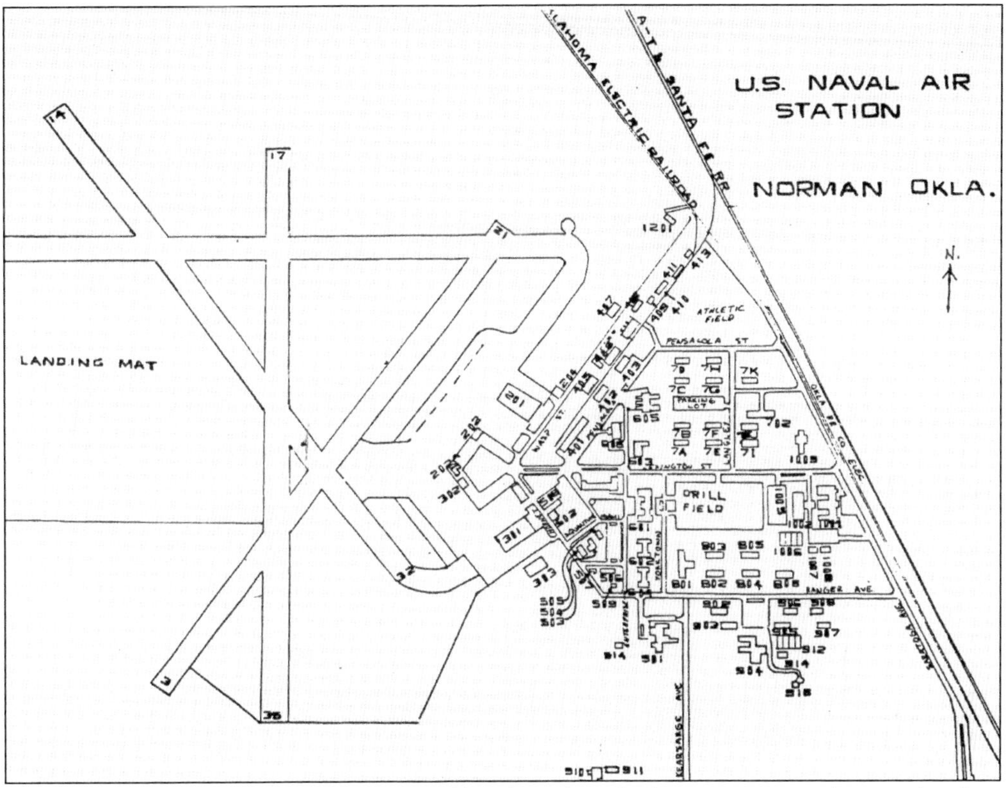


The Navy enlarged Max Westheimer Airfield and purchased 1,500 acres to provide ground and air training for combat pilots. The base was designed to train 800 aviation cadets every three months. Facilities at the north base included an indoor swimming pool, bowling alleys, and a theater. These amenities provided the cadets with welcome entertainment and physical activities. (CCHS.)

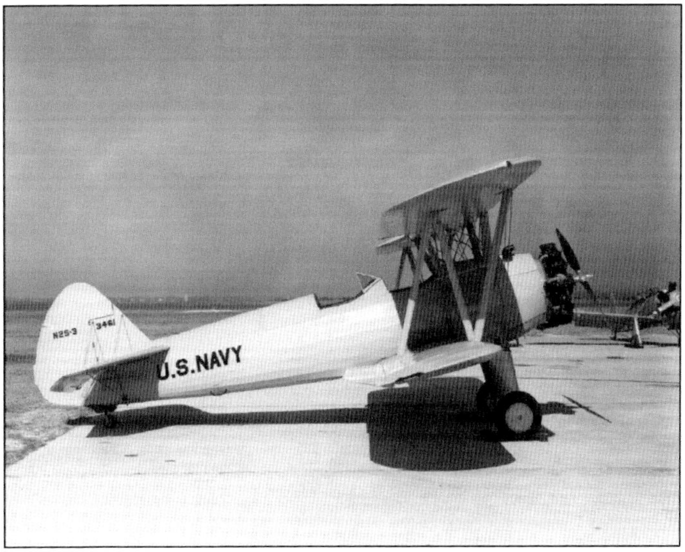


Before the men attended flight school in Norman, they received university training at one of four schools in Georgia, North Carolina, Iowa, and California. The first class of 20 cadets arrived from the University of North Carolina in September 1942. For three months, the men spent half their day in flight instruction and the other half in ground training. The men trained in the Stearman N2S-3 seen here. (CCHS.)

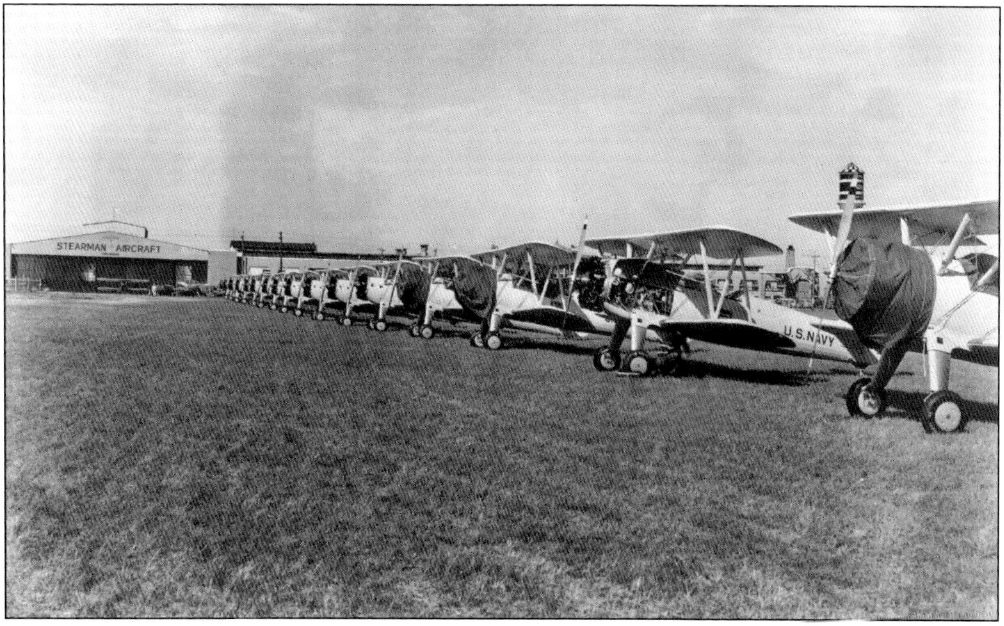


Ground training included theory of flight, navigation, communication, and air-to-air gunnery. Pilot cadets were required to land a plane on an aircraft carrier. To simulate carrier landings, instructors painted a large circle in the middle of a practice field. The men had to stop within the circle three out of five attempts. The cadets graduated from Norman as naval aviators, air gunners, and radio operators. (CCHS.)

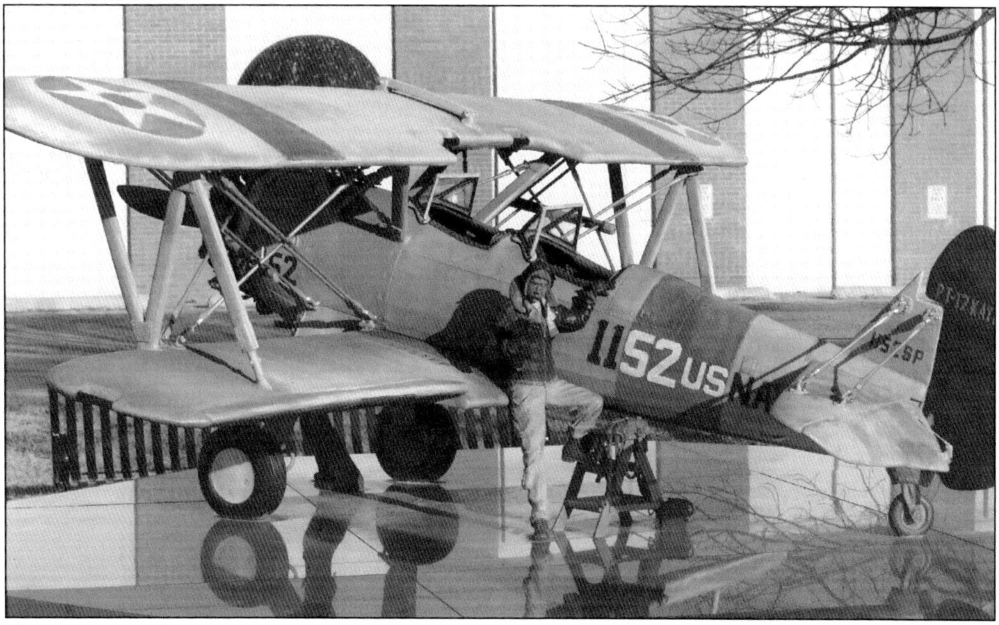


This replica of a Stearman N2S-3 trainer on Legacy Trail in Norman represents the Navy's experience at Max Westheimer Airfield, which provided flight-training facilities. For four years, the skies over Norman were filled with yellow biplanes rising and falling in aerobatic routines as the men practiced naval flight exercises. The last biplane flew over Norman in February 1946, one month before the Navy officially closed the north base. (CCHS.)

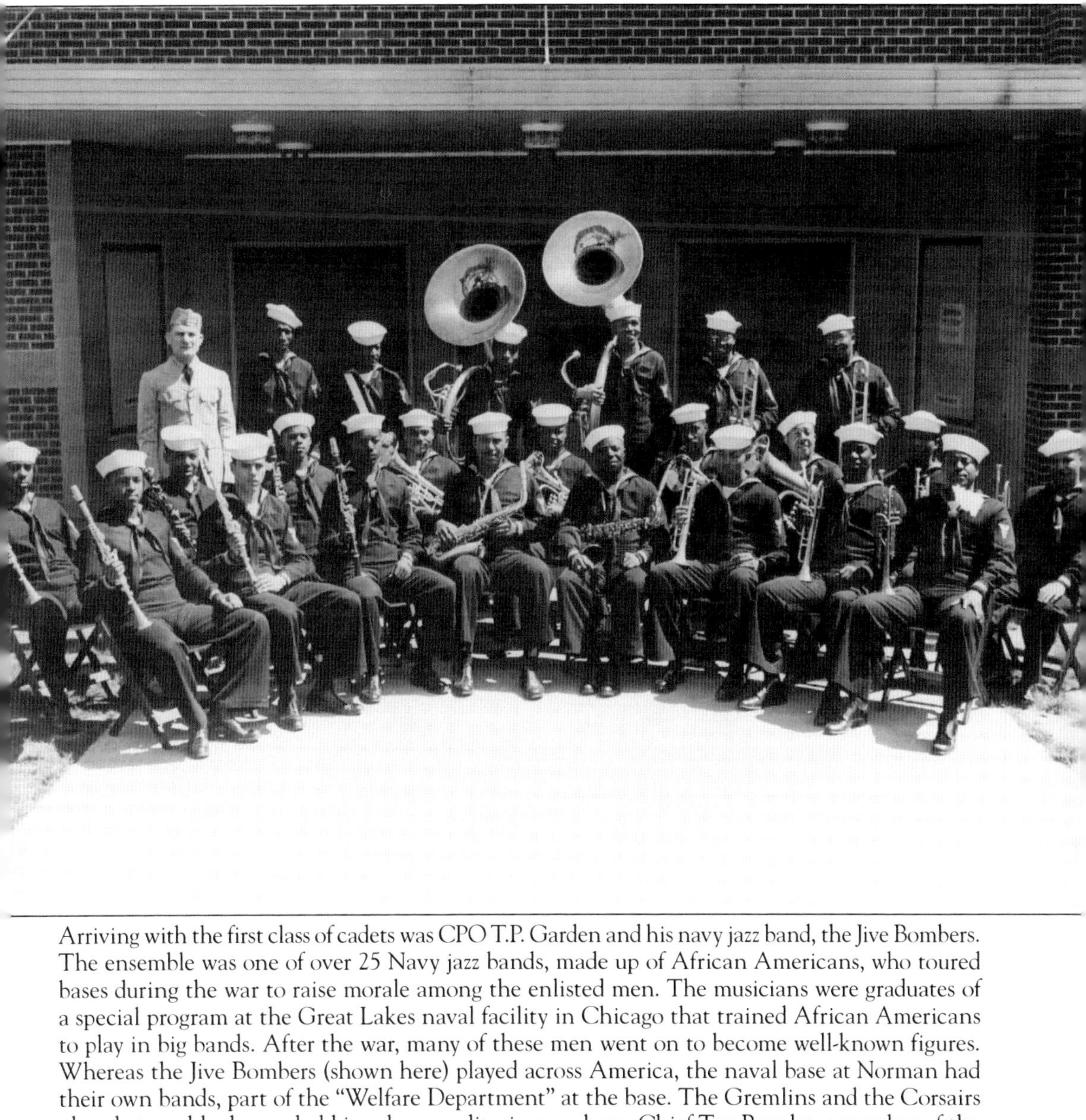

Arriving with the first class of cadets was CPO T.P. Garden and his navy jazz band, the Jive Bombers. The ensemble was one of over 25 Navy jazz bands, made up of African Americans, who toured bases during the war to raise morale among the enlisted men. The musicians were graduates of a special program at the Great Lakes naval facility in Chicago that trained African Americans to play in big bands. After the war, many of these men went on to become well-known figures. Whereas the Jive Bombers (shown here) played across America, the naval base at Norman had their own bands, part of the "Welfare Department" at the base. The Gremlins and the Corsairs played at weekly dances held in a large auditorium on base. Chief Tex Beneke, a member of the pre-war Glenn Miller Band, led the Gremlins. (CCHS.)

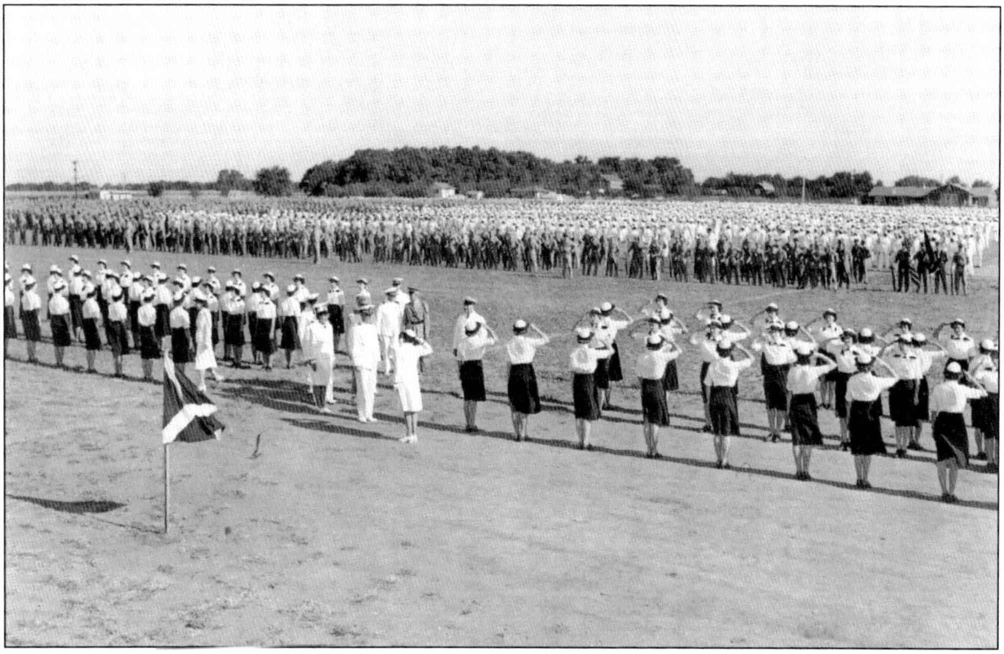

The south base trained large numbers of ground crew. When facilities became available, thousands of young men arrived in Norman to begin training as mechanics, armament specialists, and plane captains. The south base trained over 18,000 personnel, quite a boom for Norman, a city of 11,429 people in 1940. (CCHS.)

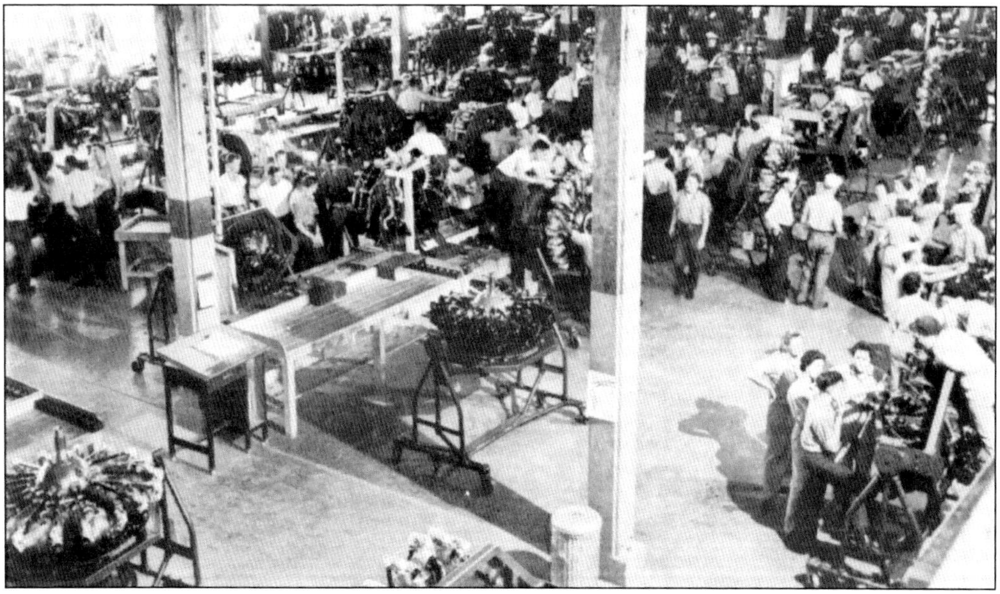

Naval air stations were important in training men as aviation machinist mates, metalsmiths, ordnancemen, rubberized equipment repairmen, and radar operators. Such training was usually accomplished at naval shore facilities or aboard ships. Ordnance education included programs in small arms, aviation loading and safety, explosives handling, firing and maintenance of aircraft guns, and chemical warfare protection and decontamination. Ordnance training took place in classrooms as well as on outdoor ranges. (CCHS.)

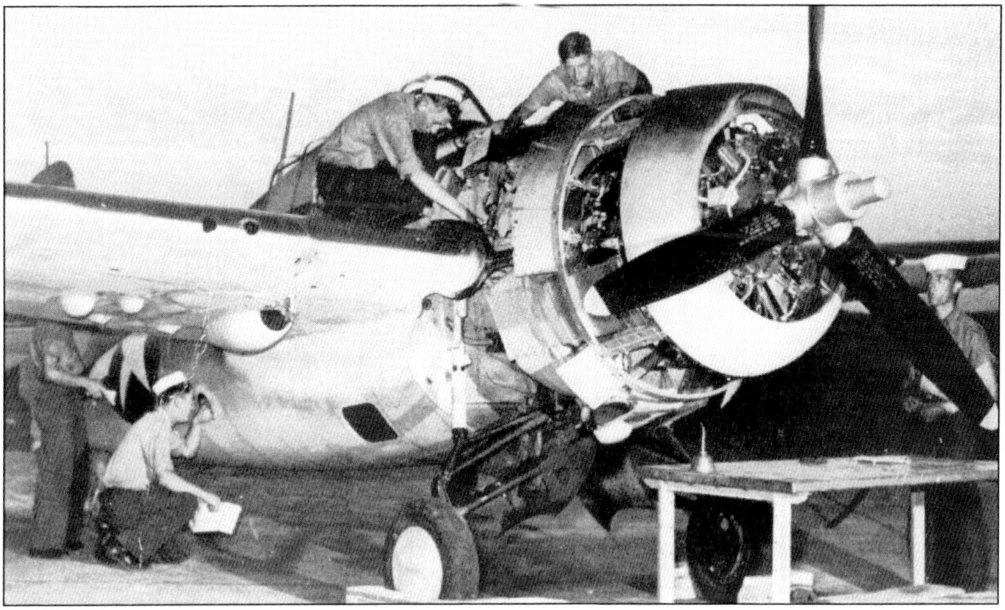

The four-month naval course trained aircraft technicians, who were needed to maintain aircraft and to keep the planes flying. The men and women who left Norman as aviation machinists or metalsmiths were assigned to naval bases and task forces, where they became part of the war effort. (CCHS.)

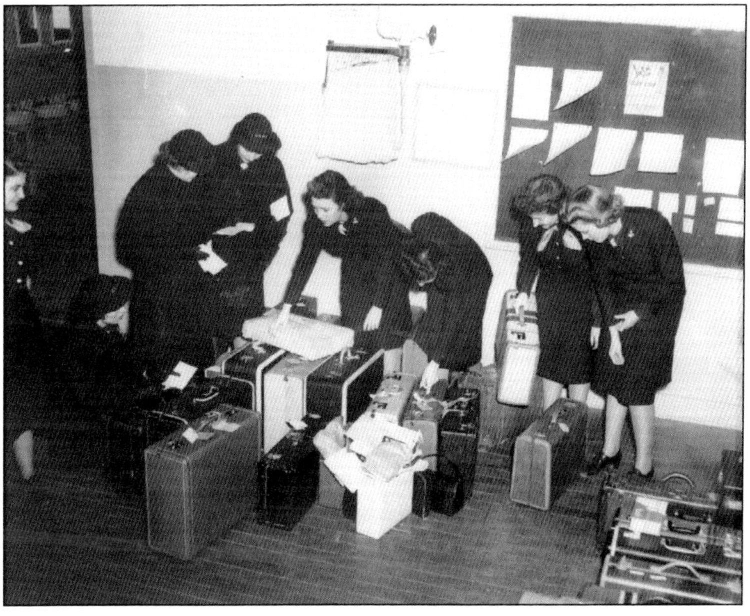

While the naval base in Norman was taking shape in 1942, Mildred McAfee was sworn in as naval reserve lieutenant commander and as first director of the WAVES. In 1942–1943, 27,000 women joined the Navy. Every three weeks at Norman depot in 1942, WAVES arrived at Naval Air Technical Training Center (NATTC) for training. (WHC.)

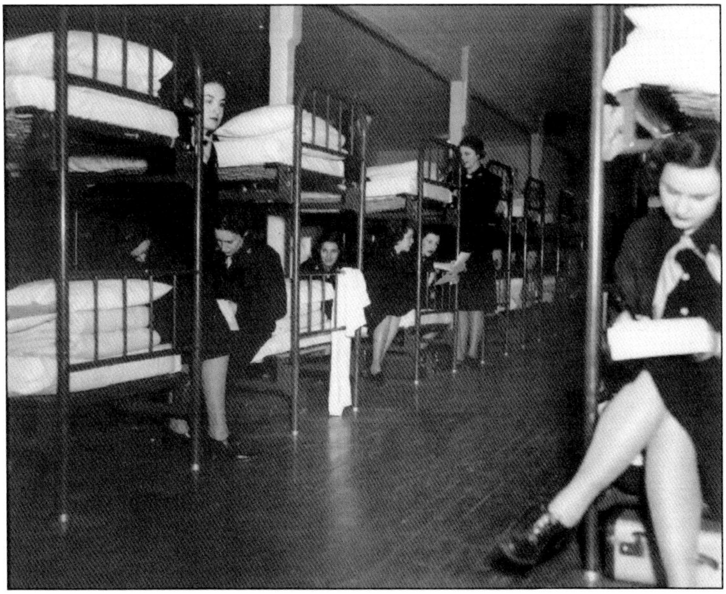

As aviation metalsmiths, women were trained to make any part of an airplane structure or engine. The goal was to acquire the skill to be able to take an airplane engine apart and reassemble it. The women were also trained as parachute riggers and storekeepers. Navy women were limited to serving only in the continental United States. Their work freed male sailors for worldwide combat duty. (WHC.)

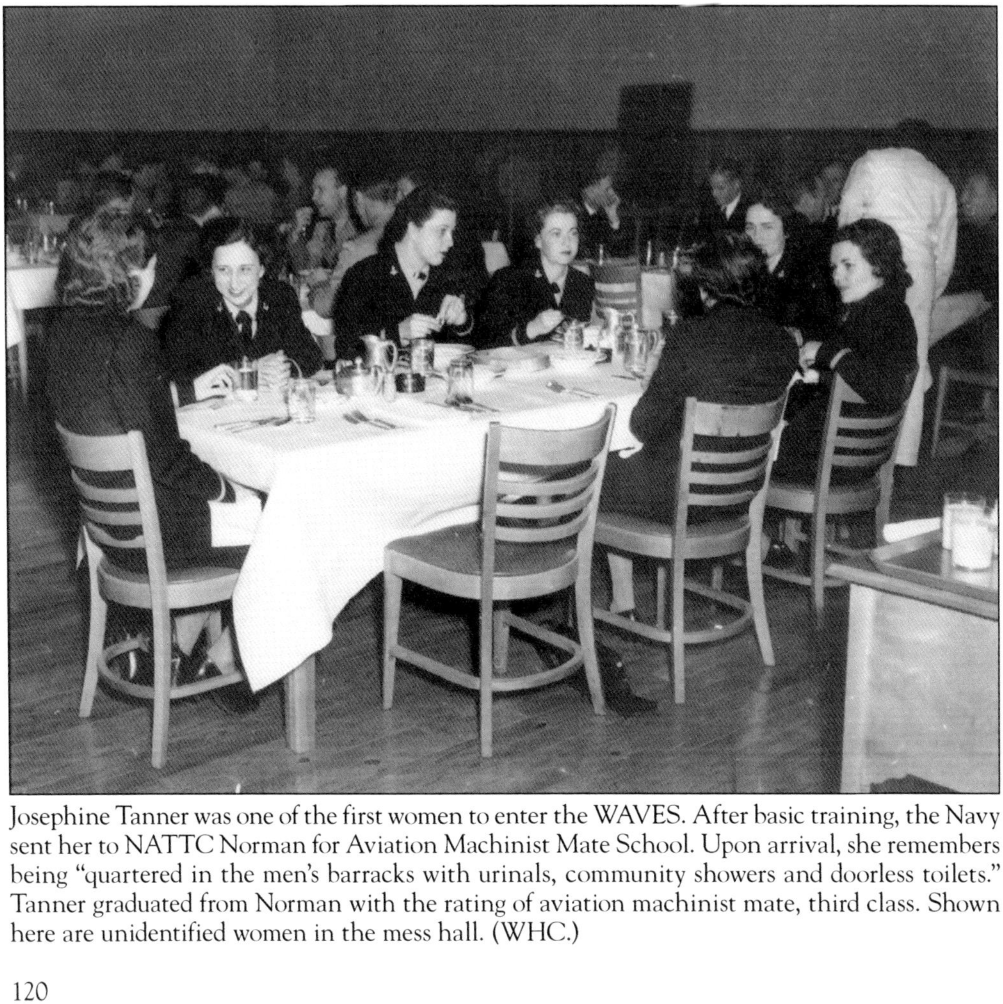

Josephine Tanner was one of the first women to enter the WAVES. After basic training, the Navy sent her to NATTC Norman for Aviation Machinist Mate School. Upon arrival, she remembers being "quartered in the men's barracks with urinals, community showers and doorless toilets." Tanner graduated from Norman with the rating of aviation machinist mate, third class. Shown here are unidentified women in the mess hall. (WHC.)

The bases were fully self-sufficient communities that offered men and women training, leisure, and recreational activities. There was a commissary, laundry, barber and beauty shops, mess halls, barracks, swimming pools, tennis courts, and an auditorium called the Great Oak Hall, with seating for 6,500 people. The hall was used for basketball games, dances, and USO shows. A base newspaper called the *Bull Horn* kept everyone informed. Shown here is the ceremony for the opening of the Naval base in 1942 in front of the administration building. (CCHS.)

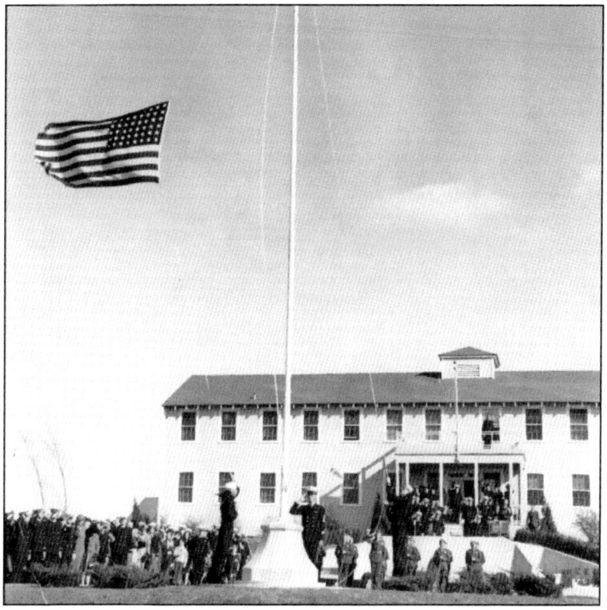

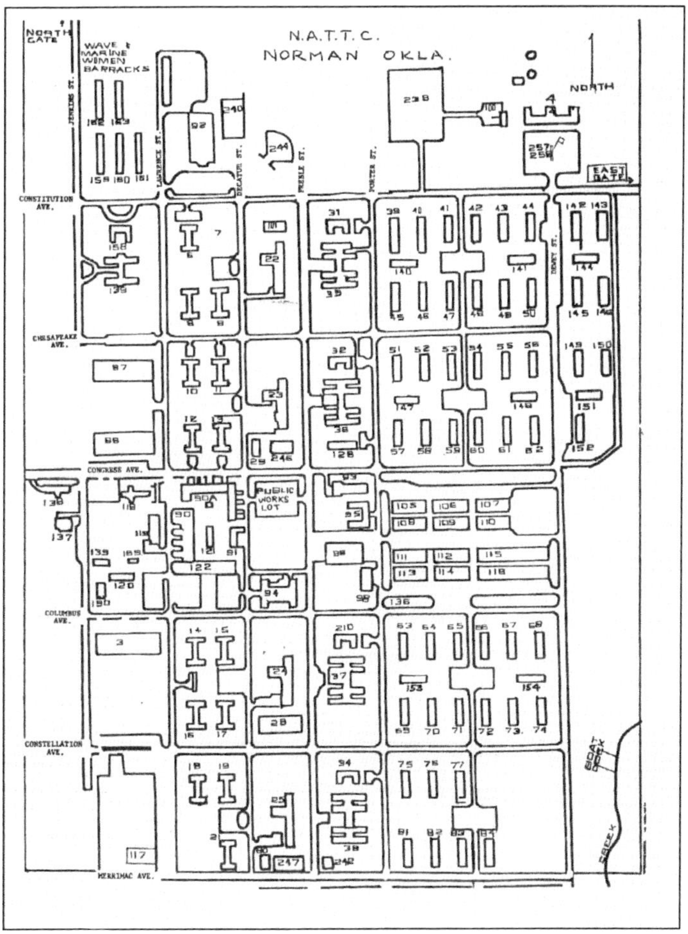


The naval training facility was south of Norman, adjacent to the university. In this map, the following buildings are identified with numbers: hospitals, 31–34 and 158; training and trade, 8–19; troop housing, 39–74 and 147–154; WAVE housing, 159–163; recreation, 22–29; swimming pools, 28, 246, and 247; tennis courts, 240; baseball field, 244; mess and galley, 35–38; fire station, 91; post office, 93; brig and guard house, 95; and bakery, 98. (CCHS.)

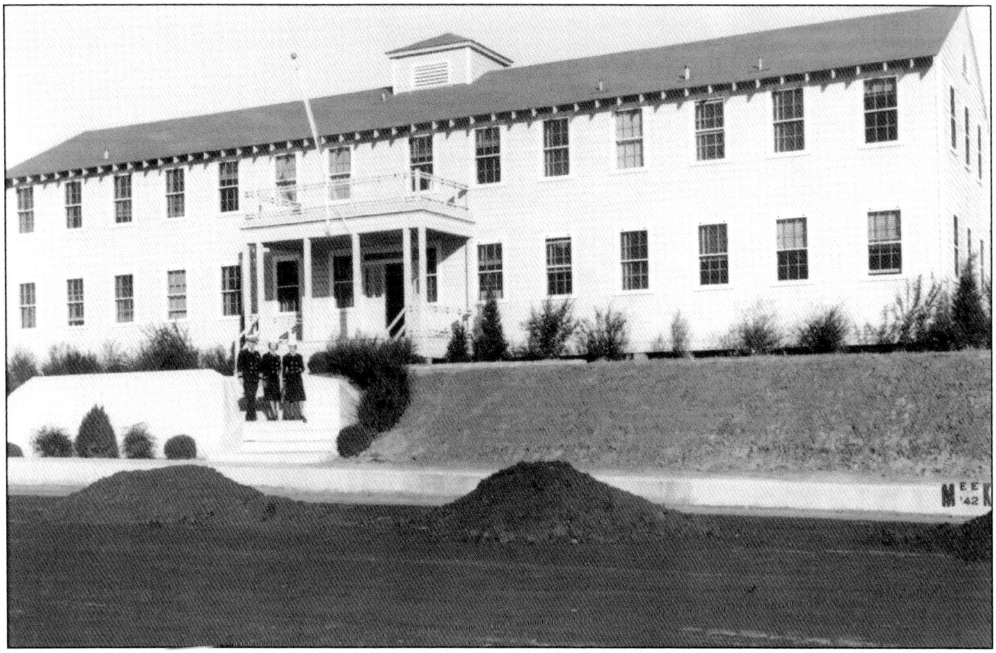

In 1942, the Navy built a hospital on the south base. The facility held 1,000 beds, but often served over 2,000 personnel. Standing in front of the naval hospital are, from left to right, Capt. L.B. Marshall, US naval medical officer in command of the hospital; Ensign Doris Anderson; and Ensign Janet Ronk.

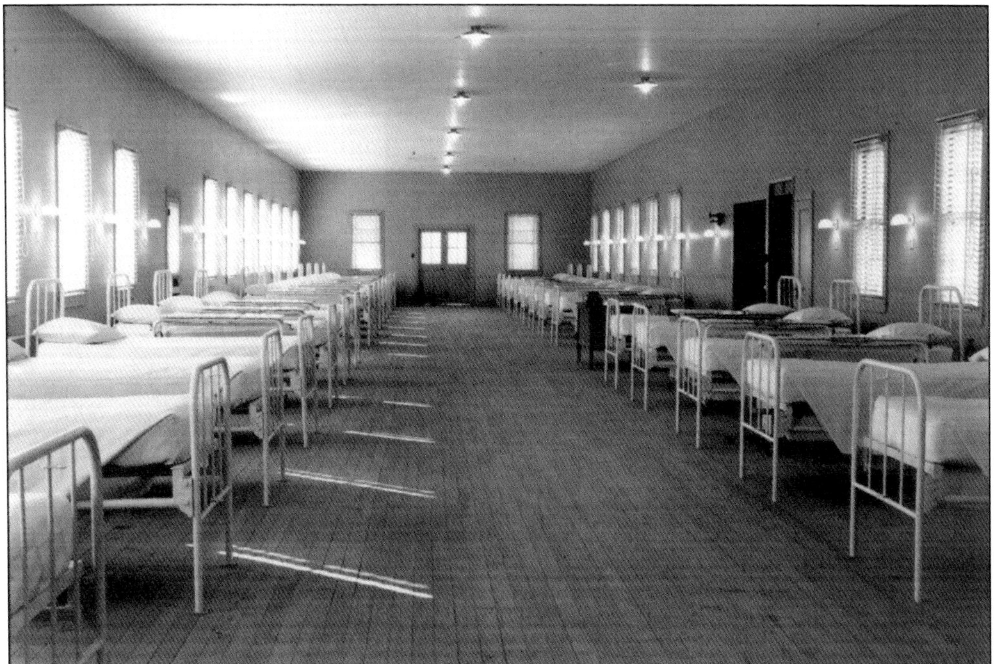

In 1943, three wings were added to the hospital; one 20-room wing for service dependents, and two wings for medical and survey WAVES. A maternity ward was opened in January 1943. Within the next six months, 100 babies were born there. (WHC.)

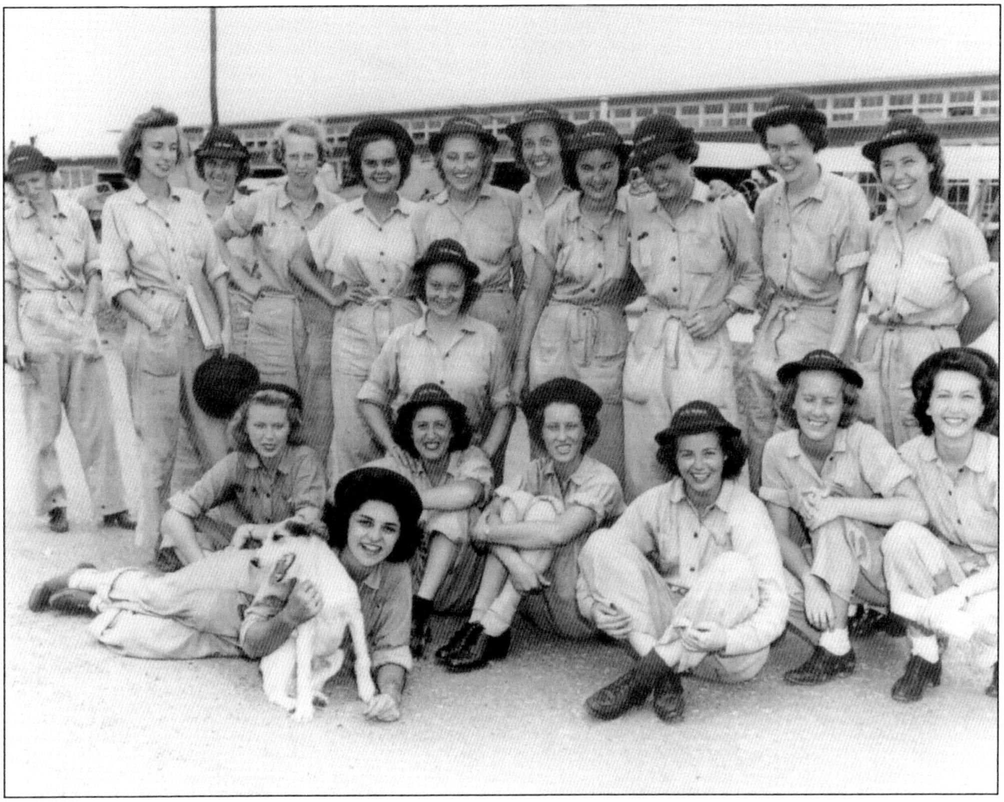

Shirley Bell's graduating aviation metalsmith class poses on July 30, 1943. Bell related that the girls in the photograph were wearing "jumpsuits made of light blue cotton denim." She commented that the girls went to "school with sailors, learning riveting and welding." After she graduated from NATTC Norman, she was assigned to Naval Air Station Seattle. "I was the only woman in an Emergency Repair Squadron of 150 men." (CCHS.)

Shown here are, from left to right, three unidentified sailors, Richard Kolonko, Fred Boblanc, and Anthony Avila. Even though NATTC Norman was the Navy's largest training center, some sailors were not impressed with the facilities. Eldon Price thought that the two-story frame buildings were stark and considered the surrounding land a red dirt prairie. The upside was that the base was within a trolley ride of Oklahoma City. (CCHS.)

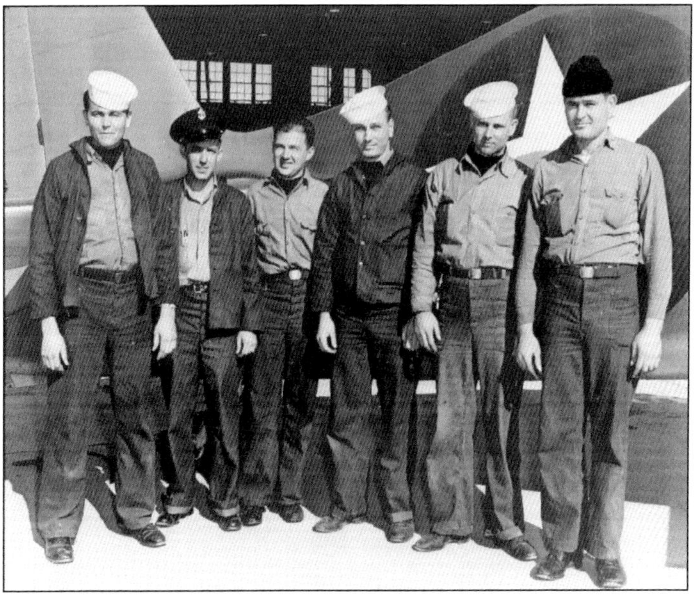

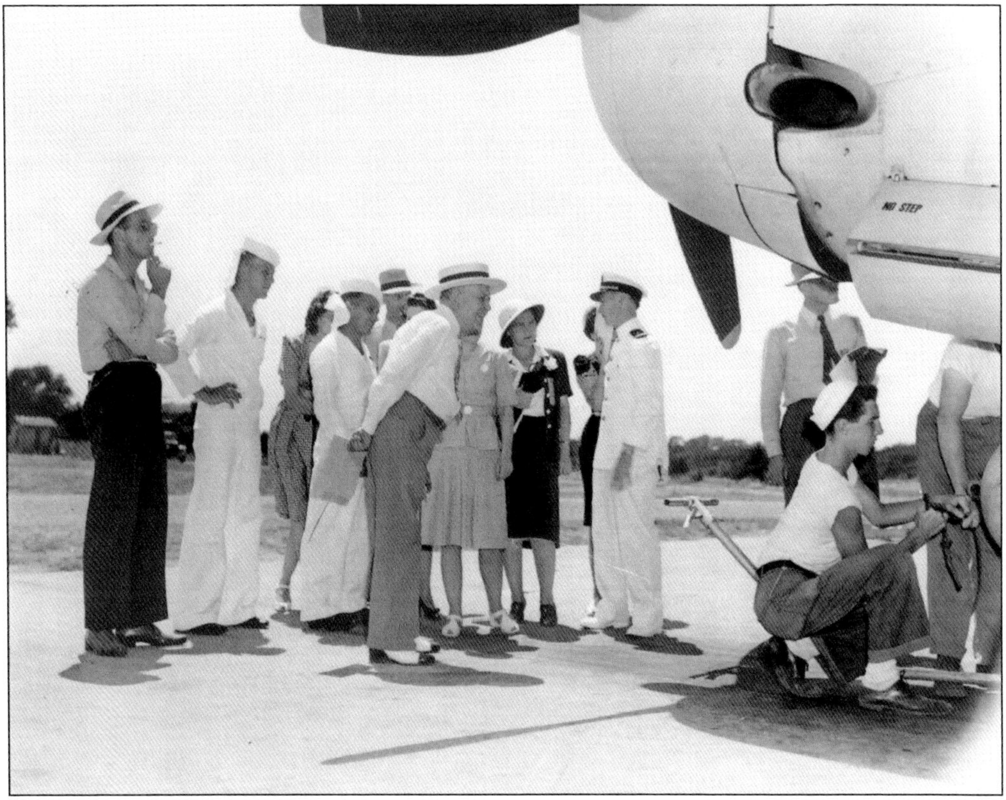


By August 1943, NATTC Norman planned an open house for local citizens to inspect the bases. Oklahomans living in and around Norman benefitted economically from the more than $7 million invested in constructing the base. Also, the boom to the economy was enhanced by the $350,000 payroll to base personnel, which was the equivalent of expanding Norman by 700 families. Citizens approved of the facility and what it meant to the city. (CCHS.)

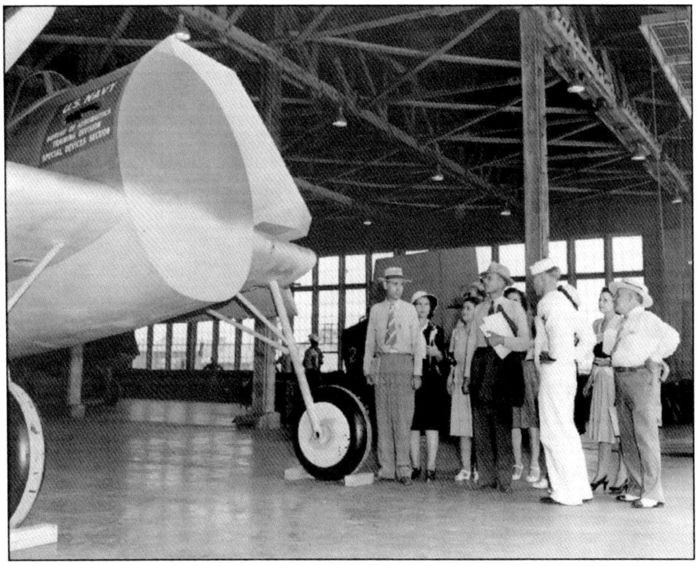

From the beginning, the Navy wanted a good relationship with Norman residents. Before base construction began, Navy personnel worked with the Norman Chamber of Commerce and the University of Oklahoma to make sure that young men and women in the Navy maintained high moral standards. The city encouraged residents to fix up their homes and rental properties in a "Clean Up, Paint Up and Fix Up" campaign. (WHC.)

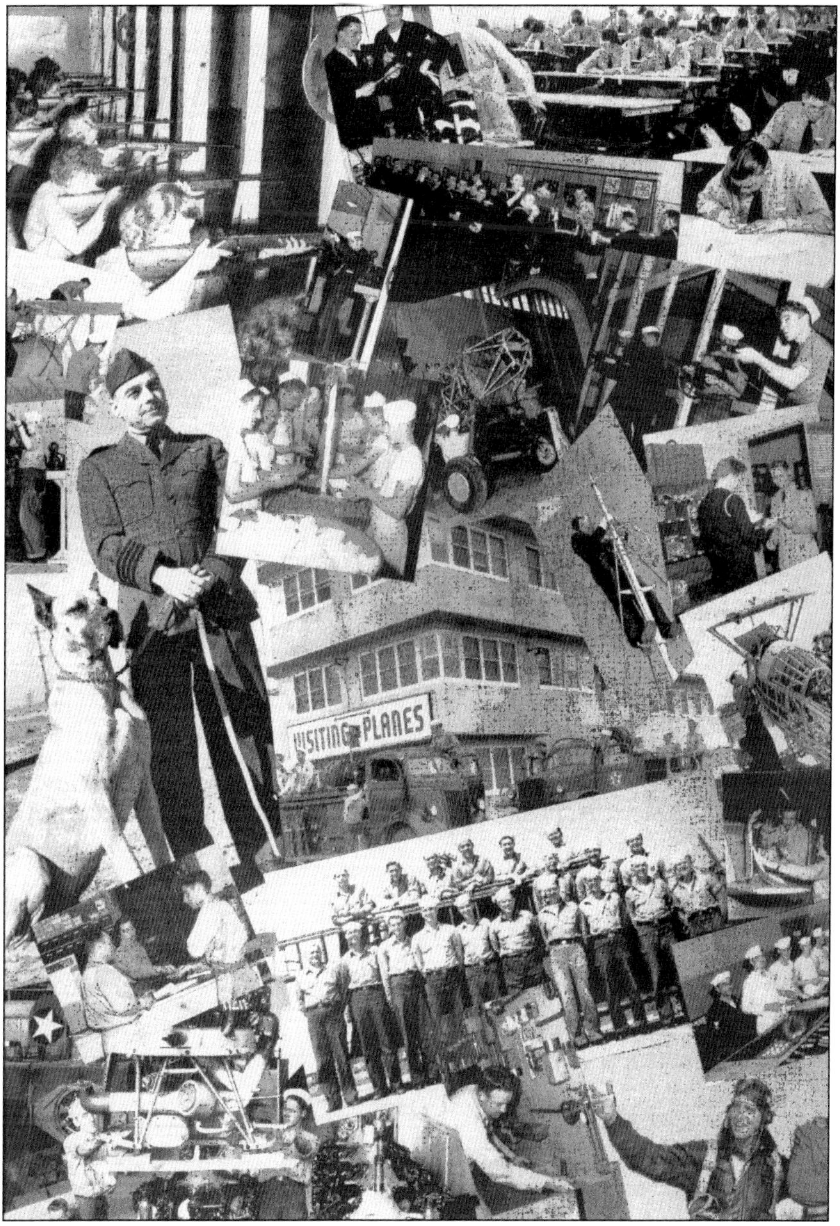


*The Smooth Log, Naval Air Station Norman Oklahoma, 1943* was dedicated to the men and women who trained at the Norman Air Station. It is a history of naval operations around the world, and the importance of training men and women to build a strong Navy to fight in the Allied effort to defeat Germany and Japan in World War II. The yearbook depicts a naval community of over 18,000 men and women who lived at the edge of the greater Norman community. The two communities overlapped, and each was perhaps the stronger because of the experience of living in their two different worlds. Servicemen and women relaxed in Norman and Oklahoma City. There were two United Service Organizations (USO) in Norman; one on Main Street and the other in an armory across from the depot. The university provided training, and Navy men and women became part of the university experience. Pictured here is one of several collages in the *Smooth Log* that promoted the men and women who spent time in the Navy in Norman. (CCHS.)

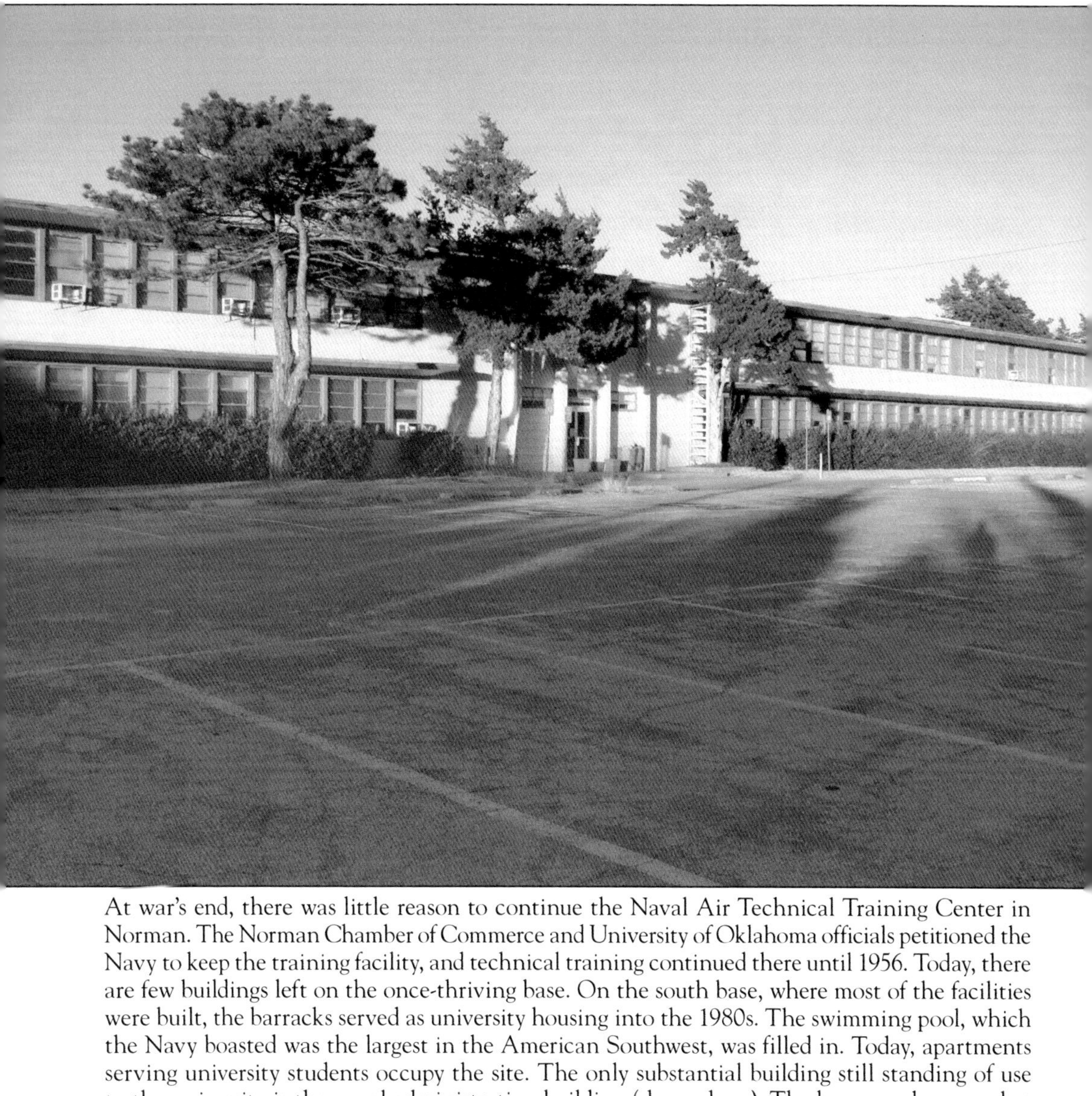

At war's end, there was little reason to continue the Naval Air Technical Training Center in Norman. The Norman Chamber of Commerce and University of Oklahoma officials petitioned the Navy to keep the training facility, and technical training continued there until 1956. Today, there are few buildings left on the once-thriving base. On the south base, where most of the facilities were built, the barracks served as university housing into the 1980s. The swimming pool, which the Navy boasted was the largest in the American Southwest, was filled in. Today, apartments serving university students occupy the site. The only substantial building still standing of use to the university is the naval administration building (shown here). The base may be gone, but memories still survive, and those who served at NATTC Norman speak fondly of the time spent in the Navy on the Great Plains. (CCHS.)

# About the Organization

The Cleveland County Historical Society (CCHS) is a 501(c)(3) nonprofit organization established in 1967, when 600 charter members pledged to "research, preserve, publicize and perpetuate the history and genealogy of Cleveland County, Oklahoma and its people," and to "assemble and display objects of historical interest and significance." In 1973, the city of Norman purchased the Moore-Lindsay House at 508 North Peters Avenue with the purpose of preserving the Queen Anne–style house as a museum that represents the settlement of Norman and early-20th-century Oklahoma. The Cleveland County Historical Society's stewardship of the Moore-Lindsey Historical House began in 1973, when the CCHS board signed a contract with the city of Norman to open the historic house to the citizens of Norman. From the generosity of the citizens of Cleveland County, through donations of artifacts and money, the historical society was able to decorate each room in the house to replicate the life of America at the turn of the 20th century. Today, the society maintains its partnership with the city as guardians of the Moore-Lindsay Historical House.

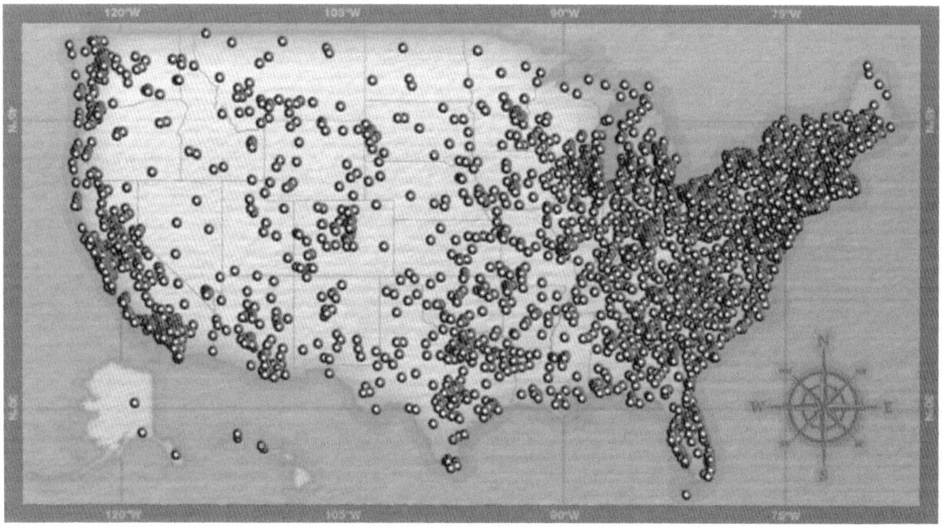